Using Financial Information in Continuing Education

Using Financial Information in Continuing Education

Accepted Methods and New Approaches

by
Gary W. Matkin

AMERICAN COUNCIL ON EDUCATION ★
ORYX PRESS ★
Series on Higher Education
1997

The rare Arabian oryx is believed to have inspired the myth of the unicorn. This desert antelope became virtually extinct in the early 1960s. At that time several groups of international conservationists arranged to have 9 animals sent to the Phoenix Zoo to be the nucleus of a captive breeding herd. Today the oryx population is over 1,000 and over 500 have been returned to the Middle East.

© 1997 by the American Council on Education and The Oryx Press
Published by The Oryx Press
4041 North Central at Indian School Road
Phoenix, Arizona 85012-3397

Published simultaneously in Canada
Printed and bound in the United States of America

∞ The paper used in this publication meets the minimum requirements of the American National Standard for Information Sciences—Permanence of Paper for Printed Library Materials, ANSI Z39.48-1984.

Library of Congress Cataloging-in-Publication Data

Matkin, Gary W., 1944–
    Using financial information in continuing education: accepted methods and new approaches / by Gary W. Matkin.
        p.   cm. — (American Council on Education/Oryx Press series on higher education)
Rev. ed. of: Effective budgeting in continuing education. 1985.
Includes bibliographical references and index.
    ISBN 0-89774-941-3 (cloth)
    1. Continuing education—United States—Finance.   2. Continuing education—United States—Curricula.   3. Program budgeting—United States   I. Matkin, Gary W., 1944–   Effective budgeting in continuing education.   II. Title.   III. Series.
LC5251.M36   1996
374'.973—dc20   96-36577
                                                                              CIP

To the memory of Milton R. Stern

CONTENTS

• • • • • • • • •

LIST OF EXHIBITS

• • • • • • • • •

PREFACE

· · · · · · · · ·

A Personal Comment

n 1985, my book, *Effective Budgeting in Continuing Education*, was published. It was the first comprehensive treatment of financial management and budgeting in the field and was based largely upon my own research and experience. The book combined a theoretical approach to the subject with practical suggestions about how theory might be implemented. At the time, I was director of administrative services for University Extension at the University of California at Berkeley. The book was well received by a small audience of CE professionals, and I was gratified by occasional compliments on its usefulness. *Effective Budgeting* went out of print in 1993, but when I began receiving inquiries from CE professionals about how they might obtain copies of the book, Milton Stern, my former dean and a representative of the NUCEA/ACE/Oryx Press publishing consortium, strongly suggested that I revise and reissue the book.

But the times and my approach to the subject had changed. A growing body of literature in the field of CE financial management was placing particular emphasis on practical applications. A steady flow of "how to" manuals and publications, often supported by workshops and professional meetings, was supplying CE professionals with the tools they needed to fulfill their day-to-day financial management responsibilities. Meanwhile, I had become associate dean of University Extension at Berkeley, charged with directing the academic program of Extension. From my new perspective as an academic manager, faced with developing a planning process adjusted to meet dramatically changing internal and external circumstances, I became painfully aware of the limitations of the budgeting and financial management information systems I had myself developed for Extension 15 years earlier. Moreover, I realized that the management fads that appear in newspaper best-seller lists (TQM typifies the genre), despite my skepticism as to their long-term value, were, simply by the force of their numbers and their constant assault upon the public consciousness, shifting management paradigms in the United States. As we at Berkeley began thinking about adopting some of these new management philosophies, I realized that new management systems had to be developed to support them.

At the age of 50, with at least 10 more years to go in the field, I found myself in danger of becoming embarrassingly out of date and out of touch. The theories and methods I had so carefully and confidently described and espoused 10 years before no longer seemed complete or comprehensive. From my new perspective, I viewed *Effective Budgeting* as somewhat old fashioned, or, to use the term I have adopted in this book for these older methods, "traditional." I began searching the literature for help both in understanding the issues I faced in my day-to-day job and in resolving the confusion I saw in contemporary management theory. In the course of this search, one concept and two developing methodologies caught my attention as being particularly relevant to CE.

The concept is "dynamic stability," which was described by Boynton and Victor, and again by Boynton, in two articles in the *California Management Review* (Fall 1991, vol. 34, no. 1; Winter 1993, vol. 35, no. 2). Boynton and Victor argued that organizations or systems that can be easily adapted to changing circumstances are both stable and dynamic. They are stable because the basic underlying structure or operating principle does not have to change radically even in the face of dramatic changes in the operating environment. They are dynamic in that they are flexible enough to support the organization through such changes. Although I mention dynamic stability only briefly in this book, it is a significant philosophical underpinning of the work.

The two methodologies that interest me are multidimensional budgeting (MDB) and activity-based costing (ABC). Because these two methods are described in detail in this book, I will not discuss them here. Multidimensional budgeting is not well known, and activity-based costing is still being defined. In both cases, I have tried in this book to be specific about how these new methods can be used by CE professionals.

As I examined my 1985 manuscript with the new publication project in mind, I realized that I faced a significant challenge. On the one hand, much of what was covered in *Effective Budgeting* was still of potential use to CE professionals, particularly to those entering the field with little management or accounting experience. These "traditional" methods are those most commonly in use in CE today and will continue to form the basis for development of new methods. Any new book had to discuss these traditional methods. On the other hand, the new methods offer exciting new vistas for CE managers—

they also had to be part of the new book. My challenge was to preserve the description of traditional methods while pointing out their limitations and describing new methods. In this process, I had to face some hard decisions about organization—what to leave out from the earlier book and how far to go in describing new methods. I hope I have made the right choices for you. I invite you to comment on this book and its usefulness. Perhaps when I retire, I will, with your help, revise it once again.

ACKNOWLEDGMENTS

• • • • • • • • •

This project could not have been completed without the help and forbearance of many friends, colleagues, and family members. I am particularly indebted to my colleagues at University Extension, University of California, Berkeley, for their help and advice, and to my family members, particularly my son Ethan and wife Maya, for tolerating my absences to complete the manuscript. Through the generosity of friends, I had a quiet place to work and help with typing and manuscript preparation. For this I am deeply grateful. The late Milton Stern, however, deserves my most heartfelt gratitude and acknowledgment. He served as editor of this book, but, more important, supported me in this project the way he had supported me ever since I began my career as a continuing educator—with sound advice, human understanding, concise insight, and the ability to convey to me his sense of responsibility to the professional field of continuing education and the students it serves. In a very real and direct way, any contribution this book makes to our field is yet another in a long list from Milton R. Stern.

INTRODUCTION

• • • • • • • • •

T his book provides an understanding of the theories related to managing and using financial information in continuing education. Because it offers practical help in developing the systems and practices needed for effective use of such information, this book meets the current needs of continuing educators for increasing levels of financial sophistication. Every CE organization needs to revise its financial management information system to keep pace with increasing competition and changing accountability and managerial requirements. This book tells you what information you need and can expect to obtain from a sound CE financial management system.

THEORY AND PRACTICE

In 1874, as he left the presidency of the University of California to found Johns Hopkins University, Daniel Coit Gilman, having narrowly averted efforts by the California legislature to reduce the level of instruction at the University of California to vocational concerns, reflected on the position he had espoused: "The most practical service which the University can render to the State is to teach the principles of science, and their application to all the wants of man— and at the same time to teach all that language and history have handed down as the experience of humanity."[1] Gilman's argument was not resoundingly endorsed by the legislature; UC's constitutional autonomy, including its control of the curriculum, survived by just one vote.

Debate over the appropriate role for theory occurs in every field of professional endeavor, including continuing education. By and large, continuing educators are a practical lot who tend to be absorbed by the day-to-day concerns of meeting self-support financial requirements and levels of service. They are impatient of theoretical approaches that are not useful in guiding practice. This book presents theories that have been validated in practice, along with contemporary examples of how those theories can be applied.

TRADITIONAL AND NEW METHODS

In this book, I make a distinction between "traditional methods" of financial management and budgeting and "new" methods. Traditional methods focus on serving hierarchical administrative structures and on establishing a planning scheme and accountability over what is termed the "responsibility structure" of the organization. In CE, these traditional methods first segment the organization into separate program departments or units, responsibility for which is assigned to specific individuals. The traditional financial management system helps planning through a budgeting process and then monitors and reports accurate financial results for the unit, including comparisons of actual results to the budget plan. Traditional CE financial management methods typically use the *course* as the most detailed or smallest common cost or budget "object," i.e., that unit or entity about which financial data are accumulated.

The new financial management methods are designed to go beyond the capabilities of traditional methods and to correct some of the inadequacies inherent in their use. Two of these new methods, *multidimensional budgeting* (MDB) and *activity-based costing* (ABC) (or activity-based management), will be described extensively. These methods are more compatible with and required by contemporary management theories that emphasize nonhierarchical management, shared responsibility, continuous improvement, flexibility, focus on customer (including internal customer) requirements, anticipation of or rapid response to changes in the operating environment, and employee "empowerment" at all levels in the organization. These new methods allow managers to view the organization from many perspectives simultaneously, including some perspectives that have little or nothing to do with the current responsibility structure of the organization. They also require managers to focus on costs in more realistic and detailed ways, using activities and customer groups, as well as products, as cost objects.

While the new methods add power and scope to managerial decision making, they do not substitute for traditional methods, which form the first phase and basis for the use of new methods. Because they are dependent on their parent institutions for information, many CE organizations do not even have a comprehensive and effective traditional financial management system. Many CE professionals do not yet fully understand what traditional methods can do to aid planning and practice. Such an understanding of traditional methods is essential for an understanding of the newer methods. This book, therefore, will describe both the traditional and the new, and how both can be used to best effect.

PROGRAM PLANNING AND ORGANIZATIONAL MANAGEMENT

All CE professionals are involved to some degree in planning CE programs. Any financial management system that does not help program planners develop programs and monitor the success of programs is failing its primary mission. Program planners at all levels need to understand the basic structure of program finance and the pattern of decision making they confront. Program finance, planning, and development are at the core of the CE enterprise, and all CE financial information systems must be developed with the needs of program planners clearly in view. However, as the scale and size of the CE organization increases, other elements of financial management also increase in importance. Managers of large CE organizations have different needs and uses for financial information than do program planners, although the needs of both have large areas of overlap.

Managers must have information about the cost and efficiencies of support services and nonprogram activities as well as information, at an appropriate level of detail, about the overall operations of the organization. They also need to manage the relationship, including the financial relationship, between the CE organization and the parent institution. Of course, CE managers need to understand program or course planning, budgeting, and financial measurements, and program planners need to understand the basic elements and philosophies of CE organization management and control. Although I make a distinction between the needs of program planners and CE managers by addressing each in separate sections of the book, I also frequently acknowledge the interrelationship between the two activities. In each section, I present examples and case studies appropriate to the target group. Readers should not limit themselves to the section devoted to the concerns of their group, but rather should view CE financial management as an integrated and interrelated whole.

TERMINOLOGY

Certain terms are used in a special way in this book to further the discussion of financial management in continuing education. *Financial management* or *financial information management* is used to indicate the deliberate use of financial information to make decisions. The importance of linking decision making to the system that generates financial information needs to be made

explicit. Much of the information generated by many CE financial management systems is never used to make decisions.

Course signifies a single instance of organized educational activity of any
kind. Course is thus a comprehensive term that can be used in the place of
more specific forms of courses, such as conferences, institutes, workshops,
seminars, lectures, or lecture series. A course is often described by the
following terms: credit, noncredit, degree, nondegree, day, evening, weekend,
on-campus, off-campus, independent study, media-based, professional, or
general. *Program* is used more generally than course because it can indicate
groups of courses or include noneducational activities. *Curricula* indicates an
articulated group of courses designed to meet a defined educational end.

Programmer or *program planner* is used in this book to indicate one who is
responsible for planning and organizing individual courses of instruction and
who is in some way responsible for the financial outcome of those courses. The
programmer may be someone whose only job is organizing courses, or someone
who is assigned, as one of his or her duties, to organize one course per year for
a museum. *Manager* or *CE manager* indicates anyone who has responsibility
for administering all or part of an organization that presents a number of
continuing education courses each year. Such a manager might be called
dean, chair, head, coordinator, administrator, director, or, more occasionally,
president, vice president, provost, or vice chancellor.

CE organization represents a wide variety of organizational entities that
present courses of instruction. A CE organization is most frequently a part of
a larger *parent* organization whose mission and activities include continuing
education.

In addition to terms related to CE, many technical terms used in financial
management, budgeting, finance, and economics are employed in this book.
All are defined in the text. These terms and their definitions also appear in a
glossary at the back of the book.

OBJECTIVES AND A REFERENCE GUIDE

This book is both a comprehensive treatment of theory and practice in CE
financial management and a handy reference useful to CE professionals in
their daily practice. The list of objectives given below refers the reader to the
sections of the book that address those objectives and provides a brief outline
of the book's organization.

Objectives of This Book

1. To describe how traditional financial management and budget theory
   can be used effectively in CE planning and administration. This objective refers to the basic concepts of accounting, budgeting, and financial

control as they apply to CE. These basics can be categorized as "static" and "dynamic." They are described throughout, but particularly in Chapters 2, 5, 6, and 9.

2. To explain why traditional theory and practice must be supplemented with new methods. Traditional methods fall short of meeting the present and future needs of CE professionals and limit their vision of the possible. Chapters 2, 3, and 4 examine the consequences of ignoring new methods when faced by new demands. This examination is then applied to the work of program planners in Chapter 7 and CE managers in Chapters 11 and 13.

3. To describe multidimensional budgeting and activity-based costing and how they apply to CE and to current popular trends in management theory. Multidimensional budgeting is introduced in Chapter 3 and then applied to the work of program planners in Chapter 7 and to organizational budgeting in Chapter 13. Activity-based costing is introduced in Chapter 4 and applied to the work of program planners in Chapter 7 and to the work of CE managers in Chapters 11 and 13.

4. To discuss the changes required in individual and organizational behavior when moving from traditional to new methods. These changes are described in Chapters 2, 3, and 4.

5. To explain how new technologies have expanded the information-gathering capability of CE managers and stimulated new thinking about ways information can be used and interpreted. Discussion of how CE managers can employ new technology is provided throughout the book.

6. To describe the specifics of CE financial management for program planners, managers, and parent institution administrators, and to present an integrated view of a comprehensive system designed to serve all managerial levels.

7. To address the financial management needs of all CE professionals in all institutional settings—large and small, self-supporting and subsidized, credit and noncredit, degree granting and nondegree granting, academic and nonacademic. While the experience upon which this book draws comes mainly from higher education, this book is based upon the premise that CE planning and organization have common elements in whatever institutional setting they occur. Museums, professional societies and associations, alumni groups, social and service organizations, health care institutions, and business organizations of all kinds commonly offer programs of continuing education. CE professionals in these organizations will find this book directly relevant to their work, and will be able to translate the examples and information provided to their local situation.

8. To describe the importance of the human side of financial management systems and the means for adjusting systems to human needs and concerns. Financial management systems are primarily human systems involving complex patterns of behavior and interpretation. This side of financial management must be given its full weight; the success of any system depends upon the willingness and the ability of people to use it effectively. This human element is particularly emphasized in Chapter 10, which describes common patterns of interaction and negotiation in the budget process.

9. To discuss such difficult and problematic aspects of CE management as pricing courses and services (Chapter 8), negotiating with faculty and other units of the parent organization (Chapter 8), evaluating long-term investments (Chapter 15), undertaking financial planning for distance education (Chapter 15), and using new instructional technologies (Chapter 15).

Organization of This Book

Using Financial Information in Continuing Education is organized in four parts. The four chapters of Part 1 establish a context for the application of CE financial management. Chapter 1 describes the most important issues facing CE administrators. Chapter 2 examines how traditional CE financial management techniques have been used and explains why they must now be supplemented with new techniques. Chapters 3 and 4 describe multidimensional budgeting and activity-based costing, respectively.

The four chapters of Part 2 define the basic terms and concepts of course budgeting and help program planners use these concepts to plan and offer courses and curricula. Chapter 5 defines and explains both the static and dynamic concepts traditionally used to describe course financial planning and behavior and introduces the important notion of portfolio management in program planning. Chapter 6 describes how programmers can prepare course budgets and the limitations of traditional concepts as they relate to program planning. Chapter 7 describes how multidimensional budgeting and activity-based costing can be usefully applied to the task of the program planner. Chapter 8 discusses special issues related to program planning, including course fees, promotion, cost alternatives, instructor compensation, overhead allocations, and cosponsorship arrangements.

The five chapters of Part 3 give CE managers (or those who aspire to such positions) an understanding of the theory and practice of financial management for the CE organization. Chapter 9 discusses the environment and operating context that shape CE financial management information systems and focuses on the important decisions that must be made in creating and maintaining a financial management system. Chapter 10 describes the application of traditional budget practices to CE financial management and presents a model for financial management and control. Chapter 11 first discusses the limitations of the traditional model and then presents the multidimensional model. Chapter 12 applies activity-based costing (ABC) to the CE organization and describes the possible uses of ABC for advancing the power and usefulness of financial information. Chapter 13 describes how to design and implement an ABC system.

The two chapters of Part 4 apply the theories and practices described earlier in the book to issues of current concern to CE professionals, particularly managers. Chapter 14 discusses how indirect costs (overhead) are defined, measured, allocated, and eliminated. Chapter 15 considers the implications of long-range financial planning with special consideration given to investments in equipment, facilities, or projects that go beyond one annual operating cycle. Chapter 15 also uses financial planning for distance education and the promise of new technologies to illustrate the decisions that must be made and to describe the information that logically supports good decision making.

This book also includes a glossary of terms, an extensive index, and numerous cross-references to help the practitioner locate specific information.

NOTE

[1] Gilman, Daniel Coit. Letter of resignation to the Board of Regents, 8 April 1874, quoted in William Warren Ferrier, *Origin and Development of the University of California* (Berkeley, CA: Sather Gate Bookstore, 1930, p. 359) and in Kathleen Rockhill, *Academic Excellence and Public Service* (New Brunswick, NJ: Transaction Books, 1983, p. 13).

PART ONE

• • • • • • • • • • •

The Context for Continuing Education Financial Management

Part 1 describes the most important issues now facing CE administrators, the essential elements of traditional CE financial management in light of the new demands to explain the limitations of such management, and the new financial management methods of multidimensional budgeting and activity-based costing. Both program planners and CE managers must understand the full context within which financial management systems operate. Both external and internal factors influence the form and specific details of financial management systems at all levels. After reading Part 1, you will be able to compare your own institutional setting and conception of important issues with those addressed in this book; describe the defining features and characteristics of traditional CE financial management systems; and understand the strengths and limitations of traditional CE financial management systems, the essentials and value of multidimensional budgeting, and the essentials and uses of activity-based costing.

CHAPTER 1

Current Issues and Institutional Settings

A s they go about their daily tasks, CE professionals face many complex issues that are common to most CE situations. The effectiveness of any financial management system can be judged by the ability of its users to respond to changes and new demands. For the purposes of the present discussion, the common set of issues and circumstances that bear upon CE organizations and their financial information management systems can be categorized as *external*, originating from forces outside the CE organization and its parent, and *internal*, coming from within the CE organization or from its relationship to the parent organization.

THE EXTERNAL CONTEXT

Today, many CE professionals see the market for continuing education as expanding and chaotic. The demand for college- and university-level continuing education, while difficult to measure, is clearly increasing, fueled by an expanded cohort of graduates of higher education institutions and by rapid changes in technology and knowledge that force people, especially highly educated people, into renewed formal learning. This demand has led to the entry into the field of a large number of new providers, including non-traditional and for-profit providers offering expanded choices in format and delivery to life-long learners. This expanding, somewhat disorderly, market has important consequences for the CE organization.

Increasing Competition

Most colleges and universities offer continuing education courses either through centralized CE divisions or through the schools and colleges that comprise the parent institution. When units of the same institution offer CE, competition often arises among them. In most urban areas, higher education institutions compete among themselves for local students. Increasingly, institutions are also competing with more distant CE providers by using technology or off-campus initiatives to offer courses to students in locations remote from the home campus.

The competitive landscape for CE is becoming more complicated as higher education institutions are joined by many other providers who see opportunities for both service and funding in CE offerings. Museums, for instance, are adopting CE as a central part of their mission to seek a new, more active role for their collections in the intellectual life of their communities. They also recognize, as do other providers, that CE is a good way to maintain positive relationships with their constituencies and to cultivate future donors. Most museums today have education divisions engaged in broad-based educational projects, including docent training, programs for school children, and conventional continuing education for adults.

Many of these same factors are behind the increase in CE sponsored by alumni groups, which see CE as a natural way to maintain relationships with graduates and friends of colleges and universities. Today, such groups do not include merely the alumni of higher education institutions; for instance, most large accounting firms, as part of their marketing efforts, have formed "alumni associations" of former employees. Professional societies, seeing opportunities to generate revenue and provide the kind of service that builds allegiance among members, have also embraced CE and entered the competition, as have community, service, fraternal, and health care organizations.

Perhaps most important, business and public organizations of all kinds sponsor or offer CE to their employees and to others. Businesses have always met most of the training needs of their own employees either through in-house training staff or by hiring outside consultants (trainers) on a contract basis to offer a particular course or set of courses. These internal or contracted employee-directed programs are usually narrowly focused on specific business-related goals. Businesses view themselves as best able to define those goals and to choose the kind of CE that will best meet them. But these days, training units designed to serve a particular business entity are seeking to sell their services to other businesses to cover some of the administrative costs associated with maintaining an in-house training staff.

Such increasing competition places the CE organization and its financial management system under increased stress. For any particular CE program, the chances of success are reduced, the life span is decreased, and the consequences of error are greater.

New Opportunities, New Markets

Expanding demand for CE presents CE professionals and their organizations with new opportunities in new markets. Evaluating these opportunities is a difficult task that must involve financial analysis. Success in serving new markets requires substantial investment in facilities, equipment, personnel, and systems, as well as relatively long lead times. New markets develop in many ways. Frequently, a new market for CE emerges from the availability or development of new technology, as in the field of geographical information systems. A licensing requirement, such as mandatory continuing professional education for psychologists, or a regulatory mandate, such as new environmental laws concerning asbestos removal from public buildings, can also lead to new CE markets. Such new markets often require changes in systems, organizational infrastructure, and, naturally, financial management.

Although contract training has been a part of the offerings of most CE organizations for a long time, the economic downturn of the late 1980s and early 1990s presented CE organizations with expanded opportunities in this area. Many large corporations, to cut costs, eliminated or sharply reduced their corporate training staffs at a time when the need for training or retraining their remaining workforce often increased. CE organizations responded by offering new services to businesses, including need assessments and specialized, focused programs. The professional development agenda for CE filled with contract training activities and conferences.

For many CE organizations, however, the promise of expanded contract activity was difficult to realize and required significant adjustments. The shift from attracting and serving individual students to obtaining contracts and serving organizational clients proved surprisingly difficult. Marketing efforts, which had typically featured direct mail and media, now had to concentrate on building and maintaining long-term relationships with client companies. Proposal writing now became an important element of the CE process, and the analysis of the client's needs and ability and willingness to pay became necessary. Clients, meanwhile, sought greater control over the content of courses, instructor selection, and course evaluation. The time frame for evaluating success of a CE product lengthened beyond the presentation of the course and its effect upon students to the survival of a positive relationship with the client from one project to the next. These new demands challenged CE managers and programmers to think in new ways about their activities and also strained existing financial information management systems.

Increased competition, the dispersal of urban populations, and the failure of the transportation infrastructure to handle the demands placed upon it have forced some CE organizations to expand geographically. Off-campus, satellite, and "downtown" CE centers have proliferated as CE organizations seek to bring courses to locations convenient to the homes, workplaces, and commute routes of their students. Although such centers expand the geographic market area of a CE organization, reaching previously unserved students, those students and the courses they take are rarely much different from the students and courses in the traditional geographic markets. Off-campus centers present the CE organization with particular problems of organizational structure and accountability, but only infrequently are they of such import to pose fundamental issues. Many CE organizations offer English language programs for international students, and some are expanding these offerings into new areas of professional continuing education. Taking advantage of the reputation the United States has for offering high quality education, they are targeting professionals in many fields for programs that combine English language instruction with technical subject matter. Serving the international marketplace requires a complex of responses from the CE organization. New programs have to be developed around the special needs of international students, including language proficiency, immigration and visa requirements, and personal financial concerns. New ways of marketing programs have to be used or invented. New and elaborate student services have to be developed and effectively provided, including immigration and academic counseling, transportation and greeting services, housing and meals, banking and financial services, entertainment, and a host of cultural adjustment services. Future investments in the program development, marketing, and student services infrastructure are likely to be substantial and require a new kind of thinking and planning.

Contract training and international programming are two examples of the far-reaching effects new opportunities and markets can have on the CE organization. New instructional technologies, which are discussed in the next section, are another example. In some colleges and universities, where CE degree programs have predominated, new opportunities in the professional and noncredit areas are beckoning. In institutions that have hitherto prohibited CE units from offering degree programs, institutional policy has shifted to allow them to do so. These opportunities have forced CE organizations and the professionals in them to change in their attitudes, work patterns, and even the structure of their enterprise.

Instructional Technologies

New instructional technologies and instructional delivery systems pose both opportunities and threats that CE organizations cannot ignore. These technologies can be placed in several categories. *Classroom technologies* enhance traditional classroom instruction; they typically involve multimedia presentations using computer technology. *Teleconferencing technologies* allow the extension of classroom instruction to two or more locations. Typically, a single instructor in a "send" location simultaneously teaches students at that site and at the "receive" sites. Two-way communication can now be achieved through a variety of technologies, and teleconferencing facilities are proliferating. *Desktop* or *workstation instructional technologies* allow individual students sitting at individual workstations, either in a classroom or in their own homes or offices, to receive instruction either in "real time" (that is, in direct, immediate contact with an instructor) or "asynchronously" (that is, without the need for both parties to be in simultaneous communication). Asynchronous instruction allows students to receive instruction at any time of the day or night and is therefore "self-paced." An extension of desktop instructional technologies may be coming soon, funded and developed by the entertainment industry. "Dial-a-movie" technology, which would allow home viewers the chance to select a particular video presentation from a giant media library, could also be used to "dial-a-course."

These new instructional technologies pose problems. The new classroom technologies are expensive and may require modifications to existing facilities. Few instructors are trained to use them effectively, although their number is growing as the technology becomes more user friendly. Because the use of these new technologies is framed by the traditional classroom and relies on instructor skill rather than specialized skills, their use is unlikely to seriously impact the CE organization, save for the finding of funds.

Teleconferencing technologies are much more expensive and often require dedicated classroom or studio space. They demand the application of specialized technical skills and often require instructor training. Logistical arrangements for the receive sites are often expensive. Instructors must devote more time to planning their courses and must adjust the material to the new medium. These new technologies challenge CE financial information systems to provide information about their real and full costs, including the cost of necessary equipment and facilities.

While teleconferencing technologies can have a significant effect on the CE organization, they usually do not alter the character of the instruction given or the relationship of the instructor to the institution. Desktop technologies, on the other hand, threaten to revolutionize both instruction and the relationship of the instructor to the student and to the sponsoring institution. Production of "courseware" for desktop technologies is extremely expensive and usually requires highly specialized technical facilities and a team effort from the course instructor, an instructional designer, and various technical specialists. The high up-front cost of course development typically means that the course must be used by large numbers of students.

The new technologies threaten the current operations of all CE organizations in that they have the potential to allow other new providers of CE to take

over current markets. Also, the adoption of these technologies raises important issues in finance, instruction, instructor relations, compensation, training, evaluation, and student services. CE professionals must face these
problems because new technologies and their promise are an undeniable and
prominent feature of the external environment we are and will be facing.

Many more external factors could be listed here, including the important
effect of economic conditions, the globalization and internationalization of
world economies, the declining state of public finance, political influences,
and environmental issues. Compiling an exhaustive listing of these features is
the work of "environmental scanners" who offer comprehensive and current
views on the nature and predicted effect of these large-scale influences on our
work. The external features listed in this section—expanding markets, the
rush of new opportunities and markets, increased competition among providers, and the opportunity and threat of new technologies—have been selected
because they are features common to many CE organizations and are most
directly relevant to the financial management of CE organizations and thus to
the discussion that follows.

THE INTERNAL CONTEXT

Because CE organizations take such diverse forms and are part of such diverse
parent institutions, it is dangerous to make generalizations about the internal
situations and issues they face. However, judging from the current literature
and from an examination of the topics featured at annual conferences, the
concerns relevant to the subject of this book fall into several main categories.

Parent Institutional Financial Imperatives

In most institutional settings in which CE is an important component, the
parent institution is experiencing unprecedented financial stress. In higher
education, colleges and universities are facing increasing costs and fewer and
more pressured sources of income. One of the many strategies these institutions are using to cope with the situation is to seek more revenue from the
"users" of the services they provide. College tuition has increased rapidly in
the last few years as students and their parents are asked to shoulder a larger
proportion of the costs of instruction. Other forms of user fees, including
ticket prices at athletic events and transcript and library fees, are also increasing. CE "users" are also being tapped. Over the last decade, CE organizations
have been moving steadily toward a self-supporting financial status. In a
typical pattern, direct subsidies of CE are eliminated, and the CE organization
is then asked (told) to assume ever increasing charges from the parent
institution as more services used by CE are identified. When this fee for
service pattern has reached its limits, the parent asks the CE unit to produce

an excess over its costs to contribute to the general fund or some other fund unrelated to the CE function. In effect, this practice taxes the CE student to pay for other services performed by the parent.

Increased recharges and direct taxes on CE are only the most visible effects of the hard fiscal times parent organizations are experiencing. The CE function is likely to be affected by many other cost-cutting efforts of parent institutions. Reduced library hours may inconvenience CE students who have to use libraries in the evenings and on weekends, increased parking rates can affect CE enrollments, and a reduction in force in the accounting department may cause a delay in the issuance of CE instructor payroll checks.

All these effects of parental fiscal difficulty have important ramifications for the CE financial management information system. Recharges from the parent require monitoring, systems of taxation need to be argued and rationalized, and the costs of making up for decreased services from the parent have to be weighed against the costs of providing services at more acceptable levels. For instance, at one major university, the costs of campus administrative computing were being recharged to the CE organization pro rata on the basis of total expenses. However, a significant portion of campus administrative computing costs was associated with student financial aid, a function not used by CE. The CE organization successfully argued that its charges should be reduced. In another case, the CE unit was being taxed 5 percent of its total income each year. Included in its income were significant "pass-through" costs created by including in the fees charged to CE students nontuition amounts to cover the cost of transportation, food, and accommodations for students on travel study programs. These costs "passed through" the income account on their way to the vendors of the services. The CE unit was allowed to reduce its income bases for these costs, thereby reducing its tax. An illustration of reduced services from the parent is the CE unit that had to set up its own, in-house accounts receivable function because the parent could not follow up in collecting overdue amounts. The CE business manager calculated that the cost of hiring an accounts receivable clerk was less than the bad debts that would occur without prompt and constant monitoring of the activity. All these examples involved using the financial information system of a CE organization in unusual ways.

Organizational Change

The financial pressure on many parent institutions is also the cause of another common concern to CE professionals—organizational stability and change. Often this issue is described as the "centralization vs. decentralization" debate. In centralized provisions, only one unit within the parent offers CE. In colleges and universities, such units might be called "University Extension" or "Continuing Education." In decentralized provisions, more than one operating unit of the parent offers CE. Financial pressures are a threat to either organizational form. Centralized extension operations in colleges and universities face threats from professional schools seeking to generate excess revenue from CE at the same time that they serve and maintain relationships with their professional constituencies. These schools argue that their subject-matter expertise and their ability to cultivate an external clientele will pay dividends not only to the professional school but also to the institution as a whole. This notion is consistent with the academic culture of universities, which normally vests academic control of courses and curricula with faculty working within the departmental structure of the academy.

Decentralized provisions also face challenges. Such provisions are usually small and fragmented, serving some external constituencies well and others not at all. They are often dependent on the efforts of faculty members who are busy with other tasks. As the assignment for CE rotates among faculty in the typical academic pattern, decentralized provisions have difficulty maintaining continuity of offerings. The programs offered by decentralized units tend to reflect more the interests of the faculty than the needs of the market. Decentralized provisions of CE frequently cannot take advantage of economies of scale in the marketing, registration, and course presentation functions. The parent has more difficulty controlling and coordinating decentralized provisions, an important consideration in so visible an activity as CE. These factors argue for greater centralization of a CE function.

In either case, change places stress on the management information systems employed for the CE function. Elaborate plans involving financial projections are often necessary and "what if" scenarios need to be developed and effectively provided, stretching most management information systems beyond their limits.

Diversification of Function

Because the CE organization is the most market-oriented, flexible, and responsive part of the parent institution, it is often called upon to administer new initiatives and projects or functions that do not fit the established organizational structure of the parent. Paradoxically, few CE organizations are devoted exclusively to CE and its directly related activities. They often administer a wide variety of activities, from reentry programs to television stations to conference centers. In colleges and universities, the CE organization is then likely to play an important role in the administration and introduction of new instructional technology. These diverse functions have diverse funding sources, with different requirements for accounting and reporting. Financial and management information systems developed for the CE function may not be suited to the management of these other activities. This diversity often results in fragmented approaches to budgeting and financial control, straining how well CE managers are able to obtain, let alone understand and interpret, financial information.

Special Financial Management Needs

The financial and management information requirements of CE organizations are often different from those of the parent institution. They are often self-supporting and must be managed in the way most businesses are managed. They have to be more market-oriented and more cost conscious than most operating units of the parent institution. Colleges and universities follow fund accounting principles, which are designed to assure appropriate use of a designated sum of money, but which frequently inhibit sound CE management and control. In an exreme but common example, the parent institution establishes an expense budget for the CE organization and then places all the revenue generated from CE into a general fund. This dissociation of income and expense budgets creates confusion and inhibits sound decision making. For instance, a successful period during which enrollments exceeded the budget might require spending in excess of the expense budget at the same time that revenue is also exceeding expectations. This "false negative" illustrates the difference between fund accounting and revenue generation accounting. Under fund accounting, the purpose of the budget is to allocate funds appropriately, and the financial system makes sure that operating units do not spend more than their budgets allow.

Self-supporting units, on the other hand, must generate the funds before or as they are spent. Under revenue generation principles, the budget defines and sets revenue generation goals and allocates expenses in accordance with those goals. Financial and management information systems are designed to help managers make the many decisions inherent in generating revenue and allocating resources to the best effect. Because they are dedicated to such different purposes, parent and CE accounting and financial management systems are difficult to reconcile. Most CE organizations establish their own systems outside the parent system, but compatible with the parent system in the important areas of reporting and budgeting. Because the CE organization gets little help from its parent in this important area, considerable responsibility falls on CE managers, who have to rely on their own knowledge and skill or that of members of their staff to develop and maintain an effective management information system.

Strategic Planning and New Managerial Paradigms

Another important and common aspect of the internal context is the prevalence of strategic planning and what might be called new managerial methods (e.g., TQM, reengineering, team building). These managerial approaches may be imposed on the CE organization by the parent or adopted and endorsed by the management of a CE organization itself. Most parent institutions employ some form of planning in which the CE organization must participate, and strategic planning is essential for the internal leadership and guidance of even small CE units. An effective management information system should both support and be an extension of the planning process. The system should not only be capable of recording, monitoring, and reporting historical data, it should also be able to project and predict future results.

New managerial paradigms also have significant impact on the structure and development of management information systems. As organization structures and reporting relationships change from a reliance on defining individual responsibilities through a hierarchical structure to shared responsibility through a team or collective process, new system structures have to be developed. For instance, the results of teams operating across functions (interdepartmentally) need to be identified and reported. Financial operations need to be segmented in several ways simultaneously to generate the information needed to evaluate the organization in several dimensions. For example, under traditional management, the financial results of a particular course could be attributed to a particular programmer. New management might want to identify that same course not only with the programmer who produced it, but also as part of management's strategic plan to expand into a new geographical or subject area, or as part of a team effort to increase interdisciplinary programming. These new management paradigms demand that more information be delivered in different forms and at different levels of detail to more people in the organization. Information systems designed to serve traditional management philosophies cannot simply be expanded to address the needs of the new paradigms; often they must be completely reengineered. CE management must set specifications and expectations for these new systems.

THE GOAL OF DYNAMIC STABILITY

The above listing of elements comprising the external and internal contexts for CE management information systems is, of course, incomplete and selective. The issues that face CE organizations can be viewed and described in many ways, and virtually every issue has financial implications and implications for the form and functioning of the management information system. The assignment to CE of multiple and sometimes conflicting goals and the breakdown of traditional hierarchical structures, without a clearly defined and generally accepted scheme for establishing responsibility within the organization, increases the level of complexity that management information systems must address. The increasing pace of change in the external environment combined with the wider use of planning models that require predictions of the future challenge CE professionals to develop systems that are "dynamically stable."

The concept of dynamic stability was developed by Boynton and Victor in 1991 and applied to information systems by Boynton in 1993.[1] Dynamically stable organizations are "capable of serving the widest range of customers and changing product demands (dynamic), while building on long-term process capabilities and the collective knowledge of the organization (stable)."[2] The key to becoming dynamically stable is the creation of a stable base of information and of information-processing capabilities that are flexible, efficient, and useful over a long period of time. Dynamically stable systems require only small modifications to respond even to significant changes in the operations or structure of the organization; they are dynamic in that they are useful in a rapidly changing environment.

Upcoming chapters will present a broad outline of a dynamically stable CE management information system that can be used in a wide range of institutional settings and, once adopted, easily modified to meet new circumstances. Chapter 2 will describe the traditional CE information system and some important basic concepts, as well as the limitations of this traditional model. It will also set the context for later chapters on two important aspects of the dynamically stable mode—multidimensional budgeting and activity-based costing.

NOTES

[1] Andrew C. Boynton and Bart Victor, "Beyond Flexibility: Building and Managing the Dynamically Stable Organization," *California Management Review* 34, no. 1 (Fall 1991): 53–66; Andrew C. Boynton, "Achieving Dynamic Stability Through Information Technology," *California Management Review* 35, no. 2 (Winter 1993): 58–77.
[2] Boynton, "Achieving Dynamic Stability," p. 58.

CHAPTER 2

Traditional Financial Management in CE Organizations

The term "traditional" is used throughout this book in conjunction with "financial management" or "management information systems" to refer to a broad set of conceptions and practices used today in CE organizations to provide financial information to CE professionals and, through the use and analysis of that information, to help those professionals plan and control operations. While significant variation exists among CE organization management information systems, common patterns and underlying assumptions can be discerned. A listing of these commonalities thus defines how the term "traditional" is used here.

THE ELEMENTS OF TRADITIONAL SYSTEMS

Traditional CE management information systems are designed to serve common *management philosophies* and *responsibility structures* through the use of *budgets* and *standard reporting processes* using the CE course (or a defined grouping of courses) as the *cost* or *budget object*. Each of these elements is discussed below.

Prevailing Management Philosophies

Traditional CE systems are designed to serve a management philosophy called "management by objectives" where the objective is singular, all-important, and defined in monetary terms. In traditional systems, the objective for a particular programmer or operating unit might be "revenue should exceed expenses by $20,000," or "don't spend more than you can make (or are given)." The management by objectives philosophy and the behaviors it requires and reinforces in individuals persist despite the best efforts of CE management to adopt and implement other management philosophies (e.g., TQM). The persistence of the objective of traditional systems is the result of several factors. First, until now, no other systems have been fully developed and described. Many traditional systems have been modified to address issues and circumstances created by the new management philosophies, but it is difficult to effect a modification complete enough to overcome both the persuasive power of the single financial objective and force of habit. Second, a single, well-defined financial objective is an easily and intuitively understood measurement of effectiveness and is, or seems, less subjective than other measures. Third, most new philosophies do not entirely eliminate the need to set clear financial goals, so there is always good reason for preserving a system that provides ways to measure progress toward such goals. Finally, radically changing financial management information systems is expensive and highly disruptive, and the need for change is often unrecognized, even by managers who are most eager to adopt new strategies. All these factors weigh against change and preserve and support the maintenance of traditional systems. Thus, traditional systems are partly defined by their inflexibility and resistance to change.

Traditional management information systems are also designed to support the management technique called *management by exception*. This technique directs scarce managerial time and attention to "exceptional" conditions where deviation (usually negative) from expectations is significant. In traditional systems, the budget usually sets expectations and the financial reporting and feedback process discloses exceptions.

Management by objectives and management by exception work together and can be easily supported by traditional methods. Clearly defined objectives are set for individuals and units of the organization and management's attention is directed to opportunities or dangers in an orderly way. The compatibility of these management philosophies with traditional methods presents a logic that is hard to dispute. However, both the management philosophies and the traditional methods that support them have limitations.

Monolithic Responsibility Structures

Traditional CE financial management information systems are designed to serve the dominant *responsibility structure* in the organization. This structure consists of a formal system of assigning and monitoring responsibility by segmenting the organization into *responsibility centers*, each of which is assigned a particular task and for which an individual (or, less often, a group) is assigned managerial responsibility. The responsibility structure serves three purposes.

- To divide an organization into smaller parts so that the work of the organization can be divided into more manageable steps
- To assign authority, resources, and responsibility for success to specified individuals or groups
- To permit objective evaluation of individuals or groups against clearly defined goals

CE organizations commonly use two kinds of responsibility centers. In *cost centers,* managers have responsibility for controlling costs but not for generating income. Cost centers in CE organizations include the registration office, the director's office, and the business office. These departments are sometimes also called *service departments.* In *profit centers,* managers are concerned with controlling costs and generating income; in a business environment, profit center managers also seek to maximize the excess of income over costs. Self-supporting segments of CE organizations are generally profit centers. These units are sometimes also called *programming* or *operating* departments. A CE organization might have its program development and presentation function divided into three profit centers—credit programs, noncredit programs, and summer sessions—each with its own budget target. Most traditional systems also allow cost centers to become profit centers through a *transfer pricing system.* Under transfer pricing, a service center establishes prices for the services provided and charges users (i.e., other departments in the same organization) according to the pricing schedule. Effective traditional management information systems provide managers of both cost and profit centers with the information they need to accomplish the objectives of the centers they manage, although, as we will see, in a relatively limited way.

Traditional systems, however, are not well suited to a third kind of responsibility center that is becoming increasingly important to CE organizations, the *investment center.* The objective of the investment center is to measure and maximize the return on investment for a defined group of assets. CE organizations involved in the management of an endowment or other asset-based funds may have investment centers. CE organizations can and should create investment centers whenever significant resources are directed toward a particular end. A computer lab or a downtown center, through lab charges or room rental fees, could become an investment center—the return on the investment could, and probably should, be calculated. Traditional systems usually are not well suited for keeping track of total investments in such facilities, particularly when the funding for establishing such a facility comes from several sources. Traditional systems usually cannot keep track of total income derived from the use of such a facility, particularly when the use extends over several years.

Traditional systems are designed to serve the dominant responsibility structure, generally as illustrated by the organization chart. The budgeting and financial reporting scheme is generally based upon the responsibility structure, and the reward system for individuals in the organization is usually based in part on the financial results the system reports for the component units. However, traditional systems are usually not well suited to the planning, controlling, and monitoring of financial results from outside the responsibility structure. For instance, in the example given above of a CE organization divided into credit programs, noncredit programs, and summer session profit centers, the traditional system could probably provide detailed and regular information about revenue and expenses for the credit program unit but would probably have difficulty providing management with a summary of income and expense for programs conducted in the new downtown center. While the operating costs of the center would usually be available, the program information might be difficult to accumulate since responsibility for programming at the center might reside in several programming departments. Even if such information were available, it might not be particularly useful or interesting to anyone but top management since no one person is likely to be responsible for making programming successful at the center.

So far, we have described the traditional system in terms of the internal responsibility structure of the CE organization. However, traditional systems are also defined by the responsibility the CE organization bears to the parent organization. Even the most independent systems must serve to fulfill whatever reporting and accountability requirements are imposed by the parent, no matter how irrelevant such information might be to the CE organization. We will next examine the influence of the parent on CE management information systems.

The Primacy of Budgets and the Logic of Reporting Methods

In traditional systems, the operating budget, supported by an appropriately structured financial monitoring and reporting system, is the primary instrument of management. Again, in effective systems, the budget is aligned with the responsibility structure. In the newer methods, budgets are also important instruments, but are used in different ways. Because budgeting is an important aspect of our time, we will begin with the following comprehensive description of the purposes, types, theories, and effects of budgets.

Definitions and Purposes of Budgets

Budgeting is a process for planning the future operations of an organization and then systematically comparing those plans with actual results. A budget is a written expression of the organization plan, expressed in dollar terms and used to communicate the plan to those responsible for carrying it out. It also becomes the standard by which the performance of the organization and its parts will be judged.

The notion that budgeting is a *process* and that the budget document is only one product of that process will be repeated often in this book. No one step of the process can be isolated from any other part, and the process is continuous. Once the written document is produced, it "lives" for the whole budget period, guiding and controlling actions and being compared with actual results. After this "feedback" comparison, the budget document serves as a basis for the formation of a budget for the following budget cycle. Robert Anthony, the author of several textbooks on this subject, describes the process as beginning with budgeting and proceeding through the stages of operating, measuring, reporting, and finally "programming"—further planning in the light of recent events and conditions.

Budgets serve many purposes simultaneously. Most of these purposes are related and overlapping, although some may conflict. Budgets often embody *goals*, or expressions of desired future results. By developing *standards of performance*, and becoming part of the sanction and reward system, budgets can be *motivators* for employees; the existence of standards of performance, consistently and continuously maintained, tends to improve morale and bring employees more into sympathy with the goals of the organization. Budgets may also become tacitly understood *contracts* between upper and lower hierarchies of an organization; the lower member agrees that the budget represents an achievable goal and the upper member agrees that achievement of the goal will be rewarded. Clearly, budgets are important in the responsibility structure—they communicate the extent and nature of the assigned responsibility, and they provide a measure by which performance can be evaluated.

As plans, budgets are also *projections of future activity*. To be effective, a plan must be realistic enough to be carried out. But the idea of the budget as a projection can conflict with the notion of the budget as a goal. Even appropriately set goals do not always result in realistic projections, especially when goals are set high with the knowledge that not every part of the organization will be able to live up to expectations.

Budgets also serve as a *means of communication*, a way for the parts of an organization to combine their experience to produce a systematic prediction of future events. Often the annual budget hearing is the only formal contact between different levels of the organization and the only time when some difficult problems may be exposed. The analysis of actual or potential deviations from the budget also often sparks important communication. Because they relate to the reward system, potential sources of deviation from the budget are likely to surface early, allowing management to make changes that will avoid negative effects.

Because they help management control an organization, budgets are also part of the organization's *control structure*. They allow managers to pinpoint problems and opportunities, and thus facilitate the management by exception philosophy.

Budgets also serve the planning process by *coordinating functions*. If programmers in the Business and Management Department have decided to double course offerings in the next year, they will need to tell the registration office to prepare for the (hoped for) onslaught of students, the promotion department to determine how to attract new students, and the person who schedules classrooms to find more space. Whenever the actions of one organizational segment have an impact on the work of another, coordination must take place. Exposure to the budget can help provide this coordination.

Most CE organizations are part of larger institutions and must prepare budgets in the form demanded by those institutions. However, the primary mission of those larger institutions is usually not continuing education, and the format of the institutional budget often does not serve the functions of the CE organization. For this reason, the CE enterprise will often need to prepare a budget of its own in a format designed to meet its particular needs.

All these purposes of budgeting should become clearer as you read through the examples and explanations in this book. Because budgets operate in the real world, contending with practical difficulties and serving practical purposes, your challenge will be to translate the theoretical ideals and illustrative examples presented here to your own concrete and unique situation.

Types of Budgets

Most CE organizations have a hierarchy of budgets. Those prepared for the smallest organizational subunits are combined with the budgets of successively larger units until the whole organization is included in the overall budget document. The discussion of traditional CE management information systems reflects this hierarchical pattern. In traditional methods, course budgets are the lowest order of budgeting; they are added together to form a budget for each programmer. The separate budgets for all programmers in the same department are in turn added together to form the department program budget. These department budgets are finally added together (along with budgets from service departments) to form the budget for the CE organization. In most situations, this organization budget will be combined with budgets from other parts of the parent institution to arrive at the institutional budget. The master budget is the highest order of budgeting, the last and most inclusive budget.

Format Types. Budgets are sometimes classified by format. *Program budgets* (and here "program" is used in its broadest sense to include an organized activity of any kind) list the income and expenses projected for a particular endeavor or, more commonly, a particular responsibility center (organizational segment). A *project budget* is a special kind of program budget for the completing of a particular task that may or may not span more than one operating period. Grants and contracts from the state and federal governments are examples of project budgets.

A *line item budget* lists the categories of income and expenses (sometimes referred to as *natural classifications*) without reference to the program or purpose with which they are associated. For instance, a line item budget might have all instructional staff payroll costs for the organization listed on one line, whereas a program budget would divide instructional costs among the various departments. Line item budgets are common in institutional budgeting, but are not particularly useful to managers of CE organizations.

Purpose Types. Budgets are also commonly designated by their primary purpose. *Operating budgets* cover the broadest range of an organization's activity and deal with income and expense related to day-to-day operations. *Balance sheet budgets,* which are not commonly used in CE organizations, project the value of assets, liabilities, and residual equity or fund balance of an organization.

Capital budgets are plans for the generation and expenditure of funds devoted to such capital items as real estate, equipment, and other assets that are expected to return value to the organization over an extended period, usually several budget years. Decisions about capital expenditures usually have important long-term significance to an organization and must be planned carefully. CE organizations do have occasion to acquire capital items, although often the budgeting for the expenditure is not complex enough to warrant a full budget treatment. Some aspects of capital budgeting are discussed in Chapter 15.

Cash budgets project the flow of cash into and out of an organization. They are designed to make sure that the organization does not run out of money to pay for its current obligations and that excess funds are invested for maximum returns. Although many CE organizations, as part of larger organizations, are not directly concerned with cash budgeting, the CE unit will have to be aware of its impact on cash flows as cash management techniques become increasingly important to parent organizations.

Cash budgets are one category of *financial budgets*, which are concerned with financing or sources of funding for an organization. Funding sources may be income from tuition and fees, subsidies from parent institutions, and so on. They may also include borrowing, gifts, and the recovery on accounts and notes receivable. Financial budgets contrast with *expenditure budgets*, which concentrate on where and how resources will be spent, ignoring where the funds come from and not explicitly calculating the effect on cash balances.

Most CE budgets are expenditure budgets; however, self-support organizations must pay attention to sources of funds.

Other Types. Budgets are sometimes categorized according to the timing of their preparation or the method underlying their evaluation of results. *Rolling* or *continuous budgets* incorporate frequent adjustments and the addition of future budgeted periods on a regular basis. Using a common form of rolling budget, one large university extension organization requires department managers to submit a budget each month covering the next 12 months of operations. In each monthly budget, the monthly budgets previously submitted may be updated and the new twelfth month added. *Flexible* or *variable budgets* establish standards for an operating entity over a range of possible volumes of activity. *Fund budgeting* takes place within the context of fund accounting and is designed to assure that individually established funds are used for the express purposes for which they were established. Fund accounting and, therefore, fund budgeting are pervasive and unavoidable in continuing education, and they often make life difficult for continuing educators by restricting their options.

Clearly, there are many types of budgets and many labels for budgets. The vocabulary of budgeting is not precise; each organization has its own names for budgets, and these names will be meaningful only within their own specific institutional context. To understand what a particular budget is intended to do, you must look beyond the label to the substance.

Theories of Traditional Budgeting

Multidimensional budgeting is presented in this book as a new method, but is in many ways really an adaptation of traditional budgeting with some important differences. Multidimensional budgeting and the differences between it and traditional budgeting are described in Chapter 3. The following discussion concentrates on traditional budgeting and on some universal aspects of budgeting that define both multidimensional budgeting and traditional methods.

Budgeting is a practical task that should occur within a theoretical framework. Many theories about the budgeting process have been formulated and named, frequently with acronyms. Knowing the meaning of these acronyms and something about what each theory involves is important to an overall understanding of budgeting.

Historical Budgeting. Because most recent theories were developed to correct defects of earlier forms of budgeting, a knowledge of the earlier forms is necessary to understand later forms.

The simplest and earliest form of budget is the line item budget, a simple list of income and expenditure categories assigned to a line on a page. Over the years, budgets have developed two parts, the *base* and the *increments*. Each established operating department receives funding for its basic operating functions and established programs for each budget period. Departments then vie for any additional (incremental) funding that might be available to the organization. Line item budget strategies thus revolve around the defense of the base from reduction and pleas or arguments for the funding of new programs from incremental funds.

Incremental funding is important because it usually becomes a part of the base as a new program is established and then requires additional funding in successive years. Typically, each department develops its own notion of what its "fair share" of incremental funding should be. Because of the importance of these incremental decisions, early forms of budgeting became known as *incremental budgeting*, and subspecies of budgets began to be known by the manner in which incremental allocations could be requested. *Open-ended budgeting* places no restrictions on the additional amount of funding that might be requested. *Quota methods* place limits how much can be requested over the base. *Alternative level budgeting* asks managers to submit budget requests assuming funding at a certain level above or below the base, say increases of 5 or 10 percent.

Incremental budgeting focuses management's attention on important changes in departmental focus and effort. It also involves little computational time and effort, since the bulk of the budget, represented by the base, is automatically defined and easily calculated. However, incremental budgeting suppresses the review of established programs, which might, by virtue of being hidden in the base, continue to be funded long after they are useful. To correct this problem, the concept of *zero-based budgeting* (ZBB) was developed. ZBB requires that the entire budget be justified for every budget period and that the value of every program be reviewed. Although laudable in its purposes, ZBB was largely a failure because it required too much time and effort.

Program Budgeting. Because early budgeting concentrated on line item control, with such categories as maintenance, payroll, and supplies, it sometimes lost track of the underlying purposes the expenditures were supposed to serve. Program budgeting requires that the budget presentation be made in such a way that a desired end result—say, the education of 100 students in the principles of financial accounting—can be related to the costs of achieving that result. With this kind of presentation, management can more easily relate ends to means and make comparisons and judgments between programs. President Lyndon Johnson required all federal agencies to submit program budgets under a system known as the *Program Planning and Budgeting System* (PPBS). This system is now considered a failure because it was expensive to prepare, and it increased dissension and discord between program staffs, who began to see each other as rivals for the same pot of money. This latter problem was less prominent in incremental budgeting, where every program was assured at least its base.

The failure of program budgeting led to the development of a number of other methods based on the same premises. *Management by objectives* (MBO), which was discussed earlier, was one of those methods. Other methods applied the "systems approach" to budgeting. Such systems approaches as the *program evaluation and review technique* (PERT) and the *management information systems* (MIS) concept, which concentrates on the kind and format of information that managers need to manage, embody much of the original program budgeting idea. All these systems use the same order of steps in the process of managing that Strother and Klus (1982)[1] have summarized in the following questions:

1. What do we want to do?
2. Why do we want to do it?
3. How will we do it?
4. How will we know whether we have succeeded?

Most organizations must adopt some form of the program budgeting system; otherwise, the management task becomes too chaotic, and too many parts of the organization remain unexamined. As described below, traditional CE budgeting is really a modified program budgeting approach. Because the nature of CE is to produce programs, the most obvious example of which is the course, program budgeting is the most natural form of budgeting for the CE organization, even if the parent institution is still enmeshed in earlier budgeting forms.

The primary difference between traditional budgeting and multidimensional budgeting is that traditional budgeting is based on only one way of categorizing the CE program, a scheme usually consistent with the organization's responsibility structure. As we will see in Chapter 9, one of the most important decisions that must be made in developing a traditional budgeting system is the choice of the primary organizational segmentation scheme. Of course, CE organizations can be segmented in many ways. For instance, the academic programs might be divided according to the responsibility structure or they might be divided and kept track of by subject matter groupings, course format types, course credit classifications (i.e., credit, noncredit, graduate, and undergraduate), geographical location, time of day offered, or any number of other bases. Although database information technology allows CE organizations to capture and report information in many ways at the same time, the technology is used mainly to gather information rather than to serve the budget process. Rarely is it used to fulfill the purposes of budgeting described above, to control, motivate, predict, communicate, or coordinate. Forcing CE managers to choose only one segmentation scheme from a number of attractive possibilities is a major limitation of traditional CE budgeting.

Budgets and Human Beings

Aaron Wildavsky defines budgeting as "the translation of financial resources into human purposes,"[2] and characterizes the budget as the heart of the political process. Although Wildavsky was referring to the federal budget and national politics, his statements hold true for budgeting in any organization, including those concerned with continuing education. We must never over-look the human factor when reviewing budgeting techniques and the steps of the budget process. Budgets are devised and carried out by people, and they cannot succeed in any of their purposes without the understanding and support of those involved in the process.

Budgets are part of the formal organizational process, and their form, content, and manner and timing of preparation are usually prescribed by formal policy. The annual budget hearing is a formal interaction between management levels. At each level of budget preparation, the process of negotiation, of discussing the fairness and achievability of targets and the resources needed to reach them, is likely to take place in a more or less formal manner.

Budgets, however, also have elements of informal interaction ranging from the most cooperative and constructive to the most petty, selfish, and destruc-tive. Budgets can be used to motivate, control, communicate with, coordinate, and punish or reward people. Much of the budgeting process is thus unavoid-ably nonscientific, subjective, and political. Although the budget is a docu-ment filled with numbers that represent a supposedly objective view of the financial target for an organization, the numbers got there through a process involving much discussion and personal opinion. When actual results are compared with budget projections, deviations will also be viewed subjectively.

Because budgets can be used in so many ways, one's view of budgeting will depend on one's experience with the process. Unfortunately, views are often negative, seeing budgets as, at best, necessary evils. Programmers often resent having to prepare course budgets, and directors dread the annual budget hearing with their superiors. Careful planning is needed to diminish these negative feelings. The process by which the budget is prepared and adminis-tered should seek to discourage distorted behavior that may impede achieve-ment of the goals and objectives of the organization.

Excessively strict adherence to budgets is a common example of distorted behavior. Budgets are estimates, sometimes accurate and sometimes not. They are based upon assumptions about future conditions. When the estimates are inaccurate or when the assumptions prove unfounded, continued adherence to a budget may not make sense. Managers who feel they must spend their entire expense budget even when savings are possible are probably engaging in behavior distorted by a budget system that penalizes efficiency by reducing future budget allocations on the basis of lower actual expenditures. The rules of this budget game should be altered to reward efficient behavior.

Distorted behavior is also likely to occur when budgets are used primarily to monitor or control employees. Employees and managers who have little to say in the budget process and who believe that the real purpose of the budget is to determine who is not performing properly are likely to begin "playing the budget game" to avoid getting into trouble rather than to advance the organization's goals. The imposition of budgets, especially unrealistic and unachievable budgets, is also likely to produce distorted behavior in the form of hostility and frustration toward the organization and the budget process.

Used imaginatively, however, budgets can facilitate the human interactions involved in guiding organizations. They can help resolve conflict by providing an objective basis for evaluating alternative actions. Budgets should be useful to everyone associated with them. The programmer should be able to review a course budget to help decide whether to give the course in the first place, whether to continue it, or whether to repeat it next term or next year. The director should view budgeting as a integral part of planning and directing the organization.

The Course as Cost/Budget Object

A *cost object* is a term used in managerial accounting to designate that entity (object) for which costs are to be accumulated. Similarly, a *budget object* is that thing for which a budget is prepared. Often these terms refer to the same object—cost accounting systems are often constructed to support and reinforce budget processes. For instance, in CE, one segment, say the credit programs unit, might be both a cost and a budget object. In traditional CE management information systems, the individual course is the most obvious and probably the best cost and budget object since it is the smallest logical segment of the CE operation. Of course, not all CE organizations have chosen the course as a cost object, either because they do not have the capacity to track costs in detail or because they have decided that the cost of tracking them exceeds the value of the information obtained. The advantage of choosing the course as the basic cost object is that it allows for flexibility in developing plans for more complex or comprehensive management systems. Financial information about courses can be aggregated in different ways to answer different questions. For instance, we might want to find out how much revenue we obtained from courses at the downtown center as well as how our courses in business did throughout the service area. If we collected information about revenue only in larger lumps, using, say, the program department as the cost object, we would never be able to answer such questions. Using the course as the budget object also helps in other ways. If we, for instance, want to know how much we will have to charge and how many enrollments we will need to cover our costs, and how much we will be able to pay our instructors, budget objects at higher levels cannot help us much.

Although the course is the most flexible cost/budget object for traditional CE management information systems, it focuses attention on the product (the course) rather than on the process of producing courses. An underlying problem posed by products as cost objects is the extent to which allocation of indirect (overhead) costs is obscured. Since indirect costs are by definition those costs that cannot be attributed directly to a cost object, some method must be devised to add these costs to the cost object in order to "fully cost" the cost object. Arguments over the fairness of these methods and the "distorted behavior" that occurs as people try to adjust the system to their advantage are the usual results of most allocation schemes. We will examine this issue in detail in later chapters.

LIMITATIONS OF TRADITIONAL METHODS

Although some of the limitations cited above arise out of natural trade-offs made in systems design, and well-designed traditional systems can provide accurate, timely information to CE managers, some inherent, hidden, and large-scale difficulties can occur with traditional methods.

First, traditional methods are based on paper-oriented, low technology thinking that conditions the form and content of the information being generated. Modern spreadsheet software programs combined with database programs have dramatically expanded the capacity of organizations to capture and report information in a variety of formats and combinations. Rarely is this capacity fully exploited. Traditional thinking and accepted patterns of information gathering and display still dominate CE management information systems.

Pre-computer thinking also conditions expectations about the timeliness of information generation. For instance, year-end closing cycles for most universities are typically six to eight weeks long or even longer. CE organization annual reports are typically issued from November to January, five to seven months after the close of the academic and fiscal year. CE managers frequently must wait weeks or even months to find out the actual costs of a particular course, or they have to rely for this information on poorly designed and administered "bootleg" accounting systems. In a world where early responsiveness to change is important, traditional systems can't keep up.

Traditional methods are usually based on a projection of historical trends and, therefore, have an underlying bias in favor of the status quo. Proper traditional budgeting does project the future, but usually only for the following fiscal year, and only in financial terms. Typically, such budgets are developed at least six months in advance of the following fiscal year and thus project financial results up to 18 months in advance. When conditions change, either a rebudgeting process is undertaken, or the original budget is maintained with large variances that have to be explained. Either way, the process is cumbersome and time consuming.

The notion of a budget "base" embeds the past in a limited projection of the future, and new ventures, because they are considered competition to established activity, are often unwelcome. Accounting and budgeting control tend to focus on incremental costs, ignoring the costs included in the base. Once a budget is established, it becomes *the* benchmark for the organization, inhibiting interim or alternative conceptions, at least until the next budget cycle. In quickly developing fields, including CE, long response times can seriously inhibit an organization's success.

This historical bias makes traditional CE budgeting unsuited to future-oriented management information techniques, those involving investment centers, large start-up costs, or the collection of data for return on investment calculations. Major capital investment decisions, say, the acquisition of dedicated classroom or laboratory space, are often neither informed by financial data nor monitored later against projected returns. Noncapital investments, those involving investments in additional staff for increased service or marketing capacity, also remain unanalyzed or untracked; they are often not even recognized as investments, but disappear into the "base" budget. Start-up costs, say, the first six months salary for a new programmer, must normally be absorbed in the current operating cycle; such costs may not be deferred to future periods when the income from the efforts of the programmer comes in. Lacking adequate and well-established processes and information sources that can inform decisions about the future or the subsequent evaluation of those decisions, traditional methods simply fall short.

Another limitation, mentioned previously, is that traditional methods are designed to support the prevailing responsibility structure and do not address alternative objectives. Most systems are designed to track financial results of individual operating units, usually through the identification of income and costs of particular programs, program groupings, or service functions. The need for comparative information, let alone the possible need to control income and expenses for organizational segments not defined by the responsibility structure (e.g., the program volume offered at a downtown center), often cannot be satisfied. Further, and perhaps more important, traditional budgeting usually fails to support strategic plans. In using the organizational or responsibility structure of the organization as the only template for the budgeting plan, traditional methods are unable to project, report, and monitor the income and costs associated with strategic initiatives that cross departmental lines. For instance, one CE organization adopted the expansion of contract training as an important element of its strategic plan. Lacking an established method and set of procedures to track its progress in fulfilling its plan, the organization had to ask each operating unit to separately identify in the annual budget those elements associated with contract training. The organization then had to develop a method for identifying each contract course and contract-related cost and a method for reporting the results of contract-related activity. This procedure added significant complexity and detail to the organization's already extensive budget and accounting process. The next year, when two more strategic initiatives were identified, the organization recognized that traditional methods were no longer adequate to support its plans.

Not only inadequate in meeting the requirements of strategic plans, traditional systems frequently fail to support day-to-day requirements for management information. An example of an addition superimposed on a existing system might be the need to determine the income and costs associated with those courses using distance learning technology. Unless they are defined as a separate group with an established budget, most CE financial management systems will not be able to provide the needed information. Traditional methods are even less adequate when the need for management information extends beyond the financial realm. For instance, traditional methods might be able to tell CE managers what the costs of a student counseling service are, but they would probably not be able to tell much about the effectiveness, even the cost-effectiveness, of the service.

On a larger scale, the most serious of the many drawbacks of traditional CE managerial information systems is the way they limit managers' perceptions of the possible, and narrow the definition of the leadership framework within which managers operate. Thus, since everyone understands that traditional methods cannot measure the effectiveness of the student counseling operation, the question of its effectiveness may never arise. Because such measurement is so far beyond the capability of most systems, few CE directors even think of trying to measure the total amount of resources, including the value of the time spent by program development staff, on the development of new courses; what could be an important index of organizational health is not even considered. In the next two chapters, multidimensional budgeting and activity-based costing are presented not only as concepts and techniques useful in the management of the CE enterprise but also as contrasts to traditional methods. Through this contrast, managerial perspectives may be broadened and the range of the possible expanded.

NOTES

[1]G. B. Strother, and J. P. Klus, *Administration of Continuing Education.* (Belmont, California: Wadsworth, 1982.

[2]A.B. Wildavsky, *The Politics of the Budgetary Process,* 2nd ed. (Boston: Little, Brown, 1974).

CHAPTER 3

Multidimensional Financial Management in Continuing Education

B y the late 1980s, the uncompetitive cost structures of American industry were apparent, made manifest by a perceived decline in our ability to compete in the global marketplace, massive capital restructuring, mergers and takeovers, and large-scale layoffs. As disturbing as this decline was the inability of our professional managers and accountants to say why we were declining or how our costs got out of line with the rest of the world. Our financial management systems were simply inadequate to the task; they had, in many cases, led to poor decisions. *Traditional cost accounting*, as developed over the last 75 years, *does not record, and, therefore, managers cannot control, the costs of nonproducing*—e.g., poor quality, machine breakdowns, waste, untimely deliveries, dissatisfied customers. Conventional budgeting, for many of the reasons cited in the last chapter, did not detect or prevent the growth of costs and the decline of efficiency. In response to this failure in the business world, two new and related techniques, activity-based costing and multidimensional budgeting, have been developed. This chapter and the next describe these two techniques and how they relate to CE.

RATIONALE FOR MULTIDIMENSIONAL BUDGETING

Multidimensional budgeting (MDB) is a process through which managers can examine, analyze, and control the operations of their organizations from several perspectives simultaneously. MDB allows managers to allocate resources to serve organizational strategies and customer needs more effectively and even allows for the introduction of apparent nonfinancial considerations into the budget process. Properly applied, MDB provides managers with new insights into the effective use of resources and can supplement existing conventional management information systems with powerful decision-support tools. Unlike traditional budgeting methods, which are designed to control and report how resources are spent, MDB focuses on the relationship between expenditures and the creation of value.[1]

The concepts of MDB and activity-based costing (ABC) are relatively new and not yet widely practiced. Although they apply equally well and with the same potential transformative force in both service and manufacturing, they have been applied primarily in the manufacturing industries. Of the two concepts, MDB is the less universally recognized, although it is so logical an extension of conventional techniques, versions of it may be more widely practiced than ABC.

MDB and ABC are closely related. While some aspects of MDB can be employed without an activity-based costing system, the full benefits of MDB cannot be realized without employing ABC. Both techniques exploit and depend upon modern information management technology, particularly database and spreadsheet software. As this chapter will illustrate, a cost-effective MDB system could not be devised without the extensive use of databases and data manipulation techniques.

The requirements for the development of a comprehensive MDB system may seem complex and costly to achieve; they depend on capturing much more detail and may strain or exceed the capacity of current systems of data collection, manipulation, and interpretation. However, they are designed to answer a question about budgeting and financial control that is rarely asked: Is the budgeting and financial management system for your organization cost-effective? In large energy, transportation, and banking companies, for instance, a study found that the equivalent of 5 percent of all staff employees were devoted full time to budgeting activities.[2] Most CE organizations invest even more resources in their budgeting and financial systems. If the use of those resources ineffectively supports decision making or, worse, leads to poor decision making, such use is a significant self-imposed liability. The use of MDB and ABC in continuing education usually has the potential both for creating cost savings and for supplying a competitive advantage through more effective managerial decision making.

THE PROGRESSION OF CONTINUING EDUCATION BUDGETS

CE budgeting systems evolved from rather primitive parent-centered budgets, with little of the detail necessary for effective CE management, to fully articulated traditional CE budgets based on detail developed from the course as cost object. This progression through increasing levels of detail and usefulness can provide a hopeful basis for what might be called the coming transformation of CE budgeting into multidimensional budgeting, in which the level of detail is expanded through reformatting to separate but related budgets.

The following section discusses the progression that has already occurred in many CE organizations.

The Institutional Line Item Budget

Because most CE units are part of larger parent institutions, they frequently are required to use institutional processes and categories to budget and account for their income and expenses. These processes and categories are usually designed in accordance with fund accounting principles, that is, they are designed to provide managers with the information they need to comply with a set of fiduciary responsibilities. The most important of these responsibilities are to make sure that the defined fund is not overspent at the end of the specified period, and that expenditures are in accordance with the stated purposes of the fund.

Funds for specific purposes, including the state and federal government funds upon which many colleges and universities depend, are often given with prescribed categories of expenditures. Thus, a grant for $50,000 to train police officers in community watch programs might specify that $20,000 was to cover teacher compensation, $2,000 for travel, and so on. Parent institutions have usually sought to keep budget categories broadly defined so as to maintain the greatest level of discretion over the funds. This means most institutional budgets have few categories or "line items." Also, it often means that income and the expenses related to its generation appear in separate budgets and in different parts of the institutional records, including the summative and controlling record called the general ledger. These line items together with the list of the separate funds accounted for by the institution and the balance sheet items (lists of assets, liabilities, residual interests in funds) comprise the institution's chart of accounts, the general categorization scheme that determines how the institution will report and keep track of its financial activities. Inevitably, budget managers become over the years more "expert" in keeping the mysteries of their own priesthood; "this is the way it's done" becomes an unchallenged rule.

Exhibit 3.1 is an example of an institutional line item budget for a university CE organization. In this budget, income has been associated with expenses of the program. Only 10 line items are shown. This limited number is typical in university charts of accounts. The organization devotes four lines to payroll-related expenses, including one designated specifically for instructor salaries as opposed to academic salaries or other salary categories. This over-representation of payroll-related costs is a logical emphasis because of the sensitive and significant nature of personnel costs. This CE organization has been able to designate two lines of the budget for itself, promotion and instructor compensation. Note the large and encompassing category for "supplies and expense," which covers everything not included in the other categories, from temporary help to items of equipment to travel and entertainment.

Fee Income		$23,981,079
Expense		
0	Academic salaries	$1,680,567
1	Staff salaries	4,581,308
2	General assistance salaries	606,602
3	Supplies and expense	8,047,353
4	Equipment	291,653
5	Promotion expense	2,693,378
6	Payroll benefits	1,531,270
7	Instructor compensation	6,380,682
8	Internal recharges	(2,081,734)
9	External recharges	0
Total expense		**$23,731,079**
Anticipated addition to fund balances		**$250,000**

EXAMPLE OF INSTITUTIONAL LINE ITEM BUDGET

EXHIBIT 3.1

Line item budgets form the basis for the most general of institutional financial management and information processes, but they are not useful to managers because such budgets lack the detail required to make decisions.

The CE Line Item Budget

CE parent institutions, recognizing the lack of detail in the line items, have developed more detailed categorization schemes that are usually supplementary to the general ledger. Using what are sometimes called "object codes," institutions code each expenditure according to an expanded list of expenses. For instance, the "supplies and expense" category would include codes for telephone, temporary help, local travel, rent, and janitorial services. While CE managers can often use these object codes to good advantage, and while some institutions have systems flexible enough to accommodate CE needs, these coding systems are usually not designed for the special needs of the CE organization. For instance, few other units of the parent organization are likely to need the kind of detail CE needs to manage and control its marketing costs. Institutional accounting systems also frequently do not have the capacity to keep track of the large number of cost objects required by CE. Thus, CE organizations usually develop a subsidiary accounting and budgeting system that runs parallel to the institutional system.

The first step in the development of a traditional CE system is to determine the line items required by CE. While the scope varies from one CE unit to another, the overall categories of expense and presentation formats are now generally agreed. Exhibit 3.2 presents a CE line item budget.

Fee Income	$23,981,079	100.00%
Direct expenses		
Promotion	$2,205,793	9.20%
Instructor compensation	6,380,682	26.61%
Supplies and expense	1,864,386	7.77%
Total direct	**$10,450,861**	**43.58%**
Gross margin	**$13,530,218**	**56.42%**
Departmental expense		
Payroll	$4,047,135	16.88%
Supplies and expense	1,345,268	5.61%
Promotion	480,585	2.00%
Equipment	94,479	0.39%
Other	(5,000)	-0.02%
Total departmental expense	**$5,962,467**	**24.86%**
Available for indirect costs	**$7,567,751**	**31.56%**
CE organization indirect costs		
Payroll	$4,352,612	18.15%
Supplies and expense	4,849,699	20.22%
Equipment	197,174	0.82%
Internal recharges	(2,081,734)	-8.68%
Total indirect costs	**$7,317,751**	**30.51%**
Addition to CE reserves	**$250,000**	**1.04%**

TYPICAL CE LINE ITEM BUDGET

EXHIBIT 3.2

In Exhibit 3.2, the budget for the organization in Exhibit 3.1 has been rearranged to meet the traditional needs for information. After income, the direct costs associated with the instructional program are shown, and these are subtracted from income to show what is called the gross margin. Direct costs are further detailed into promotion, instructional salaries, and supplies and expense. Behind each of these numbers is a possible avalanche of further detail—considerably more information is required to manage effectively, but this example presents meaningful summaries of the underlying detail. (An extensive, but by no means exhaustive listing of the possible line items is provided in Exhibit 9.2 in Chapter 9.) Exhibit 3.2 shows several categories of indirect costs. "Departmental expense" lists cost that can be directly associated with the development and presentation of courses in general, but not with particular courses. They include payroll costs for programmers responsible for developing and presenting programs and supplied with expenses to help them with their tasks. Also included are promotion costs that cannot be directly attributed to specific courses. These costs are deducted from gross margin to determine the amount "available for indirect costs."

The second category of indirect costs are those not directly associated with the development and presentation of programs. Generally, these are costs associated with serving students or with the management of the enterprise. These costs are generally summarized according to function or activity as defined by the organizational structure. In Exhibit 3.2, the CE organization's indirect costs (costs of the director's office, student registration, facilities, and other costs) are summarized and shown by line item classification (payroll, supplies and expense, equipment). In some cases, a third category of indirect cost might show the costs charged the CE organization by the parent institution.

Note that the CE line item budget, while it adds a great deal of meaningful detail to the process, does not provide some information contained in the institutional line item budget. For instance, it is not possible to determine easily how much of total payroll costs are budgeted for the CE organization as a whole, since payroll costs are shown in several places.

Traditional CE Program Budget

The CE line item budget provides some of the information required for effective management but still falls short in providing the level of detail necessary to determine how well the individual parts of the responsibility structure of the CE organization are doing. In Chapter 2, we discussed the importance of a plan of organizational segmentation. The traditional CE program budget gives expression to such a plan by analyzing the line item budget into its component segments. Exhibit 3.3 is an example of a CE program budget. The line item budget used in Exhibit 3.2 has been divided into program departments to give CE managers the ability to compare the financial results of individual units with the budget and previous periods, and to use percentages to compare one department with another.

In the example, it would have been possible to allocate CE organizational overhead to the individual program departments, but the allocation was not

Fee Income	$6,682,698	100.0%	$1,693,380	100.0%	$15,605,001	$23,981,079	100.00%
Direct expenses							
Promotion	$638,039	9.5%	$134,464	7.9%	$1,433,290	$2,205,793	9.20%
Instructor compensation	1,825,397	27.3%	329,475	19.5%	4,225,810	6,380,682	26.61%
Supplies and expense	615,634	9.2%	193,034	11.4%	1,055,718	1,864,386	7.77%
Total direct	**$3,079,070**	**46.1%**	**$656,973**	**38.8%**	**$6,714,818**	**$10,450,861**	**43.58%**
Gross margin	**$3,603,628**	**53.9%**	**$1,036,407**	**61.2%**	**$8,890,183**	**$13,530,218**	**56.42%**
Departmental expense							
Payroll	$1,020,465	15.3%	$416,522	24.6%	$2,610,148	$4,047,135	16.88%
Supplies and expense	131,000	2.0%	87,758	5.2%	1,126,510	1,345,268	5.61%
Promotion	91,000	1.4%	41,470		348,115	480,585	2.00%
Equipment	21,083	0.3%	8,309	0.5%	65,087	94,479	0.39%
Other	0	0.0%	(15,000)	-0.9%	10,000	(5,000)	-0.02%
Total departmental expense	**$1,263,548**	**18.9%**	**$539,059**	**31.8%**	**$4,159,860**	**$5,962,467**	**24.86%**
Available for indirect costs	**$2,340,080**	**35.0%**	**$497,348**	**29.4%**	**$4,730,323**	**$7,567,751**	**31.56%**
CE organization indirect costs							
Payroll						$4,352,612	18.15%
Supplies and expense						4,849,699	20.22%
Equipment						197,174	0.82%
Internal recharges						(2,081,734)	-8.68%
Total indirect costs						**$7,317,751**	**30.51%**
Addition to CE reserves						**$250,000**	**1.04%**

TYPICAL CE PROGRAM BUDGET

EXHIBIT 3.3

made. Instead, the allocation stops at the "available for indirect costs" level. This is consistent with the practice known as incremental costing (as opposed to full costing), which holds that, where possible, responsibility centers should not be held to budgets containing cost elements over which they have no control.

Course as Cost Object and the Build Up Method

The CE program budget is the most sophisticated expression of the traditional methods of CE budgeting. The foregoing discussion does not indicate that this budget format is consistent with a rather comprehensive process of obtaining management information and using that information to exercise control of the organization The advantages of this full range of control are obtainable when the individual course becomes the cost object. Because the elements of the course budgeting process are consistent with, or collapsible into, the same categories as are contained in the CE program budget, it is possible to work both forward from course budgets through an additive process or backward from the largest segmentation scheme to the individual courses that comprise it. Exhibit 10.5 in Chapter 10 illustrates this process.

Financial results from individual courses can be added together in successively larger groupings. These groupings normally correspond with the responsibility structure of the organization. In Exhibit 10.5, the first grouping level is shown on the Programmer Course Budget Summary Worksheet. In this worksheet, the budgets for individual courses are grouped by term. All the courses programmed by one CE programmer comprise one portfolio. The next level of grouping is formed by adding portfolios together to form, say, departments. Then the departments are added together to create the programming part of the organizational budget. In this way, budgets are "built up" from the detail provided by the cost object at the lowest level of detail, in this case, the course.

Handling Cross-Portfolio or Nonfinancial Goals in the Traditional Model

Previous sections have traced the progression of CE budgeting to greater and greater usefulness in line item and programmatic detail. This progression, properly applied, can yield and support a responsibility structure that assigns budget and financial responsibility according to the dimension defined by courses, defined portfolios, and departments. However, as noted earlier, traditional CE budgeting does not address responsibility assignment along other dimensions. For example, the CE organization may adopt a strategic plan for expanding its course offerings to new geographical areas or to deserving but underserved populations. If these strategic initiatives do not coincide with the prevailing short-term goals of portfolio managers, some adjustment needs to take place. For example, moving to a new area may require portfolio managers to offer courses with small enrollments until a market in the area can be developed, a practice that may run counter to the short-term budget goals. Such an initiative may also require cooperation among managers to offer a balanced program in the area and will require a method for tracking how well the collective activity across portfolios is being carried out.

Another adjustment must be made when the CE organization adopts a nonfinancial goal. For example, the CE organization may need to play a role in community efforts to deal with the closure of a military base. Such involvement may not hold much prospect for financial returns in the near future, but the CE organization and its parent institution must maintain positive and productive relationships with the community that supports them. Having one or more portfolio managers take time away from their other duties to attend community meetings and become involved in planning efforts for reuse of the base may have significant budgetary impact on the CE organization.

These cross-portfolio or nonfinancial goals require some modification in traditional budget methods. These modifications fall into several categories. The "negotiated relief" method provides for a reduction in budgetary goals for portfolio managers who will be involved in the initiatives. The budget for each manager must be calculated both with and without the initiative so that appropriate budget targets can be set. This method may or may not be combined with the "additional criteria method" for evaluating performance, which adds nonfinancial criteria to the financial criteria used to evaluate portfolio managers' performance. The "buy out" method provides portfolio managers a financial incentive for engaging in the desired activity; these incentives should be at least equal to the value of the opportunities lost because of the desired activity. For example, CE management may guarantee portfolio managers a "credit" to the gross margin of any course offered in the new geographical location that does not enroll enough students to meet normal budgetary standards. Or, the payroll budget of the portfolio managers may be reduced by the cost and/or value of the time they are expected to spend on the initiatives.

Unfortunately, these methods are too often not used. Rather, the necessary calculations of the cost of the initiatives are not made, but simply imposed on portfolio managers who are expected to meet budgetary goals at the same time they participate in the required activity. Even when the calculations are made and appropriate negotiation has been accomplished, traditional systems are frequently not up to making the necessary adjustments easily. Correcting for these adjustments requires change.

TRANSFORMING CE BUDGETING

Appropriate use of multidimensional budgeting, which is not so different from traditional budgeting, can transform the way the CE organization collects and uses financial information. Each of the several levels of multidimensional budgeting requires greater refinements and increased sophistication. The first level, in which the course is retained as the cost object, is a logical extension of traditional budgeting. The second level, in which activities become the cost object, is more complex and less intuitive, and requires a more detailed understanding of the relationship among the functions of the organization.

Multidimensional Budgeting Using the Course as Cost Object

In traditional budgeting, courses are grouped according to responsibility centers defined by the structure of the CE organization. Regrouping the courses on other dimensions yields valuable new information. Through the use of database technology, this new information can usually be obtained without significant additional effort. The cost objects (courses) can simply be coded with different attributes and then added together according to those attributes. Exhibit 3.4 takes the information from the CE Program Budget shown in Exhibit 3.3 and rearranges it by geographic location. Note that this exhibit provides differentiating detail only to the gross margin level, that is, the level of detail contained in the course budget. Thus the indirect costs, even those associated with course development and presentation, cannot be attributed to geographical locations. However, the actual operating costs of the locations can be reported, as shown at the bottom of the schedule.

Besides geographical location, many other attributes are possible—course format, subject matter, credit classification, time of day. The choice is dictated by CE organizational goals and how the unit decides to assign responsibility. The addition of attributes to the course file allows the generation of many interesting reports, but these reports are not budgets. Budgets are established in advance and used to monitor the level of attainment of the plan they represent.

Comparing Exhibit 3.3 with Exhibit 3.4 illustrates an important rule of multidimensional budgeting: the categories selected must be exclusive and exhaustive. This rule, which will be repeated in several contexts in this book, seeks to provide a discipline in the system. Under the rule, no single cost object can simultaneously be in more than one category and all cost objects (constituting the total cost) must be included in any categorization scheme. Although following this rule may place limits on the scope of any budgeting scheme, it is necessary if the integrity and the internal checks on accuracy are to be maintained.

	Downtown		South County		Other Locations		Unallocated Indirect Costs	Total	
Number of programs	841		348		1,077			2,266	
Number of enrollments	20,444		8,148		27,227			55,819	
Fee Income	$6,637,159	100.0%	$3,118,041	100.0%	$14,225,879	100.0%		$23,981,079	100.00%
Direct expenses									
Promotion	$743,362	11.2%	$327,394	10.5%	$1,135,037	8.0%		$2,205,793	9.20%
Instructor compensation	1,991,148	30.0%	779,510	25.0%	3,610,024	25.4%		6,380,682	26.61%
Supplies and expense	398,230	6.0%	258,797	8.3%	1,207,359	8.5%		1,864,386	7.77%
Total direct	$3,132,739	47.2%	$1,365,702	43.8%	$5,952,420	41.8%		$10,450,861	43.58%
Gross margin	$3,504,420	52.8%	$1,752,339	56.2%	$8,273,459	58.2%		$13,530,218	56.42%
Departmental expense									
Payroll							$4,047,135	$4,047,135	16.88%
Supplies and expense							1,345,268	1,345,268	5.61%
Promotion							480,585	480,585	2.00%
Equipment							94,479	94,479	0.39%
Other							(5,000)	(5,000)	-0.02%
Total departmental expense							$5,962,467	$5,962,467	24.86%
Available for indirect costs							$7,567,751	$7,567,751	31.56%
CE organization indirect costs									
Payroll	$370,721	5.6%	$250,000	8.0%	$340,000	2.4%	$3,391,891	$4,352,612	18.15%
Supplies and expense	920,121	13.9%	212,000	6.8%	165,000	1.2%	3,552,578	4,849,699	20.22%
Equipment	200	0.0%	1,000	0.0%	3,000	0.0%	192,974	197,174	0.82%
Internal recharges							(2,081,734)	(2,081,734)	-8.68%
Total indirect costs	$1,291,042	19.5%	$463,000	14.8%	$508,000	3.6%	$5,055,709	$7,317,751	30.51%
Addition to CE reserves								$250,000	1.04%

EXHIBIT 3.4

CE PROGRAM BUDGET BY GEOGRAPHICAL LOCATION

CE Budgeting Using Activities as Cost Objects

Budgeting plans using the product (course) as a cost object have limitations even when they are based on more than one dimension or attribute of the product. This limitation derives from the fact that not all costs can be naturally attributed to products. The largest single category of nonproduct costs are the costs of serving specific customers. For instance, the costs of serving international students, of marketing courses and curricula to them, and of serving their needs when they arrive to take a course, are self-evidently different from the costs of serving resident domestic students who take evening courses, even when the course is the same or has the same direct costs. Attempts to load differential marketing and customer service costs into the costs of courses usually fails to provide management with appropriate information. "Product as cost object" costing and budgeting systems are also not useful in identifying the costs of strategic initiatives that cross product or customer categories. An initiative for the expanded use of distance education delivery systems may involve many different course (product) categories and be intended to serve many different kinds of students (e.g., international, domestic, contract). Product cost object systems also usually provide no systematic method of identifying unnecessary or wasteful practices.

These difficulties and failures are largely overcome through the use of MDB, the full potential of which can be realized only through the adoption of activity-based costing and management. The full rationale for ABC is presented in the next chapter, but needs an introduction here. The use of a combination of MDB and ABC helps management relate spending decisions to the creation of value and leads to improved efficiency and competitive position. The use of activities as cost objects allows for the full transformation of CE budgeting.

This transformation requires that cost data be reformatted into at least four new categories of budgets: the activity budget, the product (courses) budget, the customer (student) budget, and the strategic budget. Exhibit 3.5 illustrates the relationship among each of these budgets. Creating these four new budgets allows CE management to determine resource allocations from the strategic level all the way through the operations level. At each level, the effectiveness of resource allocation decisions can be assessed.

The Activity Budget

The bottom line of Exhibit 3.5 depicts the traditional or conventional CE budget, with costs divided into separate operating departments. The first transformation of this budget is made by creating a new budget based on activities; this activity-based budget is prepared by reformatting all the costs into separate activity budgets, with one budget for each of the activities performed by the organization. The methods and rationale for doing this are

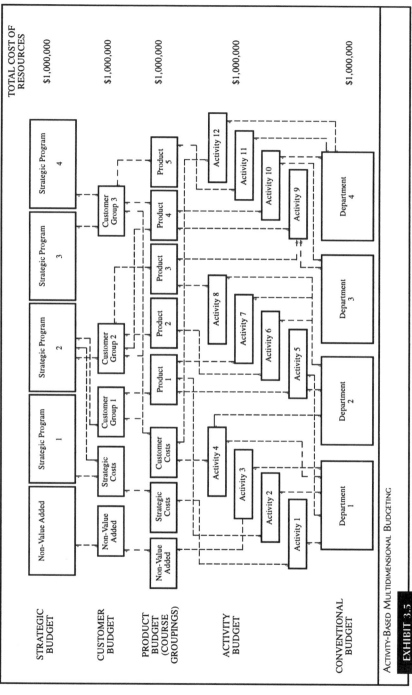

TOTAL COST OF RESOURCES

$1,000,000

$1,000,000

$1,000,000

$1,000,000

$1,000,000

STRATEGIC BUDGET

Non-Value Added | Strategic Program 1 | Strategic Program 2 | Strategic Program 3 | Strategic Program 4

CUSTOMER BUDGET

Non-Value Added | Strategic Costs | Customer Group 1 | Customer Group 2 | Customer Group 3

PRODUCT BUDGET (COURSE GROUPINGS)

Non-Value Added | Strategic Costs | Customer Costs | Product 1 | Product 2 | Product 3 | Product 4 | Product 5

ACTIVITY BUDGET

Activity 1 | Activity 2 | Activity 3 | Activity 4 | Activity 5 | Activity 6 | Activity 7 | Activity 8 | Activity 9 | Activity 10 | Activity 11 | Activity 12

CONVENTIONAL BUDGET

Department 1 | Department 2 | Department 3 | Department 4

ACTIVITY-BASED MULTIDIMENSIONAL BUDGETING

EXHIBIT 3.5

more fully explained in the next and subsequent chapters. Briefly, the rationale for this activity-based budget process is that activities consume costs, and products, customers, or managerial activities consume activities. The activity budget indicates how many resources are devoted to specific activities. For instance, activities of the noncredit program might be divided into program development, program presentation, marketing, provision of student services and information, and professional development. The activities of a service department, such as the business office, might be divided into ordering goods and services (order entry), processing invoices for payment, processing teacher payroll, and inputting data to the financial reporting system.

Creating an activity budget is a large and daunting project for most CE organizations. Later chapters will describe the methods, techniques, and shortcuts that can be applied to creating this budget and the financial information systems necessary to support the MDB and ABC processes. Such techniques include the necessary task of assigning personnel costs to activities, an additional step in the budgeting process that adds complexity, time, and expense. However, the added expense is usually worthwhile. Where these techniques have been applied, they are enlightening and reveal some surprises. For instance, most organizations using these techniques find that most of the costs of activities are incurred outside the departments that administer them. Activities rarely "map" the departmental structure of the organization, and coordination among departments is therefore required. Organizations that have accepted the challenge of creating the activity budget have benefitted even when not extending the budget process to higher levels. They can usually determine how well the processes and activities performed by a particular department conform to its mission, whether the costs of low value processes can be scaled back, whether reengineering is called for, and whether certain activities can be performed more cost-effectively outside the organization.[3]

The Product Budget

The next step in MDB is the creation of a product budget. The principles of ABC say that all activities are consumed either by products, customers, or "other" activities, sometimes (erroneously) called "nonvalue added" activities. In creating a project budget, the costs embodied in all activities needed to produce products are assigned to specific products. In the CE organization, for reasons already explained, the usual definition of product is the course or, in some cases, a defined grouping of courses. For the product budget, the direct costs of courses are assigned directly to the courses, much as in traditional budgeting. Next, the costs of activities associated with the courses are assigned. For instance, a programming department might define one of its activities as "new program development." The costs of this activity would then be assigned only to the new courses developed, and would not be associated with the continuing inventory of courses. If the cost of new program development of Department 1 was $10,000, and, if 10 new courses were developed over the period, then each course might be assigned $1,000. Certain service department activities are also associated directly with courses. For example, the business office may calculate that the cost of processing one teacher payment is $10. If a course required two teacher payments, then the course might be assigned a cost of $20 for the process.

In Exhibit 3.5, the total costs for the organization, in this case $1,000,000, are fully accounted for in each budget even when some costs do not relate to the budget category. Only a certain number of activities are related to the product budget—some "pass through" the product budget to the customer and the strategic budgets. In Exhibit 3.5, three categories of nonproduct costs are shown—nonvalue added, strategic, and customer. These costs are shown as part of the product budget to maintain the integrity of the budget process, to make sure that all costs are accounted for at every stage of the budget process.

The Customer Budget

Since all products are presumably designed to serve customers, the costs of the products are assigned to customers or, in the CE situation, student groupings. To continue our example, student grouping might be international students, evening credit course students, and summer session students. The categories of students chosen depends upon the information needs of management and on the difference in the costs of serving different categories. For instance, if the costs of serving credit and noncredit students were the same, these two categories might be combined; differentiation would not be useful. Some costs may be associated with more than one student grouping and the product costs would have to be apportioned among the student groups. In Exhibit 3.5, the full costs of the organization are again fully accounted for on the customer level by adding to customer costs the nonvalue added and strategic costs that apply to the next level above. The customer costs shown in the product budget are assigned to individual customer groups. The customer budget provides management with an assessment of the relative profitability and efficiency of the organization in serving different kinds of customers and how customer priorities are being reflected in the cost structure of the organization. The customer budget allows management to determine whether its resources are being allocated in accordance with the organizational goals as defined by the customer categories. Through the proper use of the customer budget, CE management can determine the true cost and financial return of major student categories, whether or not either the financial or educational return justifies the cost of serving each student group, what actions might reduce the cost of serving student groups without decreasing their satisfaction, and how resources should be allocated between student retention and new student recruitment.

The Strategic Budget

The strategic budget, as shown at the top of Exhibit 3.5, resorts all the costs of the organization by major organizational strategy. The first step in creating such a budget is to define what those strategies are. In most cases, those strategies will relate to serving defined groups of students and thus the ordering of the layers in Exhibit 3.5 makes sense. However, some complications are not revealed by the exhibit. For instance, one strategy might be to increase the number of students served in the south of the county. If "students in south county" was not a defined customer group, portions of the costs of serving several student groups would have to be recombined to create the customer budget. Also, certain strategies may not relate directly to customer categories. A strategy defined as improving management information systems might not lend itself to breakdown by customers. The costs associated with this strategic program would flow into the strategy budget directly without going through the intermediate product and customer budgets. These costs are associated with the strategic level the moment they are collected at the activity-budget level. The nonvalue added costs persist as a category. Ideally, these costs will be eliminated. They are shown to indicate that after the budget process has been completed the CE organization may still have some costs that cannot be justified on any budget level. This process forces managerial attention to those costs. In addition, the strategic budget allows CE management to determine if proposed expenditures are aligned appropriately with the strategic goals of the organization.

The five dimensions of budgeting shown in Exhibit 3.5 offer CE management a comprehensive way to direct and control resources in the CE organization. The interaction between these dimensions is meant to be dynamic. A change in one dimension changes all. Resource allocations can be traced from the strategic level down and from the department or activity level up in a fully related and integrated way. Using activity-based MDB allows CE managers to do the following things:

1. Create a clear relationship between budgets and strategies
2. Compare, in detail, costs across the organization
3. Measure customer value and the costs associated with providing that value
4. Make continuous improvements through the analysis of budget information aligned with the logic of business decisions
5. Readily revise the budget structure to reflect changes in strategies or structure[4]

Today, no CE organization employs a fully functioning activity-based MDB system. The preceding explanation remains a theoretical model presented to help CE managers see the possible and expand their visions of the sort of information that might become available to them. It should be clear that realizing the potential of MDB is simply not possible without a computerized management information system employing database and spreadsheet technologies. Employing these technologies for an MDB system would permit CE managers to ask and receive answers to questions that have never been asked before and to play "what if" games of speculative resource allocations in many dimensions at once. While still largely theoretical, aspects of the model presented in this chapter are readily achievable in most CE organizations.

The full expression of MDB relies upon activity-based costing. The two concepts are logically inseparable. In this chapter, we have quickly skipped over activity-based costing to present an overview of MDB. The next chapter describes ABC and its uses.

NOTES

[1] The structure and concepts presented in this chapter come largely from Jeffrey A. Schmidt, "Is It Time to Replace Traditional Budgeting?" *Journal of Accountancy* (October 1992): 103–07.
[2] Schmidt, "Is It Time," 103.
[3] Schmidt, "Is It Time," 105.
[4] Schmidt, "Is It Time," 107.

CHAPTER 4

Activity-Based Costing in Continuing Education

The previous chapter placed activity-based costing (ABC) within the context of the budget process (*see* Exhibit 3.5) and illustrated its importance for the exercise of full management control. This chapter defines ABC, describes its advantages, shows how it differs from conventional cost accounting, and explains some of its key concepts. Chapter 7 will examine how ABC might be applied to the work of a course planner and developer, and Chapter 13 will describe how an ABC system might be designed and implemented in a CE organization.

WHAT IS ABC?

Activity-based costing is a method of determining the costs of the activities performed in an organization and then assigning those costs to products, customers, or managerial functions. ABC is an essential tool of activity-based management (ABM), which relates the use of resources consumed by the organization to the results achieved by the organization. The use of ABC and ABM has been concentrated in the manufacturing industries, but these compelling ideas are now spreading into the service industries. Peter Drucker described this movement as follows:

> Traditional cost accounting in manufacturing—now 75 years old—does not record the cost of non-producing, such as the cost of faulty quality, or of a machine being out of order, or of needed parts not being on hand. Yet these unrecorded and uncontrolled costs in some plants run as high as the costs that traditional accounting does record. By contrast, a new method of cost accounting developed in the past 10 years—called "activity-based"

accounting—records all costs, and it relates them, as traditional cost accounting cannot, to value added. Within the next 10 years it should be in general use. And then we will have operational control in manufacturing.

But this control will be in manufacturing only. We still will not have cost control in services: schools, banks, government agencies, hospitals, hotels, retail stores, research labs, architectural firms and so on. We know how much a service takes in, how much it spends and on what. But we do not know how the spending relates to the work the service organization does and to its results—or of the reasons the costs of hospitals, colleges and the post office are out of control.[1]

The basic tenet of ABC, as illustrated in Exhibit 4.1, is that activities consume resources and that products, customers, or management-chosen initiatives consume activities.

Another "accounting" way of saying this is that all activities are primary cost objects. In fact, it is rare that every activity can somehow be related to a

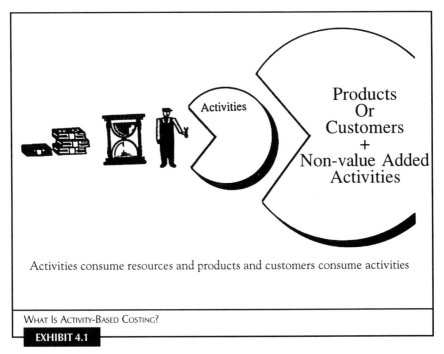

Activities consume resources and products and customers consume activities

WHAT IS ACTIVITY-BASED COSTING?

EXHIBIT 4.1

Source: Michael C. O'Guin, Activity Based Costing (Englewood Cliffs, NJ: Prentice Hall, 1991).

product, customer, or specific management or strategic objective. Organizations usually engage in some wasteful (non-value added) or unassignable activities.

To people unfamiliar with traditional cost accounting methods, ABC may not seem revolutionary; its underlying logic seems too apparent to have escaped notice for over 70 years. Yet almost every manager is profoundly influenced by traditional methods. For example, when organizations, including colleges and universities, need to reduce costs because of adverse financial conditions, the cuts are usually expressed as reductions of specific resources, such as number of employees, rather than as reductions in activities. Of course, when the number of employees (and their payroll costs) go away, some activities must be eliminated or curtailed. Managers of the curtailed departments have to reduce activities with little guidance—their supporting accounting systems do not provide information about activity costs and benefits.

Because the principles of financial and traditional cost accounting are so ingrained in information systems managers, ABC is usually defined in contrast to traditional practices and in relation to emerging conditions and new requirements. One of the clearest examples of the distortion of information created by traditional cost accounting is the widespread use of direct labor as a basis for allocating indirect costs to products. In most manufacturing businesses, choosing to use the product as the cost object had far-reaching implications. Although managers needed to know the full cost of the completed product, the methods used to calculate that cost increasingly distorted the information managers used to make decisions. To "fully cost" a product meant that the indirect costs of the operation of the business had somehow to be assigned to the product. For instance, the cost of the electricity used to run the factory theoretically had to be "loaded" into the costs assigned to many individual products, which then became "burdened" with that indirect cost. Cost accountants and managers searched for appropriate bases upon which to allocate indirect costs. It became a widespread practice to use direct labor, either in the form of direct labor hours or direct labor costs, to allocate indirect costs to products. Thus, if one product required one hour of direct labor to produce, and another required two hours to produce, the second would bear twice the indirect costs. Such a scheme made some sense early in this century when the theory that longer production times meant greater indirect costs had more validity. Under this theory, managers could lower the cost of any product by concentrating on reducing labor. For this and other reasons, direct labor as a proportion of total manufacturing costs dropped dramatically. Today direct labor probably constitutes somewhere under 5 percent of total manufacturing costs, while allocated indirect costs constitute somewhere over 45 percent! As increasing percentages of the costs of manufacturing were allocated on the basis of a decreasingly significant element, unsound decisions multiplied.

Managers began to seek lower direct labor costs overseas without fully considering the overhead costs incurred because of distance and differences in cultures, laws, regulations, and finance. Equipment and other capital investments were made to substitute for labor without considering the full effects on future operations.

Anyone who has tried to find a "fair" basis for allocating indirect costs to individual course or cost centers will recognize that the problem described above has relevance to continuing education. Distortions analogous to the direct labor distortion are almost impossible to avoid in allocation schemes. For instance, an allocation scheme that assigned registration costs to courses by charging a flat fee for each person enrolled in the course might seem fair and easy to calculate. However, such a scheme might also lead to a bias in the organization toward high fee, low enrollment courses as programmers seek to decrease their registration cost burden. If the students paying the high fees demanded increased levels of service from the registration function, a spiral of higher fees leading to higher costs might price the organization out of the market.

ABC Is Different

A new logic and a new business environment are pushing aside or changing the traditional approaches to cost accounting.

Control of Direct Costs

Traditional cost methods concentrate on the reporting and control of direct costs and assume that direct costs have a direct relation to indirect costs. The direct labor situation described above is one example. Past efforts at greater efficiency concentrated on getting workers and machines to produce more in less time. To be efficient, the production process worked to bring unit costs down, usually by increasing the scope of production and by specializing production functions into separate departments. However, as run sizes increased and as communication and coordination among departments became necessary, indirect costs increased. Inventories and inventory handling charges increased. Imbalances in departmental output rates caused increased moving and storing costs.

In the present environment, direct costs are frequently subject only to minimal control and the direct and indirect costs of production have little relationship. This is often the case in CE. Once the decision to present a course is made, there is little opportunity to control direct costs—instructor compensation and other classroom costs. In many CE organizations, instructor compensation rates are fixed by formula. On the other hand, the number of students enrolled in the course may affect the costs that, in traditional terms, are defined as indirect. ABC is a total cost system; it examines and seeks to control the full range of costs of the organization. It does not assume any relationship between costs except those disclosed through an analysis of activities.

Inventory Valuation

Traditional accounting systems place great emphasis on the "correct" valuation of inventories through the application of appropriate costing methods. ABC seeks to reduce inventories so that inventory values are not as important in financial and managerial terms. CE organizations are rarely involved in inventory valuations, but the logic of the new environment does apply if one considers the list of courses offered by the CE organization as an "inventory." If that inventory has to be updated, renewed, and changed frequently, the cost of such development becomes an increasingly significant element. ABC provides a means by which these costs can be forecast and tracked across the life of a course.

Reporting Emphasis

Traditional methods report cost performance, usually against preestablished standards; the aim is to refine the product and the production process.

The new environment calls for cost planning over cost reporting and recognizes that product profitability is determined more by decisions made prior to introduction than by refinements after introduction. While CE organizations may have several chances to refine their courses after introduction, many courses get only one chance and are therefore dependent on careful planning for long-range success. ABC is prospective in its emphasis, promoting improvement by setting ever higher goals rather than by defining success as achievement of a previously set standard.

Traditional methods assure the integrity of information by emphasizing precision in reporting. The new environment requires accurate, timely, and relevant information rather than high precision. ABC helps managers calculate the trade-off between precision and accuracy, timeliness, and relevance.

ADVANTAGES OF ABC

Now let's relate the advantages of ABC in the current environment to CE management. ABC solves many problems with traditional cost accounting methods that CE managers face daily—lack of decision-making information, strife and misunderstanding about overhead allocations, inability to clearly define and prioritize organizational goals for staff members. ABC can solve these and many other problems.

Total Cost Management

ABC includes all costs incurred by the organization in the cost accounting process. By focusing first on how the resources of the organization are consumed by activities, ABC forces an understanding of the relationships between actual costs and the goals of the organization. By using activities as a lens through which to examine resource allocations, ABC reveals three major categories of costs to be placed alongside product costs for examination and control—customer costs, overhead costs, and waste.

The emphasis of traditional methods on costing products (product as cost object) made managers aware that products are significant determinants of the structure of resource allocation within an organization. But the costs of serving different customers also drive resource allocations. The difference between the services needed by evening students in, say, professional continuing education courses and international students enrolled in daytime English language courses illustrate the point. International students generally require more elaborate and expensive systems of program development, marketing, and student services than do domestic students.

Another example illustrates the difference between product and customer costs. Students enrolled in credit courses need different kinds of services than noncredit enrollees. For credit, the cost of evaluating student work, assigning and recording grades, and creating a permanent transcript of student work are usually more significant than for noncredit, even for complex subject matter. Loading all customer-driven costs into courses (products) is illogical when the same product serves two kinds of customers. In most CE organizations, for instance, students taking a credit course may opt for noncredit status. Also, credit courses tend to undergo more elaborate review processes than noncredit courses, e.g., submission of outline, review by faculty committee. The costs of these activities are correctly classified as course (product) costs.

Traditional cost systems employ arbitrary allocation schemes and make no direct link between products and customers and the indirect costs they create. Indirect costs are considered to be "below the line" and are allocated uniformly across all products or customers. In ABC, the notion of indirect costs is either eliminated or changed significantly. ABC does not allocate costs; it assigns them. For instance, the costs of serving credit students would be assigned to the "credit students" customer category and then allocated to all credit students on some basis. This procedure may seem to be simply taking traditional methods to greater detail, but the addition of the customer, managerial, and non-value added categories into which costs may be assigned to cost objects decreases the arbitrary nature of allocations.

Isolating Non-Value Added Activity

By emphasizing total cost management and by forcing the categorization of activities as either customer, product, managerial, or non-value added, ABC forces management to identify, recognize, and deal with non-value added activity. In the strictest of definitions, non-value activities do not add directly to the value of the product from the customer's perspective, or do not directly serve the customer and create higher levels of customer satisfaction. For CE, this strict definition does not allow for the diversity of organizational activity and artifically forces certain common activities into one of the two categories. To avoid forcing costs associated with activities like employee satisfaction into the non-value added, product, or customer categories, I have developed a third category called "managerial" or "strategic."

Typical non-value added activities are related to correction, inspection, quality control, expediting, delay, storage, and some aspects of coordination and communication. Many people are confused by this list. For instance, doesn't a program of product inspection or quality control add value to the product or increase customer satisfaction by assuring high-quality products get to the market? The answer is "yes," but it would be better if high-quality products were assured by the primary process of production rather than by secondary processes designed to catch errors. Some studies have found that non-value added activities account for up to 35 percent of an organization's total costs. At one CE school, university faculty members were concerned about a few courses that appeared in the CE catalog without completely undergoing the course and teacher approval process. This already elaborate process was revised to prevent future errors of this kind. By the definition above, these activities are non-value added. Peter Drucker has pointed out that nothing is less useful "than to do a little better that which should not be done at all."

Continuous Improvement

Because ABC is a cost planning system rather than a cost reporting system, it looks to the future and to future improvements. It is not based upon the standard costing notions of traditional cost accounting systems. The standard cost is management's goal for what a cost should be and production efficiency is measured in relation to that standard. In traditional methods, the standard becomes a stagnant goal in itself and does not promote continuous improvement. Because ABC tries to project what costs will be, it forces an understanding of cost behavior and provides the basis for avoiding costs.

This forward looking aspect of ABC, which provides management the opportunity to do something about costs before they are incurred, supports effective product design. In some manufacturing products, it is estimated that more than 75 percent of the cost saving opportunities are embedded in the product design.

ABC identifies what is to be gained through quality improvement. The "cost of quality" is revealed and the size of the potential savings becomes a powerful lever for improvement. ABC reveals both the size and the location of savings opportunities. The sources of poor quality are identified, whether vendor, process, design, or department. ABC enables the organization to assign priorities to its improvement efforts. All non-valued added activities are not equal. ABC also provides management with the information needed to set improvement targets, to establish plans to meet those goals, and to monitor progress toward the goals.

Information on the Cost of Complexity

Traditional cost accounting systematically undercosts complexity in products and customer delivery systems because much of the cost of complexity is hidden in indirect costs and then allocated equally to both complex and simple products. At its extreme, this defect in traditional methods could cause an organization to drop its most profitable products in favor of its least profitable. Complexity triggers cost. Managers often intuitively understand this, but have no idea of the magnitude of the cost. Exhibit 4.2 shows the budgets for two courses to be presented in the same term. The courses are expected to serve the same number of students. Because of its higher fee, Course 1 appears to be more profitable.

	Course 1	Course 2
Fee	$450	$300
Expected enrollment	20	20
Total income	**$9,000**	**$6,000**
Promotion	$1,000	$1,000
Instructor compensation	2,000	2,000
Classroom costs	1,000	400
Total costs	**$4,000**	**$3,400**
Gross margin	**$5,000**	**$2,600**

BUDGETS FOR TWO COURSES

EXHIBIT 4.2

Exhibit 4.3 provides more information about the two courses. Course 1 is more complex than Course 2 because it involves an off-site location, more promotion planning, multiple instructors, more transactions related to classroom expense, and the physical presence of support staff at the time of presentation. Most of the elements of complexity listed here are unlikely to show up as costs in traditional course costing/budgeting systems, making accurate estimation of the magnitude of the complexity costs of these two courses highly unlikely. Yet without this information, financial comparison of these two courses is impossible.

	Course 1	Course 2
Location	Downtown hotel	Classroom on campus
Format	Two day seminar	Ten meeting evening class
Promotion method	Special brochure, advertising	Catalog listing
Number of instructors	4	1
Number of transactions for supplies and expense	10	2
Cashier required at first meeting	Yes	No

COST OF COMPLEXITY FOR TWO COURSES

EXHIBIT 4.3

Information on Course Volume, Development, and Life Cycle

Traditional cost accounting systems subsidize customized (complex), low-volume products at the expense of standard, high-volume products because traditional allocation schemes spread indirect costs uniformly among products. Product costs vary with volume as well as complexity. CE organizations face this variance when they enter a new geographical market area. Unless a "critical mass" of courses can be offered successfully, the added costs (usually classified as indirect costs) of developing market awareness for the new course offerings, locating a suitable classroom facility, making arrangements for audio-visual services, and setting up appropriate classroom support are too expensive. If these special costs of serving any particular market are simply absorbed into the overhead cost pool, the activity in that market is being subsidized by other markets.

ABC allows management to determine the cost of new course development and provides a means through which those costs can be apportioned over the length of the effective life of the course. In most businesses, the activity of new product development can be identified and tracked; such activity usually resides in a separate department or in a research and development unit. In most CE organizations, new course development is undertaken by many different responsibility centers and is not clearly identified as an activity to be tracked. In fact, information about new course development costs is so hard to obtain and summarize that most CE organizations don't even recognize the potential value of the information. In a fast changing marketplace, this information can be a significant measure of the health of the organization. CE organizations must know how much it costs to develop new products on a product-by-product (program-by-program) basis and must be able to monitor the effectiveness of the investment in new products over their lifespan. Obviously, developing a course that can be repeated is more efficient than developing a one-time course. The development effort can be spread over a number of courses—subsequent presentations of the course require less time and effort than the first presentation. This kind of assessment is an important element in the portfolio management that programmers engage in as they seek to allocate their time and energy to their many tasks. ABC treats new course development explicitly from the planning stage through the monitoring and assessment stages, thus providing programmers crucial feedback on the effectiveness of decisions relating to new course development. In ABC, "sunk costs" are important for the future because they are part of a measure of decision-making effectiveness.

ANALYSIS OF ABC

The Flow of Costs

Exhibit 3.5 in the previous chapter presented a general picture of the relationship between ABC and a multidimensional budgeting system. That same exhibit is a good illustration of how ABC works. ABC assigns the total resources of the CE organization to appropriate cost objects. Resources are all those elements the CE organization pays for and are usually described in some fashion by the chart of accounts of the organization—academic salaries, rent, supplies, marketing materials. Cost objects are any costs the organization wishes to track—individual courses, groups of students, strategic plans, specific activities. The two largest categories of cost objects are courses (products) and students (customers). However, at least two other categories are possible. One, which we are calling "managerial" because the cost objects are the product of managerial discretion, covers those cost objects that provide value to the organization without a direct association to the organization's products or customers. The other, called "non-value added," provides no value to the organization or to its customers.

Exhibit 4.4 illustrates the possible flows of cost in an ABC system. Resources can be assigned directly to one of the cost object categories or they can first be assigned to activity cost objects and then to cost objects. Since products serve customers, costs assigned to products always, in turn, are assigned to customers. Because activities always take place in activity centers, resources are first assigned to activity centers and then to activities and, in turn, to one of the four cost object groups.

Several CE examples can illustrate these cost flows. Instructor compensation is an example of a direct resource allocation to a product (course) cost object. Amounts paid to instructors can be directly and immediately associated with a particular course. Payment for an advertisement in a professional journal, because directed at attracting a specific student group, might be an example of a direct charge to a customer cost object. The costs of a staff spring picnic is an example of a cost that might be assigned directly to a managerial cost object, in this case the objective of building positive staff morale. A cost that is simply a direct waste (non-value added) is rare, but does occur from time to time.

Usually the largest segment of an organization's resources are assigned first to activity centers and then to activities as cost objects. Activity centers are logical, homogeneous groupings of functions or processes. While activity centers are usually consistent with the organizational structure, they should not be understood as service departments. An example of an activity center might be the registration office. The CE registration office usually performs a number of different activities in addition to registering students for courses. It may handle and deposit funds, provide information to students, send out catalogs on request, input student data for future use by the records department, update student records, and record student suggestions. All these activities can be identified and can serve as cost objects for further allocation.

The formation of activity centers allows for the "first stage" assignment of resources, which is similar in some respects to the assignment of costs in traditional systems. Grouping all registration office activities provides the basis upon which to create a "cost pool" associated with the group of activities. For instance, space and utility costs such as rent and electrical and telephone costs might be charged first to the activity center and then through the activity center to the activity cost object. Chapter 13 will explain the role of activity centers in more detail.

An entire activity center can serve one category of cost objects. For instance, if a program processing activity center was charged with processing approvals for credit courses, the costs of the entire center might be directly assigned to the "credit courses" product category. If an activity center was created to serve international students, its entire costs could be assigned directly to the international students customer group. Although a full activity center serving only managerial cost objects or being a complete waste of money is unlikely, these possibilities do exist.

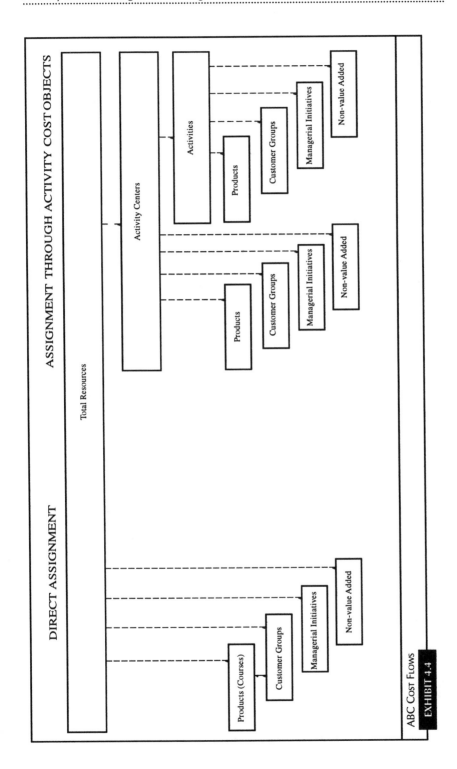

ABC COST FLOWS

EXHIBIT 4.4

Exhibit 4.4 provides an overview of how costs might flow from a simple list of the cost of resources to assignment to activities related to the ultimate purposes of the organization. However, the exhibit illustrates only a part of the richness and complexity of ABC. It shows how ABC categorizes cost objects into product, customer, managerial, non-value added, activity center, and activity classifications, but does not fully describe the hierarchical nature of costs central to ABC.

The Hierarchy of Costs

A significant difference between ABC and traditional cost accounting systems is ABC's recognition that costs are triggered by different levels of production or customer service. Traditional systems generally define a unit of production as the cost object and allocate all costs to units of production. In CE, the usual unit of production is the individual course. As we have seen, ABC expands the notion of cost objects beyond units of production to customers and customer groups, and to managerial functions. In addition, ABC reflects the hierarchy of costs that occur within both product and customer costs. In product costs, ABC recognizes that costs are incurred at the unit, batch, and product levels. In customer costs, ABC recognizes that costs are incurred at the order, customer, and market levels. Managerial costs may or may not have hierarchical levels. In ABC, costs are assigned to their incremental level, the level at which the costs would be eliminated if the level were eliminated. Proper assignment of costs to levels assures that costs are segregated appropriately for analysis. The following CE examples will illustrate these concepts.

Product-Driven Activities

In CE, the most universal definition of "product" is the individual course. Thus, CE costs associated with the "unit" level are costs associated with individual courses. Such costs include not only the direct costs associated with the individual course, such as instructor compensation, duplicating, room rent, and audio-visual services, but also those indirect costs that can be logically associated with individual courses. For instance, suppose information about each course must be entered into the CE organization's computer system. The costs associated with such entering (e.g., operator salary, computer costs) could be calculated and then assigned to individual courses by dividing the total costs of the entering process by the number of courses processed. CE costs associated with product "batches" are costs associated with natural groupings of courses. For instance, the payroll costs of a particular programmer assigned to produce and present a specified portfolio of courses are usually "batch" level costs since they cannot easily be assigned to individual courses but can be associated with a particular grouping of courses. "Product" level includes costs that support the design and maintenance of a defined product line. In CE, a product line might be a broadly defined set of courses, including several "batches" or a portfolio of courses. For instance, contract training courses might be defined as a product line. Costs associated with developing and supporting that product line, such as the acquisition of a client contact reporting system, market research, other marketing costs, and training programs for programmers seeking to develop programs for the contract market, might be defined as product costs.

Customer-Driven Activities

In CE, the customer is usually the student. Order level costs are those costs attributable directly to enrolling the student. That portion of the registration function that is directly associated with student enrollment activity is an example of order level costs in CE. Customer level costs are non-order related costs attributable directly to serving individual students. The costs of special sales or marketing efforts directed to individual customers are examples of customer costs. For example, the costs of writing a proposal for a training contract for a local company is a customer level cost. Sometimes order level and customer level costs are merged into one category. Market level costs are those required to develop, maintain, and serve a particular market. These costs do not vary with the number of customers or the number of orders. An example of a market level cost might be the cost of radio advertising designed to get prospective students to call for the latest CE catalog. In this case, the market is defined as the local market for continuing education courses as opposed, say, to the contract training market.

Managerial Level Activities

In CE, managerial level costs are those related to the organization itself rather than to products or customers. Usually managerial costs can be assigned directly to strategic objectives or managerial purposes without employing the notion of a hierarchy of costs. The salary of the director of CE is an example of a managerial level cost. One special category of managerial level activities that is sometimes treated as a separate category in itself is facility level activities. The costs of maintaining a particular facility could be assigned to either product or customers. For instance, the costs of renting and maintaining a downtown center continue despite the volume of programs or number of students attending classes in the center. CE organizations may decide to treat such facility-related costs or a certain portion of those costs in a separate category.

Cost Pools

For ease of assignment, costs at these various levels are gathered into what are called "cost pools." Whenever costs are associated with one particular level and are associated with one particular method of assignment, they may be added together and assigned at one time. For instance, the cost of entering information about credit courses into the computer system might be added to the costs of processing credit course approvals to form a cost pool that can be assigned on a per course basis to all credit courses. Defining cost pools is an important step in developing an ABC system.

Cost Drivers

In ABC, cost drivers are the bases upon which indirect costs or cost pools are assigned to cost objects. They are selected to capture the underlying cost behavior of processes and activities. Cost drivers represent the cause-and-effect relationship between an activity and a set of costs. The underlying assumption is that the cause-and-effect relationship between a defined activity and its cost driver(s) is linear—costs increase in direct proportion to the level of activity as measured by the cost driver. In ABC, cost assignment generally is a two-stage process in which costs are first assigned to activity centers or cost pools and then to cost objects at the various levels.

A simple example from CE can illustrate the ABC process. A fundamental activity in CE is the enrollment of students in evening courses. ABC treatment would require first that all the costs associated with the enrollment of such students be identified and added together to form a cost pool. This cost pool would include the salaries and wages of everyone performing aspects of the enrollment activity, including those who might be in different departments. It would certainly include the wages of the enrollment clerks who accept enrollments over the telephone, but only the portion attributable to enrolling students. It would not include providing information to students or directing their calls. It might also include costs from other departments such as the business and cashiering departments or the computer support group. Once all these costs had been formed into a cost pool, they would periodically be assigned to individual students on the basis of the cost driver, the number of students. If total enrollment costs for a quarter were $20,000, and if 5,000 students enrolled, the cost of serving each student that quarter would be $4. The cost of enrolling this category of students might be different from the cost of enrolling students in contract training courses. Contract students are enrolled through a different process involving different costs. Although many cost drivers are defined in terms of volume, some are defined by attributes. Product complexity and special customer needs often must be factors in cost driver definition. The cost of presenting a one-day special program at a hotel with six guest speakers and extensive press coverage is usually much higher than presenting Accounting 1A in the evening on campus. The cost of enrolling executive level participants in a residential three-week program is

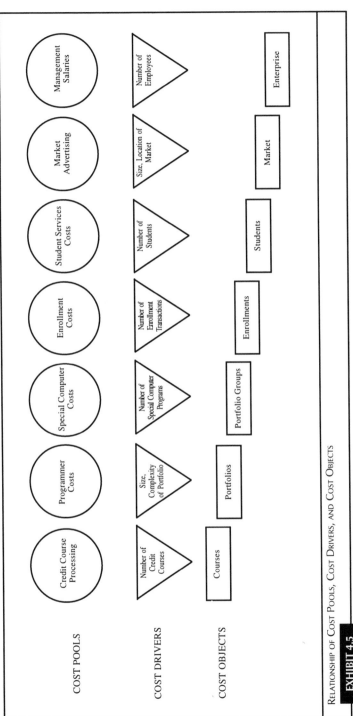

RELATIONSHIP OF COST POOLS, COST DRIVERS, AND COST OBJECTS

EXHIBIT 4.5

likely to be greater than enrolling a student in an evening French course. The executives may need or demand more information about the course, about housing and living arrangements, or about payment options and billing and invoicing procedures. To achieve the purposes of ABC, these variables need to be taken into account in the development of both cost pools and cost drivers.

Exhibit 4.5 shows the relationship of cost pools, cost drivers, and the various levels of cost objects. The descriptions given of cost pools and cost drivers are just a few of the many that might be employed simultaneously in each category. Choosing the appropriate cost pools and cost drivers are important decisions in the implementation of an ABC system. Chapter 13 will address these issues in more detail

WHAT ABC MEANS TO CONTINUING EDUCATION

ABC has some characteristics important to the typical CE organization. It is flexible and can be applied to a wide variety of situations. Although it can be applied as a complete and integrated system in an organization, it may also be applied more narrowly. For instance, as we will see in Chapter 7, some aspects of ABC can be employed productively by a single CE programmer alone, without reliance on a larger system. Also, ABC is self-reflective, allowing CE managers to assess its cost-effectiveness through its own operation. ABC can be complex and expensive, but the cost of inaccurate management information can also be high. ABC requires CE management to understand the relationship between all activities and costs, and forces an assessment of how resources are being allocated to strategic objectives. Finally, ABC prompts periodic reexaminations of an organization's strategic priorities by providing continuous information in an appropriate format for decision making. Because it is so new, ABC needs some practical tests in CE organizations. This introduction to ABC is intended as encouragement for those experiments.

NOTE

[1]Peter F. Drucker, "We Need to Measure, Not Count," *Wall Street Journal*, 13 April 1993, A14.

PART TWO

• • • • • • • • • • •

Financial Management for Course Planners

P art 2 provides course planners with an understanding of the basic financial terms and concepts associated with what they do and how they can do it better. The decisions they make about how to use their time and about what courses they offer are among the most important made in a CE organization. The amount and accuracy of information they can bring to bear in their planning decisions determine the overall effectiveness of the CE organization. Likewise, CE administrators must understand the dynamics of the financial aspects of course planning to effectively administer organizational budgets and finances. Thus, this part provides all CE professionals with both the theoretical understanding and the practical skills needed to plan courses effectively. It will help planners develop a positive attitude toward course financial planning by showing them how such planning can improve their courses, how to use their time more effectively, and how to evaluate targets of opportunity. After reading Part 2, you will be able to:

- understand the basic financial terminology and structure of the course;
- identify and use the characteristics of course costs in the course planning process;
- prepare a comprehensive course budget;
- understand when, why, and how financial decisions about courses must be made;
- understand and use the dynamic elements of portfolio management in planning and administering a portfolio of courses;
- recognize the shortcomings of traditional accounting and budgeting methods of planning courses and avoid their pitfalls;

- use the principles of multidimensional budgeting and activity-based costing in course planning; and
- apply these principles and concepts to some common issues related to course financial planning.

CHAPTER 5

The Basics of Course Financial Planning

Course financial planning begins with the preparation of a course budget. Budget preparation forces organized consideration and projection of the financial aspects of the single course. Those who prepare course budgets need to understand the possible behavior of income and expenses associated with a proposed course, and they must be able to share this understanding with others through a common vocabulary.

STATIC ELEMENTS OF COURSE BUDGETING

A traditional course budget is a snapshot of a hoped-for outcome based upon a number of assumptions, many of which are never clearly stated. For instance, course budgets rarely indicate the elements of the costs (lunches, duplicating costs) that will vary with the number of enrollments. While the assumptions can be changed to produce alternative budgets, each budget itself represents a single set of assumptions. In this respect, traditional course budgets are static representations of single points on a range of possible outcomes.

Traditional course budgets usually consist of several of these static elements: revenue, expense (or costs), and the difference between projected revenues and expenses variously called "margin," "available," "surplus," or "balance." (As my former boss, Milton Stern, warned, "Never, never use the word profit! There is *none!*") Let's examine each of these elements in turn.

Course Revenue

Revenue is usually the easiest course budget element to calculate and the most difficult to estimate. Total expected revenue is commonly calculated by multiplying the fee for the course by the number of estimated enrollments. A common variation of the calculation is to determine what total income might be, estimate enrollments, and then derive the fee. But this simple calculation requires thought, intuition, experience, and, sometimes, data.

An estimate of total revenue is often closely associated with total costs. Usually fees are set after the costs of a course have been estimated. In many contract courses—those presented in companies or agencies according to prior negotiated contracts—cost or some form of cost plus fee is the basis for determining the total contract price. In general, revenue and costs will behave the way we want or expect them to behave. When they do not, we must determine the reason for deviation.

Fixed and Variable Course Costs

Trying to estimate the costs of a particular course means having to determine how many people will attend. Certain costs can be estimated only by specifying the number of enrollees. These costs are called variable costs because they vary with the volume of the activity (in our case, the number of enrollments). Examples of common variable costs are meals, course materials and books, computer time, and lodging costs. The behavior of variable costs in one case is illustrated by the graph in Exhibit 5.1.

In this example, a one-day course on small electrical power generation plants, a set of course notes will cost $15 to produce, hors d'oeuvres at the opening no-host cocktail party will cost $8 per person, and coffee will cost $7 per person. Thus, every enrollee represents $30 in variable costs. If 40 people enroll, our total variable cost will be $1,200 (40 enrollees times $30). Line A on the graph shows that in this case variable costs vary directly and proportionally with the number of participants.

But the cost per enrollment can often be reduced if a certain volume is reached. For example, if the printer of the course notes agrees to charge only $10 per set for every set above 50, the cost per enrollee is reduced if more than 50 people enroll. This situation is shown in Exhibit 5.1 as dotted line B.

Fixed costs do not vary with volume (here, the number of enrollees). Examples of fixed costs for courses are room rental, audio-visual costs, promotion costs, and instructor and staff travel costs. In our power plant course example, the room will cost $500, audio-visual costs will be $200, promotion will cost $1,500, and instructor travel costs will be $600. These fixed costs are shown by solid line A on the graph in Exhibit 5.2.

Our total fixed costs of $2,800 do not vary with the number of enrollments. However, costs often remain fixed only for a particular level of volume. For instance, if the room we plan to use will hold only 50 people, we will have to rent a larger room at a higher cost when enrollment exceeds 50. If the only alternative room available costs $1,200 instead of the anticipated $500, our

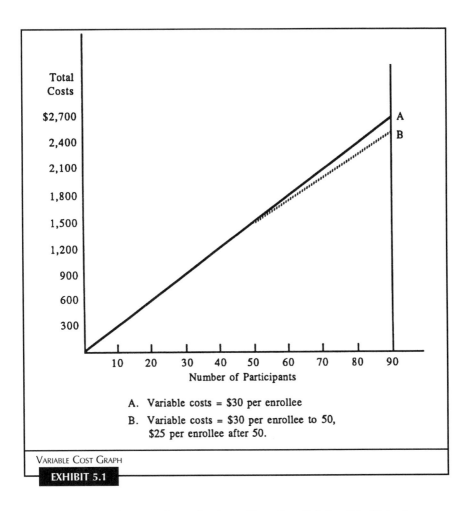

A. Variable costs = $30 per enrollee
B. Variable costs = $30 per enrollee to 50,
    $25 per enrollee after 50.

VARIABLE COST GRAPH

EXHIBIT 5.1

fixed costs jump $700 as shown by dotted line B in Exhibit 5.2. This phenomenon is sometimes referred to as the step function, since the graph has a stair-step shape.

As discussed in Part 1, fixed costs are fixed only over a relevant range of volume values. The relevant range is the range of volume values over which there is no increase in fixed costs. In our example, the relevant range is 0 to 50 for fixed costs of $2,800. In course budgeting the relevant range for each element of fixed costs must be recognized. Failure to do so can result in startling deviations from the established budget.

True variable costs vary directly and proportionally with volume. A 10 percent increase of volume of will thus produce an increase in variable costs of 10 percent. Costs that vary in the same direction as volume but do not vary proportionally are sometimes called semivariable or semifixed costs. In these

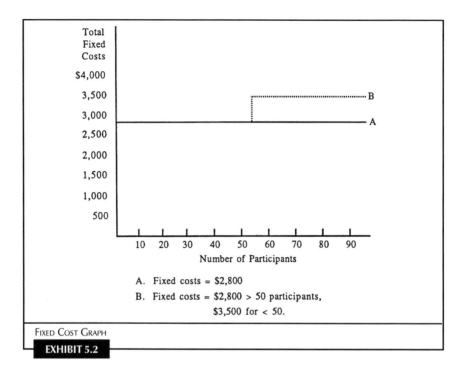

FIXED COST GRAPH

EXHIBIT 5.2

cases, an increase in volume of 10 percent will produce a smaller increase in variable costs, say, 8 percent. The volume discount on course materials shown by line B in Exhibit 5.1 is an example of a variable cost that does not increase proportionally with the number of enrollments. Semivariable costs are also called "semifixed" or "partly variable" because they contain elements of both fixed and variable costs. A semivariable cost must be broken down into its fixed and variable elements.

Instructor compensation was purposely left out of our power plant example because it can be either a fixed or a variable cost depending on circumstances. The instructor is usually paid a specific, agreed-upon amount for teaching a course, either a specified dollar amount or a rate per hour. In either case, instructor compensation is a fixed cost and will not vary with enrollment. However, instructors are today increasingly paid a certain amount per student or a certain percentage of the gross revenues received. Sometimes an instructor is guaranteed a certain amount and then paid an amount per student over a specified number of enrollments. When such arrangements apply, instructor compensation becomes a variable cost or has elements of both fixed and variable costs.

The same is true with course material costs. Course notes can rarely be bought or produced at the last minute. Such materials must often be ordered weeks in advance on the basis of an enrollment estimate. Once ordered, course materials become a fixed cost, unless unused materials may be returned for credit. If the estimate of enrollments is too low and not enough materials have been ordered, ordering additional sets on a rush basis can result in a high variable cost on those sets.

Although Chapter 6 will discuss in more detail how the costs associated with course budgeting interact and change according to circumstance, even this brief discussion shows that there are no simple formulae for developing course budgets. However, we can build a theoretical framework for understanding how the financial elements of course planning interact and how we can manipulate these elements to suit our objectives.

Direct and Indirect Course Costs

Direct costs can be directly and conveniently associated with a cost object. All the fixed and variable costs mentioned so far—instructor compensation, course materials, room rent, refreshments—are direct costs of a course. Indirect costs cannot be directly or easily attributed to a cost object. Some indirect costs are administrative salaries, utilities, secretarial and receptionist salaries, rent on administrative space, and most office supplies. Indirect costs are often simply called "overhead," and these two terms will be used interchangeably throughout this text.

Indirect costs have an impact on course budgeting when the doctrine of full costing is adopted by the CE organization. Full costing holds that cost objects should be assigned the total cost of producing them, including those (indirect) costs that must be allocated among cost objects on some basis. Indirect costs are generally accumulated (added together) in cost pools. The total of these pools is periodically distributed to the various cost objects in an easily calculated way.

However, no course budget is comprehensive or fully useful unless it deals in some manner with indirect costs. In most cases, the indirect cost range and the allocation basis are "givens" prescribed by institutional procedures or practices. The most common traditional methods of allocating indirect costs to individual courses are

- as a fixed percentage of total income
- as a fixed dollar figure per student
- as a fixed percentage of total expense
- as a fixed dollar figure per course or program

Another way of assessing indirect costs against programs is to require that revenue exceed direct expenses by either a dollar amount or a fixed percentage of either income or expense. This practice "hides" the indirect cost assessment only from the budgetarily naive. The method of allocation can be an extremely important issue. Chapter 14 contains a full description of the allocation of indirect costs.

These concepts of fixed and variable, direct and indirect costs are often confused by those unfamiliar with cost accounting and budgeting. For instance, it is often not recognized that both direct and indirect costs can be either fixed or variable. For instance, the first three allocation methods in the above list result in indirect costs being variable costs, while the fourth method makes indirect costs a fixed cost element.

A thorough understanding of the treatment of indirect costs is an important measure of the managerial maturity of a CE professional. It should be understood that there is no single correct or best method of allocating indirect costs; all methods have advantages and disadvantages. Whatever method is chosen, it will have important implications for financial decision making.

Unit Costs

The unit cost, or cost per unit, is simply the total cost of a number of units of production divided by the number of units produced. Unit costs are affected by both fixed and variable costs. In our context, the "unit" is sometimes the course, but in this part of our discussion the unit will be a participant. Variable costs, contrary to their label, remain constant per unit. In the power plant course example, the variable costs were $30 per enrollment (for now we will ignore the hypothetical cost break on materials for 50 or more). However, the fixed costs per unit decline as more and more students enroll, since each one can be assigned a pro rata share of the unchanging fixed costs, as shown graphically in Exhibit 5.3. The variable cost per unit is depicted as straight line A, parallel with the x axis at a value of $30, while the fixed cost per unit is shown as a curve with a negative slope (B). Total cost per unit is the sum of these two lines (C).

For instance, for 40 enrollments, the variable cost per unit is $30 (40 x $30/40), the fixed cost per unit is $70 ($2,800/40), and the total cost per unit is $100 ($30 + $70). Thus the "mix" of fixed and variable costs has a significant bearing on the behavior of unit costs.

Break-Even Analysis

We can now combine the concepts of revenue and fixed and variable costs in a simple graph that shows how these elements interact. This graphic presentation is sometimes known as break-even analysis because it shows the break-even point, which is the level of volume (enrollment) required for the revenue produced to equal the total costs.

Exhibit 5.4 summarizes the costs in our small power plant course and adds instructor compensation; the exhibit ignores the complications of fixed cost steps and variable cost changes and adds an indirect cost allocation as a fixed cost of $200. The bottom part of the figure shows a calculation of total

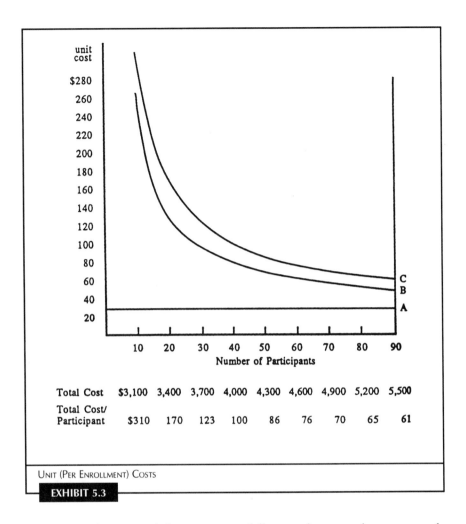

Total Cost	$3,100	3,400	3,700	4,000	4,300	4,600	4,900	5,200	5,500
Total Cost/ Participant	$310	170	123	100	86	76	70	65	61

Unit (Per Enrollment) Costs

EXHIBIT 5.3

revenue, total costs, and the margin, or difference, between these two totals for various levels of enrollment.

The break-even point (BEP), along with revenue and costs, is shown graphically in Exhibit 5.5. The BEP is an easily understood indication of success. If enrollments exceed BEP we "make money"; revenue exceeds costs. If enrollments do not reach BEP, revenue does not cover all costs.

The BEP can be calculated algebraically without reference to a graph by using the following terms and equation: Let X = the number of enrollments at BEP, TR = total revenue, F = course fee, TC = total costs, TFC = total fixed costs, and TVC = total variable costs. We know that at the BEP, TR = TC and that TC = TFC + TVC. The break-even point can thus be calculated with the following formula: xF = x (TVC) + TFC. Using the numbers from

Variable costs per student:		
Course notes		$15
Reception		8
Coffee, refreshmnents		7
Total		**$30**

Fixed Costs:		
Promotion		$1,500
Room rental		500
Audiovisual equipment		200
Instructor travel		600
Instructor compensation		1,000
Indirect costs		200
Total		**$4,000**

Enrollment	Total Revenue	Total Costs	Margin/ (Loss)
10	$1,750	$4,300	($2,550)
20	3,500	4,600	(1,100)
30	5,250	4,900	350
40	7,000	5,200	1,800
50	8,750	5,500	3,250
60	10,500	5,800	4,700
70	12,250	6,100	6,150
80	14,000	6,400	7,600
90	15,750	6,700	9,050

BUDGET DETAIL FOR "SMALL POWER GENERATION PLANTS" COURSE

EXHIBIT 5.4

our example, we get $175x=$30x+$4,000. Simplifying this equation, we get $145x=$4,000, and, therefore, x=27.6.

In other words, just over 27 enrollments equals the break-even point for this course. This kind of break-even analysis can be useful in planning courses because it incorporates many of the important variables. Where these variables (fees, costs, and the expenditures of funds) are reasonably constant, this model can yield valid results.

Although useful, this kind of analysis has limitations. Continuing education professionals need a framework that can handle several variables at once. For

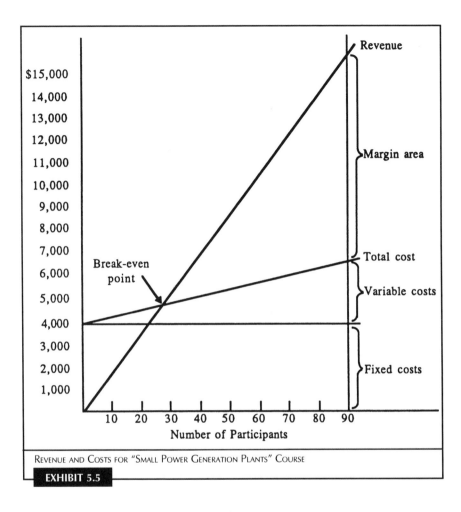

$15,000
14,000
13,000
12,000
11,000
10,000
9,000
8,000
7,000
6,000
5,000
4,000
3,000
2,000
1,000

Revenue

Margin area

Total cost

Variable costs

Fixed costs

Break-even point

10 20 30 40 50 60 70 80 90

Number of Participants

REVENUE AND COSTS FOR "SMALL POWER GENERATION PLANTS" COURSE

EXHIBIT 5.5

example, suppose a programmer decides to propose an instructor compensation scheme that incorporates both fixed and variable costs and amounts to,
say, $1,000 for up to 50 enrollments and $30 for every enrollment above 50.
This possibility, when combined with other financial decisions, such as those
relating to room size and cost, promotion schemes, and volume discounts on
the production of course materials, creates complications that break-even
analysis alone could not handle easily.

Even if all the variables could be conveniently and quickly manipulated, as
they might be with the aid of computers and appropriate software, break-even
analysis alone would not be sufficient to ensure sound course planning and
budgeting. Such planning must incorporate other elements that are difficult to
quantify and describe graphically but are nonetheless important. Experienced

programmers regularly incorporate these elements, either consciously or intuitively, when planning a course or group of courses. We call these elements "dynamic" because they represent an ever-changing process.

DYNAMIC ELEMENTS OF COURSE BUDGETING

Although the static elements described above are important to an understanding of course budgeting, they do not help in several important dimensions of decision making typical of the course planning process. They do not provide guidance in choosing among alternative course development options, and, except for the shifting between variable and fixed costs, they provide little help in assessing or altering risks and rewards associated with course development.

Few successful ventures are undertaken in a risk-free environment. Successful continuing education programmers are risk-takers but not gamblers. They estimate a balance between potential rewards and risks, taking chances when the odds are favorable. The estimates require that details of the proposed course be worked out during the planning process, which should include the preparation of a course budget. This section defines some terms and illustrates some techniques to help programmers balance the financial risks and rewards of presenting a particular course.

Programmers need to examine both their own attitudes toward risk-taking and the attitude of the management of the CE unit. A successful program that attracts enough students (however "enough" is defined) engenders goodwill toward the organization and everyone connected to it. The reputation of the programmer, the CE organization, and the parent organization is enhanced. On the other hand, a program that fails to attract "enough" students reflects badly on the organization. Students and instructors are disappointed and inconvenienced. After several cancellations, people are likely to lose confidence in the programmer and the organization. Although one cannot place a dollar value on reputation-related influences, they are as important as financial considerations in course planning.

The organization that discourages risk-taking in its members is probably on the decline and a dull place to work. Successful CE organizations reward responsible risk-taking and do not impose sanctions when it fails. Risking and winning can lead to growth by opening new markets and new opportunities. Risking and losing is costly but also provides valuable information: perhaps the market is not there or is not ready yet. The organization will not waste additional resources on it at present.

The Course Planning Process

A traditional course budget estimates the revenues and expenses associated with presenting a course and estimates a dollar outcome. It presents the relative financial rewards and risks of presenting a course according to a set of assumptions. Underlying each course budget is a planning and decision-making process.

Let us examine one model of the course planning process and see how budgeting fits in. Exhibit 5.6 lists some stages of course development; the bottom part of the exhibit is a graph of cumulative costs, including the cost of

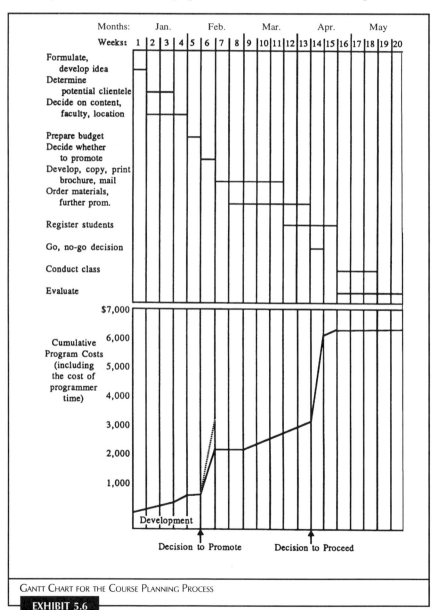

GANTT CHART FOR THE COURSE PLANNING PROCESS
EXHIBIT 5.6

programmer time. From a financial perspective, the course development process is a series of decisions about spending money. The greater the amount of expenditure, the more important the decision. In this example, two common important decision points are shown—the decision to promote and the decision to proceed. The decision to promote a course is usually the first decision in course planning that involves a major expenditure of out-of-pocket dollars, that is, expenditures for something other than programmer payroll costs. The solid line on the graph shows the actual outlay of dollars, but, in effect, once the decision to promote has been made, the commitment to expend money has been made and the cumulative cost line could be shown to jump up to include all expected promotion costs, expended or not. This situation is shown as a dotted line on the graph. Another important decision is the decision to proceed (the go/no go decision) and is usually based upon the number of enrollments in the course. Proceeding with the course, rather than canceling it, requires further investment in instructor compensation, course materials, facility and equipment rental, and so on. The cumulative cost line jumps up once the decision to proceed has been made.

Reward/Risk Concepts

Cost and Value of Programmer Time

The easiest calculation to make (and most often ignored in the course budgeting process) is the cost of programmer time. How a programmer spends time is crucial to the success of the enterprise, and yet we have no effective way of keeping track of it. We can make some helpful calculations. The cost of programmer time is defined as the value of the consideration (usually the programmer's salary and benefits) given up by the organization to secure the services of the programmer. "Time" is defined as the number of hours for which the programmer is paid. To arrive at cost per hour, subtract holidays, vacation, sick leave, professional development, and other "down time" from the normal work year of 2,080 hours. Then divide salary and benefits per time period (usually one year) by the number of *productive* hours in the time period.

The value of programmer time is the net value of the resources the programmer brings into the organization. Thus, in a self-supporting CE organization, a programmer might be expected to produce a margin (surplus of revenue over expense) of $20,000 for the year. This expectation is also usually reduced to a "value per hour" figure. This value per hour is an estimation of the opportunity cost (the net value given up by taking one opportunity rather than another) of programmer time and represents, in this case, the amount that the programmer can earn when productively engaged. This value of programmer time is a standard against which potential opportunities can be judged. To be fully compensated for the expenditure of programmer time, the organization must realize a return at least equal to the sum of the cost of programmer time and the value of the opportunities lost in the use of that time: the cost and the value must be added together. Exhibit 5.7 illustrates these calculations.

These concepts are important not only because they are usually a relatively high proportion of total course costs but also because the evaluation of rewards and risks begins when the programmer decides how to spend working time. Even if explicit calculations are not made of the time and effort required to develop a particular course, informal calculations of the relative chances for success of various alternatives are part of the daily routine of most programmers.

Time		
Total hours		2,080
Less:		
Holidays		(88)
Vacation		(120)
Sick leave (estimated)		(80)
Administrative meetings		(98)
Professional development		(80)
Productive hours		1,614

Cost per Hour		
$\dfrac{\text{Salary} + \text{Benefits}}{\text{Productive Hours}}$	$\dfrac{\$24,000 + \$6,000}{1,614}$	$18.59

Value per Hour		
$\dfrac{\text{Net Resources}}{\text{Productive Hours}}$	$\dfrac{\$20,000}{1,614}$	12.39
	Total	$30.98

CALCULATION OF THE COST AND VALUE OF PROGRAMMER TIME

EXHIBIT 5.7

Opportunity Costs

An opportunity cost is the net value given up by following one alternative over another—if you do one thing, you can't do something else. Suppose a programmer decides to develop Course A rather than Course B. After spending $1,000 on development and promotion, the programmer then cancels Course A for lack of enrollment. If Course B could have generated a net of $500, the opportunity cost of the programmer's decision is $1,500—the $1,000 loss on the failed course and the $500 foregone by not being able to develop Course B.

Opportunity costs usually cannot be calculated with any kind of accuracy; we only guess at the returns of actions not taken. But these guesses are frequent, and opportunity costs are important in evaluating the rewards and risks. A sound measure of a programmer's value is his or her success rate in course choice.

Sunk Costs

Sunk costs are associated with a particular project, say, the development of a continuing education course, and cannot be recovered or reduced. For instance, Exhibit 5.6 shows that at the end of the 13th week we must decide whether to proceed with the course; all our developmental and promotional costs (about $3,000) are sunk—we cannot recover any of them. Therefore, they have no bearing on our decision to proceed. If the income produced by proceeding will exceed the costs of proceeding, we should hold the course no matter how large the sunk costs.

The concept of sunk costs relates to evaluating the rewards and risks because, in general, the larger the investment in sunk costs, the higher the risk. For instance, a course requiring only a $500 investment in "up-front" development and promotion is likely to be "less risky" than one requiring a $5,000 investment; the consequences of failure for the first course are less severe. But this is only one side of the coin because the chances of failure must be calculated.

Enrollment Probabilities

Most programmers are familiar with the reward/risk evaluation procedure as it pertains to enrollment estimates. Most, if not all, of the reward/risk evaluation process may be contained in an estimation of the probability that a particular course enrollment level will be reached. As we have seen, other important elements in the process should also be considered. Estimating enrollment levels is the most difficult calculation to make and therefore subject to the greatest error. An ability to make this kind of estimation is really an art, depending largely on programmer intuition and not quantitative techniques. In evaluating rewards and risks, this uncertainty is a central element in the final part of the process, the estimation of up-side and down-side potential.

Up-Side and Down-Side Potential

Up-side potential is the highest return an investment might make; downside potential is the most that can be lost. Programmers may look at programming decisions in this way, seeking programs with high up-side potential and low down-side risks. These opportunities are rare. Programmers often must risk a considerable amount, in development time and effort and promotion expenditures, to realize a high reward. A balancing takes place in the decision process. Where up-front costs (the risks of loss) are large, look for a high probability of sufficient enrollment or the possibility of a high reward (higher than usual for a "successful" program). Where sunk (up-front) costs are low, accept a lower probability that "successful" enrollment levels can be achieved. Programmers often are faced with truncated up-side potentials. This happens when enrollment is limited by educational considerations, by classroom size, or by other factors. In such cases, either the sunk costs must be low, or the probabilities for good enrollment levels high.

Reward/Risk Index

Balancing the elements of reward/risk depends on the judgment, experience, and intuition of the programmer. Beyond that, this judgment is informed by calculations derived from the course budget process. Although course budgeting cannot help a programmer estimate enrollment probabilities (the probability that a particular enrollment level will be reached), it can help a programmer evaluate the appropriate proportion between reasonably estimated potential rewards and the risk of sunk costs. Exhibit 5.8 shows the budgets for two courses, both of which are expected to have an income of $3,000, expenses of $1,700, and a margin of $1,300. However, Course A will require us to "sink" $1,300 into the course before we know how many people will enroll in it—$600 on promotion, $300 on course materials, and $400 on development of the course by the instructor. Course B will require that we sink only $600 into "up-front" costs—$500 for promotion and $100 for materials. The teacher will not be paid if the course is not held. With these facts, we can create an index to help us measure the relative rewards and risks of these two courses by dividing the potential reward (margin) by the risk (sunk costs). All other things being equal (most importantly the probability that each course will indeed generate $3,000 in income), Course B, with the higher ratio of 2.16, is a better bet. This index is not, in itself, meaningful—it must be compared with other indexes similarly calculated to determine a relative order of alternatives. This example uses only financial criteria in calculating rewards and risks; many other considerations, including educational quality and service, must also be put into this equation.

	Course A		Course B	
Income	$3,000		$3,000	
Expense	Total	Sunk	Total	Sunk
Promotion	$600	$600	$500	$500
Materials	300	300	300	100
Instruction	800	400	900	
Total expense	$1,700	$1,300	$1,700	$600
Margin	$1,300		$1,300	
Index				
Margin	1,300		1,300	
Sunk	1,300	1	600	2.16

REWARD/RISK INDEX
EXHIBIT 5.8

Sharing Rewards and Risks

Using this conceptual background, we can adjust financial elements to share rewards and risks or to minimize risks. One obvious way is to shift costs in or out of the "sunk" category. For instance, if we were worried that Course A in Exhibit 5.8 might not generate enough enrollments, we might make a deal with the instructor. Instead of paying him or her $400 for course development costs and $400 to teach the course, we would pay $1,000 only if the course were not canceled. Thus we have reduced our up-side potential by $200 ($1,000 – $800) and our down-side risk by $400 (the sunk portion of the original proposal). In this way, both the risk and the reward are shared with the instructor. Again, there are nonfinancial considerations. Is this the kind of relationship we want to build with our instructors?

Another way of sharing rewards and risks is to shift between fixed and variable costs. Exhibit 5.9 shows two courses, each carrying the same fee. For Alternative 1, with low variable and high fixed costs, the risk of loss (at, say, six enrollments) and the reward for success (say, at 20 enrollments) is greater than for Alternative 2 with high variable and low fixed costs. We might, for instance, negotiate with an instructor an arrangement whereby, instead of accepting a flat fee for teaching a course, the instructor is paid on a per student basis. Thus a fixed cost becomes a variable cost and the risk of loss to the organization is reduced along with the potential return. How to share rewards and risks is easier to explain than when to share. In many CE organizations, risk avoidance is the rule, but avoiding risk often means a decrease in reward. Again, a balance must be struck.

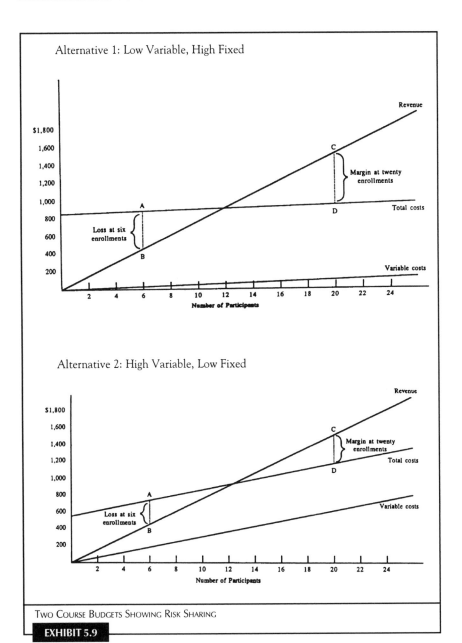

Alternative 1: Low Variable, High Fixed

Alternative 2: High Variable, Low Fixed

Two Course Budgets Showing Risk Sharing

EXHIBIT 5.9

Reward/risk sharing can also be accomplished between programmers and CE management. For instance, management may participate in the decision to develop a risky course with high reward potential that would otherwise be rejected by the programmer, who, without support from management, would be assuming too great a risk.

Portfolio Management

Evaluating the rewards and risks for a group of courses is a complex process. Such a group could be called a "portfolio" of courses when all or most of them will be presented more than once. Portfolio management is a term used in financial management to express the idea that a portfolio of investments should be frequently examined to assure a maximum gain consistent with the level of risk desired. Nonperforming investments should be disposed of and new opportunities seized upon. Most investment portfolios are diversified to spread risk and also to mix risky investments of potentially high return with less risky investments of lower return. Many programmers can view their "portfolio" of courses in the same way, seeking to mix risky, new courses of uncertain return with older, tried and true courses of relatively stable productivity. A proper balance should be struck. But what is a proper balance between the new and the old, the risky and the stable? There is no single answer, but in continuing education the notion of the product "cycle" is important in achieving this balance. Product cycle is the length of time it takes for a new product to be introduced, to gain peak market acceptance, and then to decline. In continuing education, courses and subjects follow this cyclical pattern. The programmer should be aware of and try to estimate the life span of the courses for which he or she is responsible. For instance, the product cycle for "The Concepts of Data Processing" may be relatively long (although, naturally, the course will have to be revised frequently). But the cycle for "Programming in C+" is likely to be much shorter as new languages supplant C+.

What does product cycle have to do with balancing a portfolio of courses? If we have a high percentage of courses like the C+ course, and if we determine that the cycle for these courses is three years, then we should look to renew our portfolio in three years; in other words, on the average each year one-third of our offerings should be new courses. On the other hand, if most of our courses are foreign language courses or basic business courses with longer product cycles, the rate of new courses offered each year could be less. However, usually no less than 10 percent of each year's offerings should be new, and only under unusual circumstances is it healthy for more than one-third to be new.

The foregoing analogy to financial portfolio management, with its emphasis on financial return on investment and its objective measurement standards, can be taken only so far. For continuing educators, the game is more complex.

Although the financial performance of a program is important, it is by no means the only standard of measurement, and policy and long-term planning often require that it take a back seat to other considerations. The history of continuing education highlights not the daring financial risks taken in the field, but the educational risks taken by continuing educators with the foresight and daring to try new things, from the first course in Shakespeare given at Johns Hopkins in 1876 to the computer science curriculum developed by several extension divisions in the late 1950s. Ultimately, success in this kind of educational risk-taking, with its immeasurable rewards, will obtain for continuing educators an appropriate role in higher education.

The organization that does not allow or encourage some risk-taking is taking the highest risk of all—the risk of obsolescence and decline. Unlike their colleagues in their parent institutions, continuing educators are encouraged to take risks in return for rewards and must evaluate the trade-offs involved on a routine basis.

CONCLUSION

A number of concepts are basic to an understanding of budgeting, and the proper use of a budget vocabulary is important in developing a common understanding among members of an organization. Traditional textbook explanations begin with the concept of the budget object, the entity for which a budget is prepared. The textbook approach usually concentrates on the behavior of costs, describing fixed and variable costs and the methods of determining and allocating direct and indirect costs.

These are important concepts, but continuing education professionals must usually go beyond these concepts to be effective in budgeting. Fully or partly self-supporting CE organizations must also project income, and this is often not easy. As the course development process proceeds, CE organization must be aware that the time and money they spend is being "sunk" into a course and cannot be recovered. In a sense, these sunk costs represent an investment in a course, and they are expected to yield a return.

Course budgeting contains some elements of investment portfolio management, including the important concepts of the break-even point, return on investment, opportunity costs, and the balancing of rewards and risks. Of course, not every programmer will make detailed calculations of the BEP or opportunity costs, but the theoretical background presented here can add a useful dimension even to informal program planning processes. An important aim of this chapter, and, indeed, this book, is to help make programmers' decisions more self-conscious and deliberate and to provide a theoretical framework for these decisions.

CHAPTER 6

A Practical Guide to Course Budgeting

Planning and presenting a continuing education course, as anyone who has tried it knows, is a complex process. It places considerable demands on the programmer's organizing ability. Many tasks must be performed, details carefully attended to, potential problems anticipated. How many courses have failed because the brochure was not mailed on time or a crucial mailing list was not received? How many courses have been destroyed when the lamp of the projector suddenly burned out, leaving 50 students to listen to an instructor lamely extemporizing on his subject for 40 minutes?

In the midst of trying to avoid such disasters, the programmer must also constantly assess the financial and educational viability of the course. Calculation of a course budget early in the planning process is an invaluable aid in determining financial viability—at that moment. But as conditions change and new information becomes available, the financial picture can change substantially. Ideally, a course budget should be revised for each new bit of information or at least recalculated as decisions about the course are made. Although personal computers now provide the technical capability for speedy and frequent recasting of the course budget, it is usually impractical to make more than a few budgets for a course. Infinitely more useful to the programmer is a theoretical framework that makes possible the rapid understanding of the dynamics of the course-planning process. In this chapter, we will develop this framework, building on both the traditional model of budgeting and the dynamic aspects of the process discussed in the last chapter.

COURSE PLANNING AND COSTS: AN EXAMPLE

Although no single, universally accepted course-planning model exists, a significant body of literature on the subject covers both theoretical and

Houle	Nadler
1. A possible educational activity is identified.	1. Identify learning needs.
2. A decision is made to proceed.	2. Determine objectives.
3. Objectives are identified and refined.	3. Build curriculum.
4. A suitable format is designed.	4. Select instructional strategies.
5. The format is fitted into larger patterns of life.	5. Obtain instructional resources.
6. The plan is put into effect.	6. Conduct training.
7. The results are measured and appraised.	

Buskey	Stroher
1. Analyze planning context and client systems.	1. Set objectives and select title.
2. Assess needs.	2. Determine potential clientel.
3. Develop objectives.	3. Reserve classroom.
4. Select and order content.	4. Select faculty.
5. Select, design, and order instructional process.	5. Print brochure.
6. Select instructional resources.	6. Mail brochure.
7. Formulate budget and administrative plan.	7. Order books, material.
8. Gain assurances of participation.	8. Send out news release.
9. Design evaluation procedure.	9. Register students.
	10. Conduct class.
	11. Evaluate.

Source: Houle, C. O. *The Design of Educating.* San Francisco: Jossey-Bass, 1972.

Source: Nadler, L. *Designing Training Programs: The Critical Events Model.* Reading, MA: Addison-Wesley, 1982.

Source Buskey, J. H. "Program Planning in Continuing Education" Unpublished Manuscript, 1985.

Source: Stroher, G. B. and Kit, J. P., *Administration of Continuing Education.* Belmont, CA: Wadsworth, 1982.

FOUR COURSE PLANNING MODELS

EXHIBIT 6.1

practical aspects of the process. Exhibit 6.1 gives four examples of planning models and illustrates their diversity.

These models may be used as the basis for one of three methods for controlling and keeping track of program development. The critical path method for organizing the course-planning process plots each element of course development on a chart and shows its cause-and-effect relationship to each other element. The checklist, another commonly used planning method, merely names the tasks that must be done, usually in time sequence or at least with deadlines indicated. In the following example, we will use the Gantt chart method, which has the advantage of providing a visual representation of the time dimension in the planning process.

Exhibit 5.6, on page 75, shows a Gantt chart based on a listing of stages in the development of an imaginary course called "International Stock Market Index Futures"; the chart follows development of the course from the inception of the idea to the review of the course's financial results. The chart lists only those planning steps requiring decisions with financial implications. The lower part of the exhibit is a graph showing the cumulative costs of the course, including the value of programmer time.

We will trace the development of the course on International Stock Market Index Futures by following a fictional programmer named Cindy as she follows the steps shown in Exhibit 5.6. One day, while reading the *Wall Street Journal*, Cindy ran across an article on a new investment opportunity in international stock market index futures. Intrigued, she called her broker and asked him about these futures. Her broker could add little to the information in the article. Instinctively, Cindy combined her own interest with the apparent lack of knowledge about this new investment opportunity and began to consider the possibility of offering a program on the subject for the upcoming spring term. Her course-planning process had begun.

Idea Inception and Development (Week 1)

Theoretically, the budgetary meter began running the moment Cindy had the idea for the course, however vague it might have been. The time Cindy put into reading the article and calling her broker represented the first costs that could be directly attributed to the course. During the next week, Cindy talked to as many people as she could about international stock market futures. By asking her broker and representatives of other brokerage houses in her area, she identified a number of experts on this emerging investment opportunity. Cindy spent about six hours thinking about this possible course idea during that first week. Using the method illustrated in the last chapter, we can calculate the cost of Cindy's time at $15/hour, so the cumulative cost of course development was $90 (6 hours x $15) at the end of the first week.

Determination of Potential Clientele (Weeks 2 and 3)

At first Cindy thought that the course would best be directed at stockbrokers themselves, who needed quick information about this new development to inform their clients. Judging by her own broker's lack of knowledge, she felt there might be a real need for a highly technical course taught by high-level people and directed at stockbrokers. She quickly learned, however, that most well-known brokerage houses were already doing in-house seminars and distributing literature to their employees. She therefore abandoned her first idea and turned to the users of broker services, investors like herself. Examining her own attitudes toward international stock index futures and comparing them with the attitudes of other investors, she began to develop a profile of her potential audience. She reasoned that the course would attract adventurous investors, people who were willing to gamble part of their portfolios on a relatively risky investment but who wanted to know more about the market mechanics and the risks involved. Further, it seemed that this market, as well as the brokerage community, would welcome the independent, objective survey that a university continuing education course could be expected to represent. By the end of the second week, Cindy began concentrating on investors as her market.

Decisions on Content, Faculty, Course Location (Weeks 2-4)

While trying to identify her target audience, Cindy was also making contacts with potential course instructors and learning all she could about the subject. By the end of the third week, she had formulated, with the help of several members of large brokerage firms (whom she began to refer to as her informal advisory committee), a rough outline of the course and a list of several potential instructors.

In the fourth week, Cindy decided that the course would be conducted on three successive Tuesday nights at a well-known hotel located on the outskirts of the city, between the financial district downtown and the suburban community where she theorized that most of her potential audience lived. Each session would be two hours long, counting a 20-minute break, from 7:30 to 9:30. Cindy planned to pay three instructors $500 each.

By the end of the fourth week, Cindy had spent an additional 30 hours on the course and had spent money on lunches, local travel, and reference materials. The total tab for weeks 2 through 4 was $550.

Budget Preparation (Week 5)

At this point, Cindy knew she needed a clearer idea of the financial aspects of her potential course. This was an ideal time to prepare a budget. She had not yet made any major decisions about holding the course; she had not made firm commitments to instructors and could still back out gracefully; and she had not actually signed a contract with the hotel, although she had tentatively reserved a date and a meeting room. She knew now or could figure out with reasonable accuracy what the course would cost to present. In the fifth week, therefore, she sat down and prepared the budget shown in Exhibit 6.2.

Cindy had to guess at the number of people the course might attract, but felt that 150 was a reasonable estimate. She submitted the budget to the director of Continuing Education, who discussed it with her before giving approval. She spent four hours on the course during the fifth week, incurring a programmer time cost of $60.

Income (150 @ $75)		$11,250
Expense:		
Promotion		
Brochure	$1,500	
Newspaper	300	$1,800
Teacher compensation		1,500
*Other expenses**		
Room rental ($200 deposit advance)	$1,200	
Audiovisual equipment	100	
Coffee, refreshments ($3/person)	450	
Program support ($50/meeting)	150	
Program materials ($7/person)	1,050	2,950
Total expense		**$6,250**
Margin (Income minus expense)		**$5,000**

*Cost of programmer time of $795 not shown, to be covered by the margin

Course Budget for "International Stock Market Index Futures"

EXHIBIT 6.2

Decision to Promote (Week 6)

Cindy now faced the first "natural" decision point in her planning. These points occur when a continuation of course planning, developing, or presenting means spending, or committing to spend, a significant amount of money. Until now, the development of this course had involved relatively little "out-of-pocket" expenditure, and the cost of Cindy's time had been the largest expense element. She could still drop plans for the course without suffering too much, financially or otherwise. However, the moment she decided to go ahead with the course, she was committed to spending $1,500 on the promotional brochure. The cost line on Exhibit 5.6 (page 75) thus jumps by $1,500 when the commitment to promote is made, although the actual money transaction might not occur for weeks.

Ordering Materials and Services: Further Promotion (Weeks 9-13)

In the ninth week, Cindy began to handle some of the details of course presentation. She signed the contract for the room at the hotel and paid a $200 nonrefundable deposit. (She could still cancel her reservation on one week's notice with no further penalty.) She went ahead with her plans for newspaper advertising costing $300 and ordered ads to be run two weeks before the course was to begin. She also secured materials needed for the course; she spent $500 to reproduce materials. She could return the soft cover books for credit, but she had to commit herself to the printing. She spent three hours doing these tasks. Cost commitments for weeks 9 through 13 were as follows:

Room deposit (nonrefundable)	$ 200
Newspaper advertising	300
Course materials (nonreturnable)	550
Cindy's time	45
Total	$1,095

The lower part of Exhibit 5.6 can help us analyze Cindy's decision-making process. The decision in week 6 to promote (i.e., to go forward with the course) caused cumulative costs to jump because of promotion cost commitments. Although actual expenditures have not yet been made, we might also add the costs of the room and materials deposit to that jump, since the commitment to go forward in week 6 meant that Cindy's institution had to spend that further money. In the normal course of events, Cindy would receive no new information during the later period that would cause her to reexamine her decision to proceed. The dotted line in the lower graph of Exhibit 5.6 shows this reasoning. Thus, the point we have called "decision to promote" is really much more because cost elements besides promotion are involved.

Registration of Students (Weeks 12-15)

In the twelfth week, students responded to the promotion and began registering for the course. Beyond answering a few structured questions and occasionally checking enrollments, Cindy had little to do with this course and incurred no direct costs in dollars or time during the registration process. Student registration was handled by the registration staff, whose time was paid for from the margins produced by the CE programs.

Go, No-Go Decision (Week 14)

A week before the class was scheduled to begin, Cindy had to make a final decision about whether to hold the course. If she wanted to cancel, a week would give her time to notify her instructors and students of the cancellation without too much embarrassment. She would also have time to cancel the meeting room reservation and save the $1,000 additional charge. Exhibit 6.3 summarizes the cost situation Cindy faced at this second natural decision point.

Item	Sunk Costs	Future Fixed Costs	Future Variable Costs
Promotion	$1,800		
Teacher compensation		$1,500	
Room rental	200	1,000	
Audio-visual equipment		100	
Coffee, refreshments			$3.00/person
Program support		150	
Program materials	550		3.33/person
Sub-total	**$2,550**	**$2,750**	**$6.33/person**
Cindy's time (Not budgeted)	645	150	
Total	**$3,195**	**$2,900**	

Cost Summary: "International Stock Market Index Futures," Fourteenth Week

EXHIBIT 6.3

Cindy had already "sunk" $3,195 into developing this course. If she decided to go ahead with the project, she would be committing another $2,900 plus variable costs of $6.33 per student. As explained in the last chapter's discussion on sunk costs, only these latter figures should be considered in her decision.

Cindy was disappointed to learn that only 40 people had enrolled. Experience told her to expect perhaps 20 more people to enroll in the last week, given the enrollment rate over the first three weeks. Another seven or eight people might enroll at the door on the first night. Her estimate of the final enrollment thus stood at 68, less than half the number she originally expected! Should she hold the course or cancel it?

Cindy was a veteran programmer and had faced this kind of decision before. She knew that the rational way to approach this situation was to decide whether it would cost her more in net resources (not counting sunk costs) to proceed with the course or to cancel it. She determined her approximate income from the course as follows: 68 students x $75 = $5,100. If she proceeded, the course, even with the low enrollment, would produce an excess of income over costs, where only "unsunk" costs are calculated, as follows: ($2,900 + [$6.33 x 68].) This calculation gave her $3,330.44 in total costs, which, when subtracted from her estimated income of $5,100, left an excess of $1,769.56.

Cindy decided to go ahead with the course, even though she was aware that it would not really "make money"; the cumulative costs, including the sunk costs, would probably exceed the estimated income of $5,100. When she made this decision, cumulative costs jumped by $2,900.

The decision Cindy faced was a common one and, given the numbers involved and the framework we have been developing, not particularly difficult to make, even though it was based upon estimates of future enrollments. In another situation, these estimates might not have led to so clear-cut a decision. Suppose only 30 people had enrolled? We will return to this set of circumstances shortly when we discuss break-even point analysis and levels of financial success.

Presentation of Course (Weeks 16-18)

By the time the stock market course began, most of its costs were already expended or committed, so the graph of cost behavior in Exhibit 5.6 remains flat. Exceptions to this are common, however. Last-minute events or enrollments outside the predicted range can change the cumulative cost picture. For instance, Cindy might have been able to talk the hotel into holding the conference in a smaller, less expensive room. If enrollments were greater than predicted, the production of more course materials, the need to acquire a larger room, and many other factors could require cost adjustments. These adjustments are important to the overall success of the course, but they do not require decision making based on financial considerations.

Evaluation (Weeks 16-20)

Formal course evaluations can be expensive, so evaluations are usually limited to a review of student questionnaires and discussion with the instructors. Thus, the main costs of evaluation are usually programmer time and perhaps word-processing time for transcribing student comments and summarizing results. Although most evaluations concern the educational quality of the offering and students' reactions to it, other issues can arise. Cindy, for instance, had to remember how she came up with the estimate of 150 enrollments and determine what was wrong with her enrollment-estimating process. Any major differences between actual expenses and budget projections should be analyzed to determine why and how the differences occurred. Feedback from such reviews can make the budgeting and decision-making process more useful and accurate.

To perform our own evaluation of Cindy's work, we must study the course budget in Exhibit 6.4, which combines the data shown in the earlier budgets (Exhibits 6.2 and 6.3). In this exhibit, we have multiplied all variable costs by our anticipated enrollment (150) to calculate margin, and we have added a new variable cost, overhead, which did not appear before.

Income (150 @ $75)			$11,250
	Fixed	**Variable**	
Expense:			
Promotion	$1,800		
Teacher Compensation	1,500		
Other expenses:			
Room rental	1,200		
Audiovisual equipment	100		
Coffee, refreshments ($3/person)		$450	
Program support	150		
Program materials ($3.33/person)	550	500	
Totals	**$5,300**	**$950**	**$6,250**
Margin before programmer salary and indirect expenses			**$5,000**
Less:			
Cost of programmer time	795		$795
Overhead ($15/person)		2,250	2,250
Total expenses	**$6,095**	**$3,200**	**$9,295**
Margin			**$1,955**

ELABORATED COURSE BUDGET FOR "INTERNATIONAL STOCK MARKET INDEX FUTURES"

EXHIBIT 6.4

Exhibit 6.5, our budget graph for the course, differs from the similar graph in Exhibit 5.5 important ways. Exhibit 5.5 (page 73) showed the "traditional model," in which variable costs were positioned on top of fixed costs. In Exhibit 6.5, we show fixed costs above variable. The cost of programmer time is also now shown separately from other fixed costs. Even with no students, we would still theoretically be obligated to pay the fixed costs. Therefore, fixed costs begin on the graph's zero axis at their total of $6,095 (from Exhibit 6.4) and are added to the variable costs per student to get total direct costs. Finally, we add the newly introduced overhead or indirect cost, which is here presented as a variable cost on the assumption that overhead is based on a per student rate.

Levels of Financial Success

The addition of the income line to the graph allows us to find the possible levels of financial success—the several intersections of the income and expense lines that, in effect, represent the break-even point at different levels of cost accumulation. Because we are now looking at this course theoretically, as one that might be presented in the future, it has no costs associated with it and the sunk cost situation described previously does not apply.

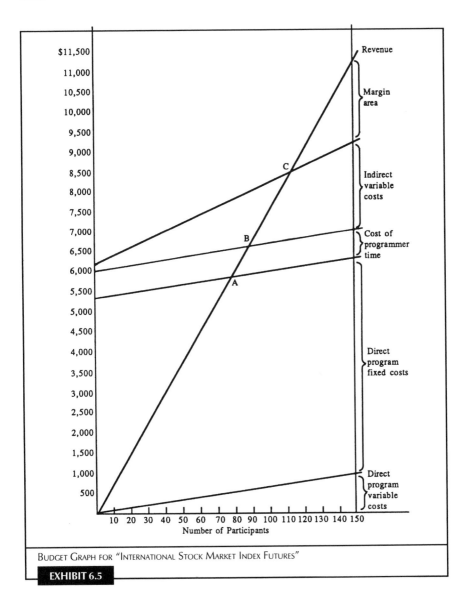

$11,500   Revenue
11,000
10,500   Margin
10,000   area

9,500
9,000
8,500   C
8,000   Indirect
7,500   variable
                                                          costs
7,000   B
6,500   Cost of
                                                          programmer
6,000   time
5,500   A
5,000
4,500
4,000   Direct
3,500   program
                                                          fixed costs
3,000
2,500
2,000
1,500
1,000   Direct
 500   program
                                                          variable
                                                          costs

     10 20 30 40 50 60 70 80 90 100 110 120 130 140 150
                    Number of Participants

BUDGET GRAPH FOR "INTERNATIONAL STOCK MARKET INDEX FUTURES"

EXHIBIT 6.5

The first intersection occurs at point A, at an enrollment of about 77 students. At this point, income from the course equals (covers) the course's direct variable costs and direct fixed costs except for programmer time. At point B (89 students), all direct costs are covered. At point C (113 students), all costs are covered; from this point on, the course begins to generate a true margin.

If Cindy ends up with only 68 students, she will not have reached even the first level of financial success. When she decided to go ahead with the course, income was expected to exceed total direct costs less those costs already paid (sunk). If Cindy continues to program at this financial level, she will end the year with a substantial deficit. If she programs at the point A level, she will cover all her direct costs but not her salary. If she reaches the point B level (on the average), she will cover all direct costs and her salary but will not have made any contribution to organizational or institutional overhead. Attaining a year-end financial result equivalent to the point C level means that Cindy is pulling her weight within the organization and meeting all costs, including her pro rata share of organizational overhead but not generating any extra. If, on average, Cindy exceeded the point C level, Cindy would be producing a surplus for her organization.

Although no graph can show the dynamic elements of the budgeting process, these are also important. Let us consider, therefore, two dynamic elements discussed in the last chapter: reward/risk ratio and opportunity costs.

Reward/Risk Ratio

When Cindy prepared her first course budget, she took a wild guess at the number of participants expected and came up with 150. As things turned out, this was much too optimistic. But 150 students would have generated a margin of almost $2,000. By renting a larger hall, she could have accommodated even more people at little additional cost or trouble. Her up-side potential was open ended, but her risk was high. As Exhibit 6.3 showed, Cindy did not get a clear reading on enrollment until the fourteenth week, by then, she had already "sunk" $3,915 into planning and development, including $645 (43 hours) worth of her own time. She had to risk over $3,000, not including the opportunity cost of her time, to make a potential $2,000 or more on the program. In simplistic notation, the reward/risk ratio might be stated as follows: $2,000/$3,000 = .66.

We can compare the stock market course with Principles of Accounting I, a small course that Cindy presented in a local insurance company last year. The company asked her to give this course in its offices two nights a week to help its employees upgrade their skills and perhaps use as credit toward a degree. The class was limited to 10 people by the size of the classroom and the requirements of the company. Each time the course was presented, Cindy spent three hours establishing the course and dealing with the instructor, plus another two hours at the award ceremony following completion of the course. The company guaranteed full attendance. Exhibit 6.6 shows the budget for this course.

Even though the success of this course is more or less assured, the promotion money (used to publicize the course in the company's in-house newsletter) and the value of Cindy's time before the course starts could be "sunk" and thus "at risk." This "at risk" money amounts to $145 ($100 in promotion plus

Income (10 @ $160)				$1,600
	Variable		**Fixed**	
	Per Person	**Total**		
Expense:				
Promotion			$100	$100
Teacher Compensation			700	700
Materials	$20	$200		200
Subtotal	**$20**	**$200**	**$800**	**$1,000**
Margin before programmer time and indirect costs				**$600**
Less:				
Cost of programmer time			$75	
Indirect costs (@ $15/person)			150	225
Margin				**$375**

COURSE BUDGET FOR "PRINCIPLES OF ACCOUNTING I"

EXHIBIT 6.6

three hours of programmer time at $15 an hour). The reward/risk ratio for this course might therefore be computed as follows: $375/$145 = 2.59.

Of course, we do not need this calculation to tell us that the accounting course is much less risky than the stock market course. The problem with the accounting course is that the most Cindy will ever make on it is $375. These two examples illustrate the typical trade-offs that programmers encounter: high risk is often coupled with potential high reward, low risk with low reward. If Cindy had a sufficient number of courses like Accounting I, she would be in good shape at the end of the year, but spending the time to develop similar courses with other companies would require the expenditure of further at-risk, up-front money and thus would decrease the courses' reward/risk ratio.

These two examples also illustrate two elements of risk measurement that are usually present in course development. The first element—the risk of losing development costs—can be measured in dollar terms. The higher the development costs, the higher the risk. The second risk, which is usually impossible to measure accurately, is the risk that not enough people will enroll. Programmers usually make an estimate of the probability of enrolling enough people to make a course financially viable. These two elements of risk are, of course, interrelated. A programmer would be willing to spend a great deal in development costs if a sufficient number of enrollments was guaranteed, as was the case with the accounting course. If development costs were low, the programmer might be willing to try a course even if there seemed to be a relatively low probability of sufficient enrollments.

Opportunity Costs

If Cindy is brimming over with good program ideas, she must choose among those ideas to develop only a small portion of them. She spent 40 hours on the stock market course in the hope of making $2,000 or more, while she spent a mere five hours on the accounting course in order to make $375. Again, the small accounting course looks like a better opportunity, since Cindy can gain $75 per hour of her time there ($375/5) and only $45 per hour on the stock market course ($1,955/43). The difference narrows a bit, however, when we add to the margin the contribution to overhead (indirect costs) of the two courses, which is higher for the stock market course because of the larger number of possible enrollments. Also, if the stock market course had proven successful, Cindy might well have been able to repeat it with less time and effort and a higher assurance of success than were possible the first time, thereby increasing the return on the investment of her 43 hours. Assessing the relative opportunities presented by a number of alternatives is perhaps the most difficult kind of judgment a CE programmer must make. Our "surplus per hour" calculation is merely a crude attempt at measuring opportunity costs; so many variables are involved, including variables not measurable in dollar terms, that no single formula can be used.

COURSE BUDGET FORMAT USING THE DECISION/PROCESS MODEL

With a new understanding of the behavior of course costs and levels of financial success, we can begin to use more elaborate budget formats. Exhibit 6.7 presents a course budget format that incorporates the elements of fixed, variable, indirect, and sunk costs. Most CE organizations use a simpler, less comprehensive document, and they might not need some of the features included here. On the other hand, certain other features of possible importance are not included on this form. Some of those features have been incorporated in expanded option tables (Exhibits 6.8, 6.9, 6.10) that could be applied to budget systems that use computers. Computers allow input screens to be developed easily and recalculations to be performed rapidly. Without these machines, extremely elaborate or frequently redrawn budgets usually do not represent a cost-effective use of programmer time.

Exhibit 6.7 shows the budget for a course entitled "Exploring the Sierra Nevada." This atypically complex travel course illustrates the use of this course budget format in its broader sense. In this course, between 19 and 40 students will spend two weeks hiking in the Sierra Nevada mountains in the company of three naturalists. The naturalists will give lectures on the flora, fauna, and geology of the region. The course has been approved for five hours of credit from the Department of Biology, and a final examination will be given. For most of the distance, a mule train will carry the supplies and gear for the group. A shuttle bus will bring the group back to the starting point when the trip is over.

Description

A budget's description should include whatever information is most important for identifying the course properly. Choice of the proper description is particularly important if the budget is going to serve as an input document to a data system. For instance, if statistics on courses by location were important, say,

---

Description

Course name:	Exploring The Sierra Nevada	Credit/noncredit:	Credit
Course I.D.	EDP 232	Semester units:	5
Programmer:	Joe Jones	CEU'S:	0
Assistant:	Bill Smith	Contact hours:	75
Term:	Summer '96	Minimum enroll:	19
Date begins:	June 1, 1996	Maximum enroll:	40
Date ends:	August 31, 1996	Go, no-go:	May 1, 1996
Location:	Sierra Nevada	Budget preparer:	Jones
Department:	Biology	Budget approved:	
Teacher name:	Muir		

Financial Summary

Item				
Expected enrollment	35			

Income	$14,000			

		Variable	Fixed	Sunk
Expenses				
Promotion	$900		$900	$900
Instructional costs	2,700	$1,050	1,650	
Other expenses	3,561	2,240	1,321	800
Cost of programmer	1,000		1,000	500
Indirect costs	3,150	350	2,800	
Total costs	**$11,311**	**$3,640**	**$7,671 (A)**	**$2,200 (D)**

Margin (income - expenses)	$2,689 (C)			

Break-even point:	$\dfrac{A}{\text{Av. fee - G}}$ =	$\dfrac{7,671}{400\text{-}104}$ =	25.90
Reward/risk ratio:	$\dfrac{C}{D}$ =	$\dfrac{2,689}{2,200}$ =	1.22

Income

Type fee	Fee	Enrollment	Gross	Pass-Through	Total
Type 1	$450	20	$9,000	$1,000	8,000
Type 2	400	15	6,000		6,000
Type 3					
Type 4					
Totals	**$850**	**35**	**$15,000**	**$1,000**	**$14,000**

COURSE BUDGET FOR "EXPLORING THE SIERRA NEVADA"

EXHIBIT 6.7

Expenses

Item	Variable Costs Per Person	Total	Fixed Costs	Total Costs	Sunk Costs
Promotion					
Catalogue (per cost guide)			$250	$250	$250
Brochure printing			150	150	150
Brochure mailing			200	200	200
Paid advertising			300	300	300
Other					
Subtotal promotions			**$900**	**$900**	**$900**
Instructional costs					
Instructor compensation					
Muir			$1,000	$1,000	
Guest/Lect.			500	500	
Guest/Lect.	$25	$875		875	
Subtotal	**$25**	**$875**	**$1,500**	**$2,375**	
Instructor travel			150	150	
Reader fee	5	175		175	
Subtotal inst. costs	**$30**	**$1,050**	**$1,650**	**$2,700**	
Other Expenses					
Room rental					
Audiovisual equipment					
Course materials	$18	$630	$300	$930	$300
Meals, coffee, etc.	46	1,610		1,610	500
Staff expenses			96	96	
Other					
Pack train			750	750	
Insurance			75	75	
Shuttle Bus			100	100	
Subtotal	**$64**	**$2,240**	**$1,321**	**$3,561**	**$800**
Total direct costs	**$94**	**$3,290**	**$3,871**	**$7,161**	**$1,700**
Cost of programmer time			$1,000	$1,000	$500
Subtotal	**$94**	**$3,290**	**$4,871**	**$8,161**	**$2,200**
Indirect costs					
Registration fee	$10	$350		$350	
Other (20% of income)			$2,800	2,800	
Subtotal indirect	**$10**	**$350**	**$2,800**	**$3,150**	
Total expenses	**$104 (B)**	**$3,640**	**$7,671 (A)**	**$11,311**	**$2,200 (D)**

Course Budget for "Exploring the Sierra Nevada"

EXHIBIT 6.7 (CONTINUED)

courses held at a downtowñ center as compared to on-campus programs, the location of each course might be specified at the top of its budget. Exhibit 6.8 lists the number of data items, including those shown in the example, that might be important to place in the description of a course budget. (Of course, only a few items could be chosen in any given instance.) Exhibit 6.8 is also a comprehensive listing of course attributes that might be included in a database.

Financial Summary

The financial summary section summarizes the detailed income and expense sections appearing in the income and expense sections of the schedule. In addition, the summary shows some important calculations that are useful in judging the financial viability of the course. The most important calculation is for margin (income – expense), which in our example is $2,689. Exhibit 6.7 shows only two of the many other calculations that could be made. Remember that course budgets are most useful when they are compared with something. They can be used as a standard against which actual results may be judged, or they may be compared with similar programs or other opportunities for programming. If a course has been presented before, its budget can be compared with the financial statement of the previous years' course.

Exhibit 6.7 includes a calculation of the break-even point at one of the three success levels described earlier in the chapter. We could compare the results of these calculations with those for other courses or with our own ideas about the chances of achieving various enrollment levels.

Income

Because a course will often have different fees, our budget format (Exhibit 6.7) provides four lines for "type fee." In our example, students who need transportation to the trailhead (Type 1) are charged $50 more than those who arrange to get to and from the trailhead on their own (Type 2). The number of estimated enrollments at each fee is shown, and the "gross" amount of income (enrollments x fee) is calculated.

The next column, labeled "pass-through," is useful in limited situations. It is included mainly to make a further point about the nature of income and expense and the impact of certain types of transactions on the behavior of costs. For courses that involve significant student travel and accommodation costs that are built into the fee of the course, the multiplication of fee times enrollments can present a significant distortion of income and margin as compared with other courses. Such costs can be said to "pass through" to the vendor; that is, we collect the fee from each student and immediately pass some of it on to a vendor (airline, hotel, and so on). These costs may be

Course identification number
Course name
Term
Programmer name
Course academic number
Section number
Enrollment minimum
Enrollment maximum
Go, no-go decision date
Prerequisites
Fee(s)
Schedule:
    Date course begins
    Date course ends
    Day(s) of week
    Dates
    Time of meeting
    Exceptions to schedule   (Holidays, other exceptions)
Academic department   (Where course approvals are required)

Credit designation   (Undergraduate, graduate, noncredit, ceu)

Number of units   (Credit only, semester, quarter)
Number of continuing education units
Course contact hours
Number of meetings
Hours per meeting
Format description   (Workshop, seminar lecture series,
                                performance, traditional course)
Subject matter name or code
Mailing list interest code
Location:
    General description
    Address
    Building
    Room
    Other
Capacity of room
Is teacher compensation dependent on enrollment?
Date(s) course roster required
Teacher:
    Name
    Address
    Home phone
    Work phone
    Social security number
    Highest degree
    Business affiliation
    Payroll status
    Title
    Academic department(s)

COURSE BUDGET HEADING ITEMS

EXHIBIT 6.8

necessary to the course, but they are peripheral to the instructional process and do not really represent tuition or fee income. If, for instance, the students had to arrange and pay for these items themselves, as is often the case, these costs would never be recognized in the financial records of the sponsoring organization. In our example, the $50 transportation charge is treated as a "pass-through" cost, since it really has nothing to do with instruction.

Expenses

The expense section of our example course budget (Exhibit 6.7) adopts the columnar arrangement. I believe this is the optimal arrangement for a comprehensive course budget. It shows first the variable cost per person, then the total variable costs based on the projected enrollment, than fixed costs, and finally the total of both fixed and variable costs, to arrive at total course costs. The last column is reserved for sunk costs and requires that the programmer, at the time the budget is prepared, estimate the costs that will be expended or obligated before the decision on whether to hold the course is made. Most CE organizations do not require this calculation to be made in the course budget process, but, as we saw in the financial summary, estimations of sunk costs can be important in analyzing prospective courses.

The order in which expenses are presented is entirely a matter of custom. However, it is important to group related expenses together so that they can be subtotaled. Most of the entries on this budget are self-explanatory, but a few comments may be useful. For instance, the arrangement we have made with the guide/lecturer is the first variable cost in our budget. He is a graduate student familiar with the area and has agreed to share his knowledge with students on a one-to-one basis throughout the trip, as well as provide support for the leaders, for $25 per student. Our budget shows the $25 per student multiplied by the anticipated 35 students to get a total of $875 for his total estimated payment. Note that if the course is canceled for any reason, we owe the instructors nothing, so there is no instructor compensation entry in the "sunk" column.

Our example shows only a few other expenses, but there could be many more. Exhibit 6.9 is an expanded list of possible promotion expense categories, and Exhibit 6.10 shows other expenses.

We have already discussed the desirability of calculating and showing explicitly an estimate of the amount and cost of the time that the programmer will spend in developing a particular course, and we set one of the levels of financial success at a point that included this cost. In our current example, the programmer estimated that the cost of the time he would spend on this course was $1,000, of which $500 would be "sunk" (spent before the final decision about holding the course is made).

Category	Notes
Media Categories Print Catalog	
Brochure	This can further be described in terms of brochure size or degree of finish.

Flyer
    Poster
    Newsletter
    Personal letter
    Internet, electronic commerce costs	

Advertising Radio	These can be further broken down by the name of the station or publication.

Television
    Newspaper
    Magazine	

Cost categories Printed materials Editing	Most of these categories could be broken down as provided either in-house or from the outside.

Layout, composition
    Illustration
    Cover design
    Author fees
    Copyright fees
    Typesetting, electronic preparation
    Printing
    Paper costs
    Envelopes
    Staff time
    Mailing costs:
      Postage
      Mail list purchase
      Label extraction charges
    Mailing house (handling) charges
      Folding
      Binding
      Stuffing
      Sorting
      Affixing labels
      Delivery costs
      Warehouse and storage costs	

PROMOTION COST CATEGORIES

EXHIBIT 6.9

Advertising
    Press releases
        Writing
        Printing, distribution costs
    Production costs
        Actor fees
        Equipment
        Other
    Space costs, spot costs

Electronic commerce
    Homepage creation, maintenance
    Updating services
    Equipment, software

Public relations
    Displays, exhibits, fairs
    Press kits
    Hospitality, entertaining
    Press relations

Other
    Telemarketing

PROMOTION COST CATEGORIES

EXHIBIT 6.9 (CONTINUED)

As we learned earlier, indirect costs can be applied to individual courses in a number of ways. In our example, registration indirect costs are applied on a per student basis, and other indirect costs are applied on the basis of a percentage of total income. Thus, this indirect cost calculation has both fixed and variable elements. However, most CE organizations use only one method of assigning indirect costs.

The budget format given in our example is intended only as a suggestion. It was designed partly to illustrate concepts presented earlier in a different form. Once a programmer understands this budget's theoretical framework, he or she should be able to adapt this budget format to the requirements of particular situations. This format can also be adapted for use on computers with commonly available spreadsheet programs.

SUMMARY

Developing a course involves making a series of decisions. The preparation of a course budget helps decision making by presenting a financial standard against which changes can be judged. The explanations and examples in this chapter are intended to render course budgeting more useful by giving programmers the facility to manipulate and understand the financial effects of new or changed conditions.

Audiovisual equipment
    Film, videotape rental, purchase
    Equipment rental, use charge
    Delivery, mailing charge

Course materials
    Textbooks, other books (including freight)
    Materials reproduction costs
        Copyright license fees
        Printing and assembling costs

Reader fees
Lab fees
Room, facility rental
Security service
Janitorial service
Ushers, crowd, traffic control
Coffee, refreshment
Lunches, meals
Staff expenses
    Couriers
    Cashiers
    Programmer on-site time
    Travel, per diem
    Meals
    Incidentals
Entertainment
Registration costs
    Registration packet
    Hotel charges
    Name tags

OTHER COSTS

EXHIBIT 6.10

The dynamic nature of the course development process means that traditional course budget processes will fall short of the ideal. Most of the time, a course budget will be prepared only once, with changes and adjustments being mentally factored in. Even so, a properly prepared and formatted budget can bring together a number of the considerations necessary for careful course planning.

CHAPTER 7

Multidimensional Budgeting and Activity-Based Costing for Programmers

Multidimensional budgeting and activity-based costing are organization-wide initiatives; their implementation requires that the financial management infrastructure be adjusted. Part 3 describes how such an organization-wide application of MDB and ABC might be designed and implemented. Individual programmers working in such an environment will find that many of the dynamic factors described in the previous chapters will be more clearly defined; more information will be available to programmers as they make the day-to-day decisions so important to the organization. They will not have to rely as much on intuition to decide, for instance, the opportunity costs of developing one course over another. However, even where such a comprehensive environment does not exist, a knowledge of MDB and ABC can be employed to advantage.

WHAT'S MISSING IN THE TRADITIONAL PROGRAMMER FINANCIAL PLANNING MODEL?

In the typical CE organization, the cost of programmer time is not assigned to individual courses or, if so assigned, is usually based on an allocation formula rather than an actual measurement. However, the cost of programmer time is a significant percentage of most CE organization budgets; ignoring this cost means that financial statements are either uninformative or, worse, misleading. Programmers, because they lack information or guidance, must struggle to make rational decisions about the way they spend their time. The failure to fully account for this cost occurs because collecting information in any meaningful way about how people spend their time is considered a burdensome task, often antithetical to the culture of educational institutions.

The use in traditional systems of the course as cost object is another source of limitation. First, there is no way of accounting or valuing noncourse costs devoted to serving customers, administrative tasks, supervision, professional development, or even vacations, no way of determining what costs are waste or non-value added. Second, traditional systems do not provide information about the real cost differences among courses because the largest cost—programmer time—is either not assigned or assigned equally to each course. Thus the cost of complexity is not calculated. Third, traditional systems do not reflect the important concept of course life cycle. A new course usually takes more time to develop and present than an existing one. Development costs, an important element in the portfolio management process, are rarely captured in traditional systems. In addition, these costs are not available for comparison against either the expected, or the actual, "shelf-life" of the course, crucial determinants of the wisdom of engaging in course development.

Finally, traditional accounting and overhead allocation systems hide or distort the cost to the organization of programmer decisions about courses. For instance, a programmer may decide to develop a course requiring that four instructors be paid a flat fee plus a percentage of the enrollment fee for every enrollment over 25. This decision requires the business office to make special calculations and take care that the instructors are paid correctly. This special handling represents a cost to the organization that most systems would not recognize. How are such shortcomings overcome by the application of MDB and ABC?

TYPICAL PROGRAMMER ACTIVITIES

Most CE programmers have interesting, complex, and varied jobs. Categorizing these activities in a meaningful way, the first step in developing an ABC system, presents a challenge to programmers and their CE unit. Defining a hierarchy of costs within the three classifications of costs—product, customer, and strategic or managerial—offers a framework for listing programmer activities. Categorization schemes should conform to organizational initiatives, which will vary considerably from one to another. For instance, a CE organization might have the increased use of distance education as a strategic goal. One activity category for this organization might be distance education course development. The nature and extent of programmer time spent in distance education could then be tracked, measured, and compared with the results. In another organization, even one using distance education, this might not be an important category.

Despite the possible variety in categorization schemes, some general categories will be used by most programmer-related ABC systems.

Product (Course) Related Activities

In CE, the product is usually synonymous with the course. Some CE organizations provide services, say, counseling or small business advisory services, and these may also be considered products. However, these and other services are more likely to be considered "customer" costs associated with particular groups of students or potential students. For this discussion, product costs will be considered to be primarily course costs.

Program Development

Most CE programmers engage in some form of program development. On the *unit* level, program development means the development of a single, identified course. Course development costs, including the cost of programmer time, theoretically can be assigned to individual courses, although sometimes, when a group of courses is being developed, the total costs of development might be assigned to the group. On the *batch* or *portfolio* basis, program development costs cannot be identified with individual courses but are, nevertheless, associated with an identifiable group of courses. For instance, a programmer might attend the meeting of the Society of Facilities Managers with the purpose of obtaining information about the needs of the group for continuing education. The costs of attending this meeting, including the cost of programmer time, might be considered a portfolio level product development cost associated with the development of a certificate program in facilities management. The cost of curriculum advisory boards are also typically portfolio costs. On the *product* level, development costs are associated with the development of a broadly defined group of programs usually encompassing more than one portfolio of courses. Development costs at the product level are less common than levels lower in the hierarchy, but are possible. For instance, subscriptions to business trade magazines and other periodicals related to business trends might be considered a product level cost for the business department.

Program Marketing

Marketing is an important activity for most CE programmers. Marketing activities might include researching markets, designing campaigns, developing direct mail pieces, determining distribution methods, and personal selling by the programmer. Although considered here as product costs, marketing costs can also be considered customer costs, i.e., the cost of obtaining and retaining a customer or group of customers. Thus, marketing costs may legitimately appear in two of the three broad categories of programmer activities.

In some cases, marketing costs are easy to identify and assign. For example, the costs of printing and mailing a particular brochure advertising a particular course are easily assignable to an individual course. In other cases, however, the costs are not easily identifiable or assignable. The cost of the programmer's time in planning for a marketing campaign is sometimes difficult to obtain and assign. Again, activities may be assigned at the unit, portfolio, or product level, depending on the situation. The brochure mentioned above is at the unit or course level, an ad in the newspaper mentioning the facilities management certificate program and asking people to call or write for more information is at the portfolio level, and a radio advertisement informing people about the programs in business may be at the product level.

Program Presentation/Implementation

Once the course has been developed and effectively marketed, it must be delivered to the students. CE programmers typically take the major responsibility for course implementation—assigning and setting up rooms, making sure audio-visual needs are met, answering questions from the instructor, and getting the instructor paid. Because some programs are more expensive to present than others, this is an important category. Although most costs here are at the unit or course level, there may be some at the portfolio and product levels as well.

Program Evaluation

Program evaluation is an important but sometimes undervalued activity. Most CE programmers use student questionnaires to evaluate courses. The review, processing, and communication with instructors about the results are all activities at the course level, even if assignment of costs is from a cost pool on a standardized basis. In some cases, portfolios of courses are reviewed by accrediting teams or internal academic review teams. The cost of these reviews are portfolio level costs. Again, there may be some similar costs at the product level. ABC often elevates the importance of evaluation because evaluation fosters ongoing improvement.

Customer (Student) Related Activities

Customer-related activities are associated with obtaining, retaining, and serving particular customers or groups of customers. Recognizing these activities and assigning costs to them helps programmers determine the relative costs of serving particular groups of students. Such activities can be categorized as being at the order, customer, or market levels, although for CE programmers the order and customer levels are frequently merged. Most of the categorization at the customer level has to do with different kinds of students or CE clients. For instance, a programmer might want to keep track of how much it costs to serve contract training clients, credit students, noncredit students, and international students. Each of these groups may have distinctive requirements and make special demands on the time of the CE programmer. Activities associated with these customer groups can take many forms.

Marketing Activities

Marketing was mentioned above as both a product and a student-related activity. Costs of marketing to different student categories can vary greatly. Since product costs eventually become customer-related costs (see Exhibit 3.5, page 41), marketing costs are usually deemed to be product costs. However, where more than one category of student can take a particular course or program, marketing becomes more logically a customer-related cost than a product cost. For instance, marketing costs might be related to customers for a course delivered in the evening that is open to public enrollments even though offered under the terms of a contract signed with a company. However, many marketing activities at the market level are customer costs. For instance, contract training may require considerable time and effort on the part of the programmer in relationship building with potential clients. This kind of activity might be considered marketing and the costs of it might be collected in a pool assigned to contract training.

Order Obtaining and Enrollment Activities

Programmers are sometimes involved in obtaining orders or enrolling students. In contract training, for instance, marketing efforts frequently require that a proposal or contract be written. The costs of this time-consuming requirement should be assigned to the particular customer or at least to the contract customer group. In some cases, programmers might also be directly engaged in enrolling students or in supervising the enrollment of students. Thus, a group of international students might arrive together and need special help in enrolling in a course of study.

Post-Enrollment Services

Once students enroll in courses, they may need services beyond those provided in the classroom. They may need information about the course, accommodations, or payment methods. The extent of this post enrollment service can vary widely among student groups. Again, international students typically need a great deal of post enrollment service, including housing, health insurance, transportation, and other logistical help. Programmers may be involved in providing these services.

Managerial Activities

CE programmers are involved in many activities that cannot easily be classified either as product or customer related. These activities are "managerial" in two ways. First, they may involve managerial or coordinating functions within their responsibility areas or on behalf of the CE organization as a whole. Supervision of staff supporting the programmer's portfolio is an example of an "inside" responsibility; being a member of the organization's space planning committee is an example of "outside" activity. Second, an activity might be "managerial" by virtue of a policy decision by higher management to encourage it. Professional development activities might be in this category—they are supported by management but do not relate directly to products or customer groups. Because the range of managerial tasks and possible initiatives is extremely wide, this category is difficult to characterize and describe. It is a useful category, however, because it provides direct information about the real costs of some of the activities closest to the interest of the professional management of the CE organization.

Non-Value Added Activities

This category belongs in every programmer's list of activities. It is not intended to disclose time wasted by the programmer or the normal "down time" that exists in every person's day. Rather, it seeks to point out the nonproductive use of time imposed on the programmer by the organization or by circumstances. For instance, programmer time spent dealing with student or instructor complaints or producing useless reports is "non-value." Programmers should have the opportunity to report activities according to their own definitions. This reporting can direct the organization to greater efficiency.

MULTIDIMENSIONAL BUDGETING FOR PROGRAM PLANNERS

Chapter 3 described two forms of multidimensional budgeting—one using the course as the cost object, and one using activities as cost objects. In that chapter, the first transformation from traditional budgeting to MDB involved a reclassification of the cost objects into groups to obtain group totals. The next and largest transformation occurred when activities were used as cost objects. We will use one example of a programmer's budget to illustrate this progression from a programmer's perspective.

Course as Cost Object Reclassifications

Exhibit 7.1 shows the annual budget for a particular programmer. The programmer expects to offer 95 courses, of which 10 will be canceled due to lack of enrollment. The 85 remaining courses will produce $1,120,675 in income. Direct (classroom and marketing) expenses will be $488,235. Departmental costs will be $133,163, including payroll costs (salaries and benefits) of $105,213 for the programmer and her assistant.

Number of programs planned	95	
Number of programs cancelled	10	
Cancellation rate	11%	
Programs carried	85	
Enrollment (carried programs)	2,351	
Average Class Size	27.66	
Fee Income	**$1,120,675**	**100.0%**
Direct expense		
Promotion	$47,750	4.3%
Teacher compensation	218,460	19.5%
Direct supplies and expense	222,025	19.8%
Total direct	**$488,235**	**43.6%**
Course margin	**$632,440**	**56.4%**
Departmental expense:		
Payroll	$105,213	9.4%
Supplies and expense	17,030	1.5%
Departmental promotion	10,920	1.0%
Total departmental	**$133,163**	**11.9%**
Total expenses	**$621,398**	**55.4%**
Available for indirect cost	**$499,277**	**44.6%**

EXAMPLE OF A PROGRAMMER'S ANNUAL BUDGET

EXHIBIT 7.1

Traditional budgeting would assign all costs of this program budget to individual courses. For the purposes of this illustration, departmental costs have not been allocated to courses. Multidimensional budgeting would re-group the courses according to one or another classification scheme. This portfolio of courses might consist of three types of courses—public courses, contract courses, and courses for international students. Exhibit 7.2 shows the same programmer's annual budget restated to illustrate each of the three selected categories. We call this transformation "first stage" because it still uses the course as cost object—the transformation is achieved by classifying courses into one of the three groups.

	Public	Contract	International	Total	
Number of programs planned	80	10	5	95	
Number of programs cancelled	10	0	0	10	
Cancellation rate	11%			11%	
Programs carried	70	10	5	85	
Enrollment (Carried programs)	1781	450	120	2351	
Average Class Size	25.44	45.00	24.00	27.66	
Fee Income	**$852,175**	**$148,500**	**$120,000**	**$1,120,675**	**100.0%**
Direct expense					
Promotion	$29,750	$10,000	$8,000	$47,750	4.3%
Teacher compensation	131,910	44,550	42,000	218,460	19.5%
Direct supplies and expense	175,690	16,335	30,000	222,025	19.8%
Total direct	**$337,350**	**$70,885**	**$80,000**	**$488,235**	**43.6%**
Course margin	**$514,825**	**$77,615**	**$40,000**	**$632,440**	**56.4%**
Departmental expense:					
Payroll				$105,213	9.4%
Supplies and expense				17,030	1.5%
Departmental promotion				10,920	1.0%
Total departmental				**$133,163**	**11.9%**
Total expenses				**$621,398**	**55.4%**
Available for indirect cost				**$499,277**	**44.6%**

PROGRAMMER FIRST-STAGE MULTIDIMENSIONAL BUDGETING

EXHIBIT 7.2

The obvious advantage of the multidimensional budget is that it allows the programmer and CE management to budget for major strategic initiatives adopted by the organization. Exhibit 7.2 shows just three initiatives. However, the possibilities are unlimited and many more initiatives could be specified. Of course, each additional category adds complexity to the budgeting and accounting process.

Activity as Cost Object MDB

Although MDB using a reclassification of cost objects, as illustrated above, provides useful information, it leaves the "departmental expense" category, about 12 percent of total expense in our example, unassigned and unexplained except in what is called the "line item dimension." The use of activity-based costing principles would allow these costs to be assigned to typical programmer activities as shown in Exhibit 7.3.

In this example, the product and customer categories are the same (public, contract, and international), and all departmental costs have been

Total to be distributed:	$133,163				
Activity	**Total**	**Public**	**Contract**	**International**	**Managerial**
Product related					
Development	$46,607	$23,304	$11,652	$11,652	
Marketing	17,311	6,016	8,374	2,920	
Presentation	13,316	10,966	1,566	784	
Evaluation	2,663	2,193	313	157	
Total product	**$79,898**	**$42,479**	**$21,905**	**$15,513**	
Customer related					
Marketing	$11,985	$1,198	$3,595	$7,191	
Order getting	13,316		13,316		
Post enrollment	7,990	799	2,397	4,794	
Total	**$33,291**	**$1,997**	**$19,308**	**$11,985**	
Managerial related					
Happy workforce	$2,663				$2,663
Efficient operations	13,316				13,316
Other	3,995				3,995
Total	**$19,974**				**$19,974**
Non-value added	**0**				
Total	**$133,163**	**$44,476**	**$41,213**	**$27,497**	**$19,974**

PROGRAMMER DEPARTMENTAL EXPENSE DISTRIBUTION BY ACTIVITY

EXHIBIT 7.3

allocated based on our estimate of how the programmer and her assistant will spend their time. For instance, they expect to spend 35 percent of their time engaged in product (course) development. Thus, 35 percent of $133,163, or $46,607 will be budgeted for this activity, half of which, or $23,304, will be devoted to developing courses for the public market. The total cost of each activity is distributed to the product/customer categories or the "managerial" category. Ten percent of the total effort of this programmer team will be devoted to "order getting" in the contract area.

In this example, the managerial category has three elements—"happy workforce," which might be an effort to raise staff morale; "efficient operations," perhaps a study of how things could be made more efficient; and "other." This worksheet could be made more complex by adding product and customer categories and activity definitions.

Once departmental expense is distributed to activities, the programmer activity budget can be constructed. Exhibit 7.4 shows the same information as Exhibit 7.2 except that departmental expense has been reclassified by activity category.

More detail could be provided on this worksheet. Instead of summarizing departmental costs under the three general headings of product, customer,

	Public	Contract	International	Managerial	Total	
Number of programs planned	80	10	5		95	
Number of programs cancelled	10	0	0		10	
Cancellation rate	11%				11%	
Programs carried	70	10	5		85	
Enrollment (Carried programs)	1,781	450	120		2,351	
Average Class Size	25.44	45.00	24.00		27.66	
Fee Income	**$852,175**	**$148,500**	**$120,000**		**$1,120,675**	**100.0%**
Direct expense						
Promotion	$29,750	$10,000	$8,000		$47,750	4.3%
Teacher compensation	131,910	44,550	42,000		218,460	19.5%
Direct supplies and expense	175,690	16,335	30,000		222,025	19.8%
Total direct	**$337,350**	**$70,885**	**$80,000**		**$488,235**	**43.6%**
Course margin	**$514,825**	**$77,615**	**$40,000**		**$632,440**	**56.4%**
Percent margin	*60%*	*52%*	*33%*			
Departmental expense:						
Product related	$42,479	$21,905	$15,513		$79,897	7.1%
Customer related	1,997	19,308	11,985		33,290	3.0%
Managerial related				$19,974	19,974	1.8%
Total departmental	**$44,476**	**$41,213**	**$27,498**	**$19,974**	**$133,161**	**11.9%**
Total expenses	**$381,826**	**$112,098**	**$107,498**	**$19,974**	**$621,396**	**55.4%**
Available for indirect cost	**$470,349**	**$36,402**	**$12,502**	**($19,974)**	**$499,279**	**44.6%**
Percentage of income	*55%*	*25%*	*10%*			

PROGRAMMER SECOND-STAGE MULTIDIMENSIONAL BUDGETING

EXHIBIT 7.4

and managerial, we could have provided all the detail contained in Exhibit 7.3.

Our view of these three program areas might change as a result of applying activity-based accounting. At the gross margin line, public programs and contract programs appear relatively close in percentage contribution at 60 percent and 52 percent, respectively, while international programs are a smaller but acceptable 33 percent. However, once departmental costs are assigned, the percentages are different. The percent of income available for overhead produced by contract programs is less than half that produced by public programs (25 percent compared to 55 percent), while the international program produces only 10 percent of its income to common costs.

Each of the total costs shown in Exhibit 7.4 become in effect cost pools, which then can be the basis on which costs are assigned either to courses, groups of courses, students, student groups, or other activities. For instance, the $7,900 estimated on Exhibit 7.3 for the activity "program representation" for public programs becomes a pool to be divided equally among all public courses.

As against traditional accounting, the combination of MDB and ABC accounts for the true source of costs through the careful assignment of all costs, including programmer's time. The combination provides much more useful information and data than traditional methods and forces programmers to undertake a sometimes painful examination of how they spend their time.

ACTIVITY-BASED COSTING FOR PROGRAM PLANNERS

Besides not accounting for the full costs of programmer activity, traditional systems fall short in accounting for complexity and for product or course life cycles. ABC can address these issues through the establishment of appropriate cost pools and the identification of appropriate cost drivers (see Chapter 13). Although programmers know intuitively and through their own experience that certain kinds of courses take more effort and make more demands upon the organization than others, they rarely have any way of quantifying these differences. ABC provides the measurement tools.

Exhibit 7.5 describes two courses. At the bottom of the exhibit is a budget summary for each course. Although the courses are different in their financial structures, they are expected to produce roughly the same "bottom line" or margin. The upper part of the exhibit lists some attributes of each course. Introduction to Macroeconomics appears to be a standard evening credit course. It is not new and is being taught at the CE downtown center by a teacher who has done so before. Global Positioning Systems is a new three-day noncredit course presented off campus by a person who hasn't taught for the CE organization before.

An ABC system identifies the costs associated with differences in cost objects no matter where they are in the organizational structure. It establishes cost pools and then assigns costs out of those pools to cost objects. It

	Intro. to Macroecon.	Global Positioning Systems
Type of course: credit, non-credit	Credit	Non-credit
Brochure: yes, no	No	Yes
New course: yes, no	No	Yes
Number of meetings	15	3
Number of meetings presence required	0	3
Number of hours	45	28
Location	Downtown Cntr.	Hotel
Room capacity/enrollment limit	60	No limit
Number of instructors	1	1
New instructor	No	Yes
Instructor US citizen	Yes	Yes
Instructor graduate student	No	No
Instructor payment initiated by	Bus. Office	Department
Special payment instructions	Yes	Yes
Book sales	Yes	No
Estimated enrollment	35	20
Fee	$345	$995
Budgeted income	$12,075	$19,900
Expenses:		
Promotion	$500	$1,900
Instructional costs	2,600	4,000
Supplies and expenses	200	5,100
Total expenses	$3,300	$11,000
Margin	$8,775	$8,900
Percentage margin	72.67%	44.72%

COMPARISON OF TWO COURSE BUDGETS

EXHIBIT 7.5

provides information about how costs should be assigned through lists that might be called "cost driver scoring tables." Exhibit 7.6 is an example of a course cost driver scoring table. This table indicates that it costs about $50 each to process a credit course but only $25 each for noncredit courses. Behind these figures is a calculation that totaled all the costs associated with processing courses—entering them into the computer system, preparing and distributing approval documents, and following up on contradictory information—and then divided those costs by the estimated number of courses processed. In this case, the cost driver was the number of courses—costs rose and fell in direct proportion to the number of courses offered. The next line of the scoring table identifies another cost driver—costs associated with the production of "special" as opposed to "standard" brochures or promotional treatments that do not get recharged to the job directly. The estimated unrecharged costs associated with the processing and production of special brochures vary with the number of such jobs. Each line indicates another cost driver and assigns a cost to that driver. The cost driver "new course" is listed as "variable" on the table because that cost driver might be different from one part of the organization to the other. Developing a new course in the humanities might cost more than in engineering. Cost pools for new course development might be developed for each programmer as was done in Exhibit 7.3, which shows $23,304 allocated for the development of public courses. In this case, the programmer intends to develop eight new courses at about $3,000 per course. Significant variation might occur among the courses chosen for development. The programmer would still have to make some opportunity cost calculations, but at least some guideline has been established.

Using the scoring table, we can now compute the full cost of each course and make more informed comparisons, as shown in Exhibit 7.7. The exhibit allows us to see some significant differences in the two bottom lines, primarily due to the large charge against Global Positioning Systems because it is a new course.

This example illustrates the scope and power of ABC, as well as its potential for misuse and misunderstanding, particularly where it is not combined with a MDB approach. One interpretation that might be derived from Exhibit 7.7 is that a programmer should never develop new programs—the charge is too high. This conclusion is counteracted by the MDB process in which a *goal* for new program development is set for the programmer and funds are, in effect, allocated for such development.

A remaining issue is course life cycle. The $3,000 charge against Global Positioning Systems is a one-time charge that will not be repeated if the course is held again. In effect, this charge should be amortized over the life of

Course initiation fee:	
Credit	50
Noncredit	25
Produce special brochure	100
New course admin. fee:	
Credit	400
Noncredit	200
New course departmental fee	Variable
Cost per meeting	5
Extension presence required per meeting	50
Cost per hour	1
Location cost (non-direct):	
On campus	25
Off campus	50
Monitor limit	10
Cost per instructor	15
Surcharge new instructor	20
Surcharge foreign instructor	15
Surcharge grad. student instructor	20
Instructor payment initiated by	
Business Office	15
Department	10
Special payment surcharge	20
Book sales	50
Cost per enrollee	5
Grade processing/student records	15

SAMPLE COURSE COST DRIVER SCORING TABLE

EXHIBIT 7.6

the course. If the course will be offered only once, the current course should bear the full cost and the budget is accurate. If the course will be offered many times, then the per course amortization charge might be small and the current course is being unfairly charged with the full amount. In Part 3, we will explore how the life cycle effects of development costs are treated by building on the examples given here to describe the amortization process.

	Intro. to Macroecon.	Global Positioning Systems
Type of course: credit, noncredit	$50	$25
Brochure: yes, no	0	100
New course admin fee	0	200
New course departmental fee	0	3,000
Number of meetings	75	15
Ext. presence required at _ meetings	0	150
Number of hours	45	28
Location	25	50
Room capcity/enrollment limit	10	0
Number of instructors	15	15
New instructor	0	20
Instructor US citizen	0	0
Instructor graduate student	0	0
Instructor payment initiation fee	15	10
Special payment instructions	20	20
Book sales	50	0
Estimated enrollment	700	100
Total cost driver charge	$1,005	$3,733
Fee	$345	$995
Budgeted income	$12,075	$19,900
Expenses:		
Promotion	$500	$1,900
Instructional costs	2,600	4,000
Supplies and expenses	200	5,100
Total expenses	$3,300	$11,000
Margin before cost drivers	$8,775	$8,900
Cost driver charge	1,005	3,733
Margin after cost driver charge	$7,770	$5,167
Percentage margin	64.35%	25.96%

COST DRIVER SCORING FOR TWO COURSES

EXHIBIT 7.7

Programmers and CE managers have to reorient their thinking when they use MDB and ABC. An exposure of the full resource allocation scheme for the organization means that everyone must understand the interaction between costs and results. Misunderstandings or misinterpretations of complete data can lead to distorted behavior as surely as lack of information can. Programmers are key elements in the CE organization and crucial to the success of any financial management information system. While they must understand how MDB and ABC apply to their day-to-day planning and operation, they also should have an understanding of the full process used by the organization. Part 3 is designed to provide that understanding.

CHAPTER 8

Special Issues in Course Planning

The course-planning and budgeting models outlined in the previous chapters have immediate practical applications. Sound budgeting practice based on the concepts that have been discussed will help a programmer decide whether to offer a particular program or which of a number of possible programs represents the best investment opportunity. These are the most important financial decisions in a CE enterprise, for the financial and educational health of the CE organization rests upon them. But many other decisions go into the presentation of a course, and the models can also be of help in these decisions. In this chapter, we will examine the following issues faced by programmers during the course development process:

- *Fee determination:* How much should we charge for a course?
- *Promotion costs:* How can we make better decisions about the way a course is promoted?
- *Cost mixes:* What is the effect of different proportions of fixed to variable, or sunk to unsunk costs?
- *Instructor compensation:* How much should an instructor be paid, and how should negotiations with instructors be conducted?
- *Indirect cost allocation or assignment:* How do different methods of applying indirect costs affect our decision-making process?
- *Cosponsorship and partial services:* How should we split costs and income when two or more agencies are presenting a program, and how should we price services to outside agencies?

Finally, we will discuss how a programmer in a continuing education enterprise can develop an overall strategy to achieve the organization's goals and objectives. The recommendations in this chapter accept the desirability of maximizing financial return, even in educational settings where financial return may be a secondary goal. The purpose is to indicate where and how entrepreneurial and educational interests may be unified to mutual advantage.

DETERMINING FEES

Deciding how much to charge for a course is usually one of the more difficult tasks a programmer faces. In organizations where fixed rates per unit or per contact hour have been established, the fee-setting process is simple; in a less structured environment, arriving at the fee can be as troublesome as it is important. The process must take into account several factors, some of which must be estimated on the basis of little information. These factors include the cost of the course, the market (or competition in supply and elasticity of demand), and price as a perceived indicator of quality. From the student's perspective, the fee is only a part of the total cost of the course; different ratios of course fee to total cost can affect fee determination. Consumer surplus is also a useful concept in setting fees, as are the desirability of consistency in fee setting and the effect of ethical considerations on fees.

Cost

In Chapter 6, we described the way programmers usually set course fees. In this "cost workup" method, they determine the cost of the course, estimate the number of enrollees, and divide the cost by the estimate to arrive at the fee. This rather poor way to establish a fee has the advantage of being easy to compute and explain. This method does not consider the market factors of supply and demand or of competition, and may not take into account the "full cost" of presenting a course or the effects of the "hidden subsidies" (*see* Introduction). Not accounting for these items can lead to a distorted financial picture and a budgetary shortage at the end of the accounting period. On the other hand, a course's indirect cost allocation may include charges for elements from which the proposed course will not benefit. Still, this method of calculating a course fee is a useful first step in the fee-setting process because it establishes a floor beneath which the fee should not fall after market factors are considered.

Market

To obtain a true proportional relationship between the cost of a course and its fee, we must consider competition and demand. Competition affects the supply side of the traditional market model, in which market equilibrium occurs when supply equals demand. Supply is the quantity of a good or service available in a certain specified market and includes all goods or services that can serve as substitutes for the good or service being offered. In our case, other continuing education courses being offered in our area on the same general subject or directed to the same people are part of the supply that competes with us. These courses might be offered by other agencies or might even, in restricted markets, include some of the same courses we offer. If the fee charged for our course is markedly higher than the fees for other courses that our market views as equivalent, how the fee was developed does not matter; other things being equal, no one will come. On the other hand, if the cost workup method produces a fee considerably lower than the cost of alternatives to our course, we will not realize the full potential margin on our course. Too low a fee also has a psychological impact—potential students may ask "why?" and stay away.

The programmer must consider the cost and availability of alternatives to a given course in a broad and realistic context. For example, the market for weekend programs during the winter may be considerably influenced by the size of the snow pack on nearby slopes; potential students may weigh the price of a weekend course against the price of lift tickets. We are competing for the time of a potential student who has many other choices.

Elasticity of demand also has a considerable influence on the fee-setting process. Elasticity of demand, in our context, is the relationship of course fee to the number of enrollments. Consider the following demand table for Course A:

Fee	Participants	Estimated Income
$80	20	$1,600
75	30	2,250
60	40	2,400
55	45	2,475
50	50	2,500
40	60	2,400

As we decrease the fee, we entice more people to enroll in the course. Despite the reduced fee, this increased enrollment increases gross income until the fee in our example course drops below $50. Beyond that point, further reductions in the fee will not attract enough additional students to result in higher gross income. Some courses are more elastic than others. In an elastic course, fee variations will have a significant affect on enrollment. In an inelastic course, a change in the fee does not significantly change the number of students enrolled. When a course is the only one of its kind and all potential students must take the course, it is "inelastic."

Price as Perceived Indicator of Quality

Until now we have presumed a certain rationality in the choices students make among educational alternatives. However, some factors in buyer decision making hardly seem to warrant scientific analysis. When a buyer is unfamiliar with a product or when the item being purchased cannot be inspected or approved in advance, price may become a symbol or anticipator of quality. This factor can affect choices of restaurants, over-the-counter medicine, and continuing education courses. Charging a higher price than the competition may attract students who view higher price as an indication of higher quality. This effect can be reinforced by a high-quality brochure or by the careful choice of course location and instructors. Because such measures may increase cost and, therefore, risk, we again see that balancing such cost factors leads to success in course development.

Percentage of Total Student Cost

Often ignored in discussions of setting course fees are the other costs, both out-of-pocket and opportunity costs, that students or their sponsors must pay. If substantial, these costs can make the course fee seem trivial in comparison.

	Amount	% of Total
Cost of course	$ 750	14.1
Round-trip airfare	680	12.8
Per diem expenses—$50/day	300	5.6
Cost of employee time (salary)	1,000	18.8
Value of employee time at est. billing rate ($500/day)	2,500	46.9
Other costs	100	1.8
TOTAL	$5,330	100.0

The example in the above table shows the total value given up for a professional engineer to attend a six-day seminar; the course fee is a small percentage (14 percent) of the total cost of this education to the engineer's company. An increase of $50 in the fee would increase the total cost to the company by only 1 percent and would probably not influence the company's decision about whether to send an engineer to the course.

In addition to these quantifiable monetary costs, other costs of importance to the student are often hidden or not measurable in terms of dollars. Time away from work and family are valuable personal considerations. Courses that tie up too much time or require an extended commitment might well be viewed by students as priced too high in terms of lost opportunities even if the monetary fee is reasonable. Recreational activities can have an important effect on the timing of courses. Some programmers avoid scheduling courses on Monday nights in the fall because of Monday night football and on Friday nights at any time of year because weekend recreational alternatives exert too strong a pull on potential students.

Consumer Surplus and Differential Prices

The concept of consumer surplus is closely allied to the concept of elasticity of demand. If we return to the demand table for Course A and set the fee for this course at $50; the 20 people who were willing to pay $80 have, in a sense, been given a "surplus" of $30 each. A surplus could also be computed for any other students who were willing to enroll at a price above $50. The realization of this fact has led to the creation of differential prices aimed at allowing providers to recapture some of this surplus for themselves. The introduction of different prices is generally accompanied by an attempt to differentiate between customers. Airlines, in requiring advance reservations and week-long visits to qualify for lower fares, are trying to differentiate between the business traveler (with inelastic demand) and the recreational traveler (with elastic demand). In continuing education, this differentiation may take several of the following forms:

- *Reason for enrolling in the course.* Students who take the course for credit, presumably to apply that credit toward a degree, may pay a higher fee than those who take it for other reasons, even though their enrollment does not cost the organization more.
- *Student categories.* Since some people will always be willing to pay more than others for the same course, it is desirable to isolate those people in some way, charge them the higher fee, and charge a lower fee to those who are willing to pay only the lower fee. Usually the best way to do this is to set a relatively high price and then give discounts, scholarships, or partial scholarships to those unwilling or unable to pay the full fee.
- *Geographical location.* Fees are sometimes set differently for out-of-state students or students who reside outside a particular district to discourage outsiders from taking advantage of a service paid for by and intended for a specific constituency.

- *Enrollment type.* It is often useful to try to influence the pattern of enrollment and even the means of payment by setting different fees. It is desirable to be able to determine early whether a course is going to succeed or not, before too many costs have become sunk and to get an early count of enrollments to speed up the ordering of books and materials, lunches, and rooms. For these reasons, people who enroll early are often charged a lower fee, while enrollees at the door pay a higher fee. Those who enroll in an entire lecture series may pay a lower fee per lecture than those who attend and pay for only selected lectures. To encourage word-of-mouth promotion and to spur enrollments, people who enroll as part of a group may be charged a lower fee than single enrollments.

Consistency in Fee Structure

Many continuing education organizations have preset fees per units, per hours, or per course. There are good reasons for setting fees in advance, but there are also some dangers and disadvantages. The main advantage in setting fees according to a prescribed schedule is that such consistency enables students to remember the fees charged by the organization and to view those fees as consistent and rational. The disadvantage of a preset fee structure is that market factors, and sometimes even differences in costs, cannot readily be considered. Established fee schedules work best when the courses to which they apply are relatively homogeneous in cost and market appeal.

The hard-boiled market approach to fee setting may seem, and probably is, inconsistent with the goals and purposes of many continuing education enterprises, especially those dedicated to helping the educationally disadvantaged or with a policy requiring them to price their services at the lowest break-even level. However, most public service CE organizations are held accountable for some measure of results—number of adults trained, or number of adults placed in jobs. They will therefore want to recruit adults motivated to learn in areas where jobs can be obtained; market principles will still apply.

Clearly, setting the fee for a course is not an exact science and must be done with a feeling for the market and the intended audience. A programmer who understands the factors involved can become more skillful in setting fees. Giving up a blind attachment to the cost workup method of fee setting is the most important step in achieving this skill.

PROMOTION: DECIDING HOW MUCH TO SPEND

The decision to promote is one of the most important early decision points in the process of course development. The manner in which a course is promoted and the amount of money spent on promotion are crucial to the course's success. Unfortunately, decisions about promotion are difficult to make and involve much ambiguity and lack of information. Most of the information needed for promotion decisions cannot be gathered by a single programmer but must flow out of a general, systematic information system provided by the organization.

Two characteristics of promotion costs make them important in course budgeting and financial planning. First, they immediately become "sunk" costs and are therefore "at risk." Second, they have a functional relationship to income—the amount of money (and time and effort) spent on promotion has (or *should* have) a direct effect on the number of participants attracted to a particular course and, therefore, on the amount of income the course generates.

Determination of Promotion Costs

Although programmers will choose the forms of promotion they feel will be most effective, they lack a definitive measure of promotion effectiveness. Effectiveness is hard to measure because promotional expenditures are difficult to isolate. If we use the broadest definition of the term promotion, we will realize that many line items on the typical course budget have elements of "promotion" in them, especially programmer time. The most successful programmers are always looking for opportunities to promote their courses and spend much time themselves in direct promotional efforts. Telephone calls to training directors or others with whom the programmer has developed relationships are often the most effective possible promotion. Yet, the time thus spent usually is not added to or computed in the promotion budget of the course, even through the opportunity cost of such promotion can be high.

Marginal Cost

Another reason why promotion expenditures are difficult to isolate is that some portion of promotion expenditure can be viewed as marginal cost. The calculation of several levels of financial success in Chapter 6 indicated that, assuming a relatively low variable cost, additional enrollments beyond a certain point will produce a significant contribution to margin. Suppose we have a course that will reach its break-even point (level C on Exhibit 6.5, page 93) at 25 enrollments, that the variable costs per student total $15, and that the fee is $100. Each student contributes $85 ($100 - $15) to fixed costs and, once the break-even point is reached, to margin. If we are confident the proposed promotion budget will attract 25 students, how much more should we be willing to spend to attract the twenty-sixth student?

This is the concept of marginal cost. Since the twenty-sixth student will bring an extra $85, we should be willing to spend up to a limit of $85 to generate more margin. In other words, once we reach the break-even point, we can calculate a new break-even point for the justification of further expenditure.

Suppose our original promotion budget is $400, but we have an opportunity to advertise the course in the local paper for an additional $500. If this additional expenditure produces six or more enrollments, it is worth making, since at six enrollments we would be taking in more than we spent on the additional promotion ($85 x 6 = $510).

Suppose 10 additional enrollments resulted from the newspaper advertisement. Our original promotion plan was more effective (and more cost-effective) than the newspaper advertising because it produced 25 enrollments at a cost of $400, while our newspaper ad produced only 10 enrollments for $500. However, the expenditure of that extra $500 produced a contribution to margin of $850 ($85 x 10), leaving us $350 ahead ($850 – $500).

Applying the marginal cost concept to the measurement of promotion cost-effectiveness can make measurement difficult; for instance, in the preceding example we had to apply different standards of effectiveness to different promotion methods for the same course. Using the marginal cost concept to justify additional promotional expenditures is also dangerous. Predicting the exact number of enrollments any particular promotional scheme might produce is difficult, and promotion money is risk money. The more a programmer spends on promotion, the higher the risk. Because promotion money spent in pursuit of a marginal return is not as effective as that spent to produce the full return, the risk associated with marginal promotion costs is higher.

Quantitative Methods

In confronting promotion decisions, programmers often rely at least partly on quantitative methods that try to measure promotion effectiveness in hard dollar terms. The following are examples of quantitative measures:

- Promotion cost expressed as a percentage of income
- Cost per thousand (cost of reaching 1,000 households)
- Cost per inquiry (cost divided by number of inquiries received)
- Cost per enrollment
- Number of times margin earned (course margin divided by promotion cost)

These measures are useful only when compared to a tested standard of performance, and must be interpreted with great care. For instance, some courses are "promotion intensive," depending more on promotion than on other cost elements for success, and thus might logically have a greater percentage of total cost in the promotion category.

Quantitative measures have some inherant limitations. They usually depend to a large extent on some sort of "tracking" system whereby enrollments, inquiries, and so on are traced to the promotional method that produced them; yet, even the best tracking methods seldom track more than 70 percent of the enrollments. Another limitation is that quantitative measures usually are directed only at the short run, calculating the effectiveness of the promotion for a particular course without incorporating the possible future effects or the institutional effects of such promotion.

In spite of the ambiguities involved, risk related to promotion can be reduced, and the return on the investment of a particular promotion expenditure can be increased when time and effort are spent in setting up promotion evaluation measures. Programmers may establish tracking systems, ask enrollees and inquirers how they heard about a course, interview training directors about advertising effectiveness, and seek information about promotion effectiveness in many other ways. Evaluation is especially important when new promotion techniques are used. Evaluation of promotion effectiveness is worth the effort because promotion costs are crucially important.

EVALUATING COST ALTERNATIVES

Fixed and Variable Costs

Programmers must sometimes decide whether to make a particular cost fixed or variable. Take, for example, an instructor who is willing to (or demands to) negotiate his compensation. The instructor is willing to take a flat (fixed) $300 or $25 per student (making instructor compensation a variable cost). In suggesting the latter scheme, the instructor is offering to participate in the rewards and risks of the course. He is gambling that the course will attract 12 or more students, since at 12 students his compensation will equal his offer of a fixed $300 ($300/$25 = 12). The programmer must decide whether to accept that same gamble.

This example illustrates the most important aspect of differing mixes of fixed and variable costs: The higher the variable costs, the lower the risk and the reward; the higher the fixed costs, the greater the risk and the reward. The programmer in the preceding example will have to estimate the chances of achieving the break-even position and then will have to determine the desirability of accepting the risk involved.

Sunk and Unsunk Costs

The mix of "sunk" and "unsunk" costs may also sometimes be altered. A programmer may be able to postpone spending or committing certain funds until after the final decision about holding the course has been made. If, for example, a programmer can avoid or reduce the amount of nonrefundable meeting room deposits (a good example of sunk costs) or arrange to pay the deposits after the go, no-go decision, the amount of potential loss (and the risk) is reduced. In this case, the net benefit to the program comes with no compensating trade-off. That is not always the case. For example, a programmer may pay $20 per student to order materials three weeks in advance of a course and $30 per student for a rush requiring a two-day turnaround. The programmer may decide either to order ahead and gamble that enough people will show up to make the lower rate pay off or play it safe and pay the higher rate when a much better estimate of final enrollments can be made, thus reducing unneeded copies.

DETERMINING AND NEGOTIATING INSTRUCTOR COMPENSATION

In many organizational settings, programmers are not required (or allowed) to negotiate with instructors about compensation; instructors are paid according to established schedules. This is more likely where the educational program is relatively homogeneous and compensation can be based on credit hours. The scheme saves time and reduces irritation. For noncredit courses, or courses by instructors who are well known or in high demand, this scheme may be too inflexible.

Where programmers do negotiate instructor compensation, such negotiations are often difficult. Cold-blooded dickering over compensation may seem inappropriate in an educational, service-oriented setting. By the time such discussion takes place, the programmer and the instructor often have already worked together for some time, with the instructor providing valuable ideas at no charge. Quibbling over compensation at this point is awkward for the programmer; offering the job to someone who has not invested the time but is willing to teach the course for less is equally difficult. In addition, many programmers have not developed negotiation skills and are uncomfortable with the bargaining process. However, our decision-process model, combined with some common sense negotiation strategies, can make the process easier.

Ways to Calculate Instructor Compensation

Fixed Rate

An instructor can be paid a fixed amount established ahead of time. The amount may be arrived at by negotiation, reference to a schedule of published compensation rates, or some other means. This is probably the most common compensation method.

Per Student Rate

Instructor compensation can be tied to the number of students who enroll in the class. The rate may be the same for all students, or may vary according to the category of student or the number of students. For instance, an instructor may be paid $25 for every regularly enrolled student and $15 for each student who audits the class, or the instructor may be paid $25 for each student up to 30 students and $15 for every student in excess of 30. Many variations are possible.

Percentage of Income

In this variation on the per student method, an instructor is paid a stated percentage of the gross income generated from the course, say, 25 percent. This method may be preferred over the per student method where the number of students is more difficult to determine than the total amount of income or where several fees apply to the course.

Percentage of Net

In this method, the instructor is paid a stated percentage of the net margin of a program. This scheme requires a careful definition of net margin and accurate bookkeeping. Net may be defined as income minus direct expenses, income minus both direct and indirect expenses, or in any other way that makes sense and is clearly understood by both parties.

Sharing Development and Sunk Costs

Where extensive development costs are involved, higher risks can be shared in a number of ways. Suppose an instructor is willing to develop a course for $500 and to teach the course, if it meets enrollment standards, for an additional $500. Alternatively, she is willing to develop the course at no immediate charge, but asks $1,500 to teach the course if it meets enrollment standards and is presented. Under the first alternative, the instructor will be certain to receive $500 and will have a chance to receive a total of $1,000 if the course is successful. Under the second alternative, she is not certain to receive anything but has a chance of making $1,500 if the course is successful. Thus there is a trade-off between sunk and subsequent costs, and the programmer will have to estimate the risks involved and the potential for reward. Under the first alternative, the programmer will have to risk $500 in the hope of gaining a return of $500 later if the course is successful; under the second alternative, no up-front risk (no sunk costs associated with program development) means the eventual return will be lower.

Combination Methods

Two or more of the methods just described may be used together. For instance, the fixed rate may be combined with the per student rate; an instructor may be paid $300 plus $25 per student for every student in excess of 30. Alternatively, the instructor may be paid a fixed rate of $300 plus 15 percent of net margin. Combination methods are frequently used to produce more equitable reward/ risk sharing.

In addition to these varied compensation arrangements, an instructor might be on an established monthly salary and given course assignments according to established work load standards—an increasingly common circumstance where continuing education is integrated with traditional instructional programs. This variation of the fixed rate method presents some particular problems. First, allocating salary and fringe benefits appropriately to the CE course may be difficult, especially where work load standards are complex. Faculty teaching assignments may vary from one term to the next, and faculty may be assigned nonteaching duties, such as counseling and committee work, to which assigning a value is difficult. Second, compensation varies among faculty, so each faculty member will have a different rate. Both these circumstances make teacher compensation difficult to compute and to assign to the CE course, and therefore difficult to budget. Also, teacher compensation under these circumstances, fully burdened with fringe benefit costs, may be too high for CE courses in self-supporting enterprises.

Considerations

How, then, can a programmer decide which compensation method is best in a given situation? The determination of a fair compensation rate requires consideration of several factors, most of which are not quantifiable. These considerations involve both the programmer's perspective and an estimate of the instructor's attitudes.

Reward/Risk Ratio

If an instructor demands a share in the possible rewards of a course, he or she should usually also expect to share in the risk of presenting the course. This reward/risk sharing is best accomplished by using either the per student method or the percentage of net income or percentage of net margin method. The proportion of the reward/risk ratio that the instructor shares can be adjusted by setting the rate at different levels or by using a combined method.

Relative Contribution

This factor involves estimation of the relative value of contributions to the success of a program. In some courses, promotion is the most important factor in their success. In other cases, the idea for the course may be the contribution of greatest relative value. On the other hand, some courses rely to a great extent on the name and reputation of the instructor(s) for their success. In these cases, the programmer might be more inclined to offer or accept a relatively high instructor compensation rate and also to assume what would otherwise be a disproportionate share of the risk. Continuing education, like the motion picture industry, has "stars" whose appearance reduces risk and assures success.

The contribution of the organization to the course's success also should not be undervalued. A competent organization, one that can answer students' questions, organize promotion efforts, and handle the many details of course development and presentation, has considerable value; yet, at times, it is taken for granted both by instructors and programmers.

Supply and Demand

Supply and demand issues are closely related in some ways to relative contribution. The same supply and demand factors that applied to course pricing also apply to instructor compensation. For many courses, the supply of instructors exceeds the demand for their services. In other subject areas—e.g., computer science—instructors are in short supply. Those who are capable are often busy with other projects, so the opportunity cost to them of teaching a course is high. Programmers can expect that these scarce instructors will demand and receive a premium for their services.

Nonmonetary Considerations

Programmers should be aware of the motivations of potential instructors and should structure compensation schemes and negotiations to maximize the potential benefit these motivations can generate. After all, teaching bestows a number of psychological rewards. Many people enjoy imparting knowledge to others and expounding on their favorite subject. Instructors may also take pride in being associated with a particular institution or organization or in fulfilling an impulse to serve the community. Whether ego-serving or selfless, these motivations are part of the implicit equation programmers should use in calculating instructor compensation.

This "nonmonetary" category might also include another important consideration with financial implications that are difficult to compute. For a number of professionals—accountants, lawyers, architects, insurance salespeople, dentists, physicians—teaching a course, especially one promoted widely and prominently featuring the instructor's name and qualifications, is a form of advertising. The value of teaching the course to these people may thus far exceed the direct compensation they receive. This value should be recognized by the programmer and maximized in compensation negotiations.

Opportunity Costs

In bargaining with instructors, programmers should establish limits beyond which they will not go. This is called the walk-away position. Two main opportunity costs are connected with walking away from negotiation with an instructor. First, the programmer might have to abandon the program, losing all potential for return. Second, he or she will have to spend time, effort, and perhaps money to find an alternative instructor. That instructor may be less qualified than the first choice, which in turn has its cost to reputation, to established standards, and possibly to the direct financial return of the course if the change of instructor results in a decrease in the number of participants. As with all opportunity costs, these difficult-to-calculate costs must be calculated in some way.

Organizational Considerations

Most CE programmers work for organizations, and are expected to support their organizations' purposes. Furthermore, the very existence of the organization, as noted earlier, has a value for individual programs. Effective programmers recognize this value and can place their own programs and program development in the broader context. They recognize that the relationships they establish with their instructors influence the way the organization as a whole is viewed and that the organization's reputation in turn has a direct effect on its ability to attract competent instructors and, ultimately, participants. They see real utility in maintaining consistency in instructor compensation policies, even if such consistency is maintained at the expense of a particular course. Programmers in the same organization who pay different rates to instructors, unless they can show good reason for doing so, can threaten the entire fabric of instructor relationships, cause instructor dissatisfaction, and ultimately produce higher costs.

In a related vein, instructors who have taught regularly for a particular organization in the past and who have demonstrated institutional loyalty are likely to expect that their faithfulness will be recognized by an increase in pay. Increases in pay for past loyal service may serve an organization's future interests by encouraging such loyalty.

Present compensation negotiations may also be influenced by considerations of the future. A programmer may agree to pay an instructor at a lower rate for her first few courses in anticipation that, as the program builds, she will have a heavier teaching load and will be paid more. On the other hand, an instructor may be paid more than standard in the beginning to establish a continuing relationship that will result in substantial returns over the long run.

Other organizational reasons may exist for paying "above scale." For example, regular faculty of an institution are often paid at a higher rate than are outside or adjunct faculty. This scheme establishes a distinction that many faculty members, some of whom may exercise some review function over continuing education, find congenial. There may be other categories of people to whom it is organizationally desirable to pay higher rates even if these cannot be justified on the basis of the course budget. These extra costs should be considered simply as part of the cost of belonging to an organization.

Negotiation Strategies

The art of negotiation is currently a popular subject and many books on it have appeared. Lack of space presents a full discussion of strategies for negotiating instructor compensation, but several points arising from the preceding sections are worth noting.

Mention Compensation Early

Address the subject of compensation rates early in discussions with potential instructors. The process can begin with a professional negotiating technique called "lowering expectations." This technique can use such oblique remarks as "I'm not sure we'll be able to get anyone to teach this course for what we can afford (are allowed) to pay," or "I'm concerned that we will not be able to pay the instructor for this course what he or she is really worth. "You can also use more direct comments, such as, "I'm excited about this course, but I'm wondering if a competent instructor such as yourself would be willing to teach the course at our established rate of $30 per contact hour."

This sort of early warning serves several purposes. First, it tells potential instructors that a great investment of time and effort does not necessarily mean high compensation. Second, it says that there are rules regarding instructor compensation that the programmer cannot be expected to alter. This knowledge may subtly lower the expectations of the instructor who, caught up in the enthusiasm of the early stages of course planning, may begin to see unwarranted dollar signs. Third, such frank, early introduction of the subject may clear the air for future discussions, eliminating much beating around the bush that can be embarrassing and frustrating to both parties.

Do Your Homework

In every negotiation, knowledge is power. The more knowledge a programmer has about the financial structure of a proposed course and about the personal financial situation and teaching motivations of the potential instructor, the more successful a negotiator that programmer is likely to be. The decision/process model, combined with the considerations and options discussed earlier in this chapter, can give the programmer a substantial advantage in instructor negotiations. Prior to discussions with the instructor, the programmer can compute the course's break-even point under varying assumptions, establish a rough calculation of the reward/risk ratio and the amount of risk the organization is willing to assume, determine the instructor's relative contribution to the program's success, and assess the supply and demand situation. The programmer should then be able to establish both the maximum compensation that the organization would be willing to pay (walk-away position) and the amount of compensation with which to open negotiations. Having established these two points, the programmer can proceed with confidence, knowing when to yield and when (and how) to argue.

Plead Limited Authority

A common tactic in negotiations is pleading limited authority to gain time, reorganize strategy, rethink alternatives, and put pressure on the other party. To plead limited authority, simply say that all agreements must be reviewed and approved by a higher authority. Since virtually every programmer has some kind of boss and belongs to some kind of organization, such a plea will sound (and usually is) legitimate. Even if a programmer has authority to determine instructor compensation, it is usually a mistake to admit this in negotiations. Since an instructor, who presumably has the authority to make his or her own decisions, can rarely counter with a similar tactic, the programmer can get the instructor to commit to a position revealing real motivations and an initial bargaining position. The programmer can then retreat and compute at leisure a counterproposal that tries to address the instructor's concerns but results in a compensation basis more favorable to the programmer's organization.

Talk About Reward/Risk Options

Although talking about risk and reward rations during compensation negotiations is sometimes counterproductive, some instructors may force the issue. Usually, in arguing for higher compensation, they will select an estimate of the total enrollment in a course (the higher the better, from their point of view) and then show, using a low estimate of total course costs, how unconscionably high the net return to the organization will be compared with the relatively paltry compensation the instructor will receive. If the programmer has a clear notion of the relative risk of the course and has the latitude to negotiate, he or she can answer this ploy by suggesting a risk-sharing plan. Since the instructor has already revealed his or her own notion of a reasonable enrollment figure (which is likely to be high), a bargaining position has been established around which a per student rate can be set. This launches a discussion of reward/risk considerations and forces the instructor to take those factors into account. Although it has dangers, the reward/risk concept can be a powerful tool in the hands of an astute programmer.

Know When to Defend the Budget

If negotiations necessitate a discussion of the course budget, the programmer is often placed in an inferior bargaining position. Remember that most course budgets are prepared on the basis of an enrollment number that means success for the program. The dynamic factors—reward/risk, opportunity costs, and the informal subsidization of losers by winners—do not appear on most budgets. Further, the concepts of cost and value of programmer time are completely foreign to most instructors. The instructor, by carefully ignoring or minimizing these factors, may attempt to persuade you by reference to the budget that he or she is being offered too small a share in the course's financial rewards. The instructor may also argue that the overhead is too high or that the pools upon which the overhead rate is based do not apply to this particular course. The only effective method of dealing with such tactics is to keep from assuming a defensive attitude about the budget and remind the instructor of the counterarguments. Again, a clear understanding of the issues is invaluable in dealing with instructors who insist on going into the course budget in detail.

THE EFFECTS OF INDIRECT COST ALLOCATION AND ASSIGNMENT

In traditional systems, in which all indirect costs are allocated to courses as cost objects, the danger is great of inadvertently distorting the behavior of programmers away from organizational goals. This is because loading all costs into a course burdens it to the extent that programmers seeking to maximize financial returns may make their decisions upon an arbitrary method of cost allocation rather than the true underlying financial structure. However, such distorted behavior may be present even where ABC is used and where it fully discloses the costs of operations and distinguishes between courses and activities as cost objects. Thus, programmers must have a clear understanding of how nonpromotion and nonclassroom costs are treated in the CE financial management systems; they must be alert to the effect that either allocation or assignment methods have on all course planning decisions. Chapter 5 introduces the notion of direct and indirect costs; Chapter 6 illustrates one method of allocating indirect costs to particular courses; and Chapter 14 includes a more detailed discussion of the methods of allocating indirect costs and the effect on behavior of these methods.

Since all indirect cost allocation methods are to some degree arbitrary and inequitable, programmers must understand the methods and the reasons behind allocation schemes and the effect they may have on their financial decisions. The programmer who constantly tries to beat down the overhead rate or avoid its full impact usually does the organization a disservice. The programmer who can understand the reasoning behind an overhead allocation method and the compromise it implies can help the organization minimize the difficulties of dealing with indirect costs.

ARRANGING COSPONSORED PROGRAMS AND PRICING PARTIAL SERVICES

Cosponsored programs present the programmer with a special set of problems. Cosponsorship usually requires careful definition of the roles and responsibilities of each of the sponsoring agencies and often means that considerable time and effort must be spent in coordinating activities and in negotiating programmatic and financial issues.

Programmers are also sometimes asked to provide consulting services or conference services to others outside their unit. For example, an internal campus department that is sponsoring a conference may look to the continuing education organization for logistical help. Such situations involve considerations outside the scope of our analysis so far, but the concepts we have covered, particularly those relating to negotiating with instructors, can clarify some of the issues and provide a straightforward course of action. The concept of relative contribution (where each party is rewarded proportional to its contribution to the success of the venture) comes crucially into play.

Sponsoring a program with another agency can have real advantages, and programmers should be alert to cosponsorship opportunities. Continuing education enterprises can often gain market exposure and reach special markets easily and cheaply through cosponsorship arrangements. Other agencies often possess the subject matter knowledge required to organize the content of a course and the ability to attract competent instructors. For instance, a local Department of Public Health may have considerable experience in dealing with alcohol abuse in the community. It may welcome another qualified agency's offer to represent a public course on alcohol problems and, because education is one of its missions, might want to lend its name and its support to such a program.

The issues involved in arriving at a cosponsorship agreement are usually fairly clear.

1. Which agency will do what, when?
2. Which agency will pay for what, when?
3. How will student enrollments and processing be handled? Who will collect the money?
4. How will the decision about holding the course be reached? Who will make the decision and on what basis? If the decision is to be made jointly, what process will be used to arrive at the decision?
5. How will losses or margins be divided, and by what date will settlement take place?

Working out the first issue usually involves a realistic appraisal of the strengths and weaknesses of each agency and the coordination of contributions to ensure the success of the program. Such decisions are necessary preliminaries to working out financial arrangements, since they will normally hinge in part on the relative contributions of each agency.

The second issue is often determined by the availability of resources to each agency. Usually agencies are reluctant to pay for elements over which they have little control.

The third issue is really an elaboration of the first. The agency to whom the student must send the course fee is more likely to be identified with the course than other cosponsors, but such an identity carries the cost of handling enrollments, and this cost (normally covered through an overhead allocation) should be included in the overall financial arrangement.

Determining the go, no-go point is a crucial element of any reputation since the consequences of cancelling are likely to be different for each party.

Working out financial arrangements is usually the most difficult and time-consuming issue confronting cosponsors. Defining financial relationships aids in defining programmatic relationships; the two are intertwined. A desirable first step is the preparation of a course budget. This budget should be prepared in as much detail as possible, preferably in some version of the format shown in Exhibit 6.7 (page 97). The initial goal should be simply to list all costs and all sources of income, regardless of which agency is ultimately made responsible for them. Costs should include the costs of programmer time, programmer clerical support, and staff time, as well as the cost of the time of those from other agencies who will be involved in the program. In some situations, including the value of programmer time may also be appropriate, although this concept is sometimes difficult to explain. In addition, it is usually appropriate to have the initial budget provide for indirect costs at whatever rate and upon whatever basis each of the sponsors customarily uses. This procedure at least puts the overhead issue on the table for consideration and can help the negotiators arrive at an equitable arrangement.

After the initial budget is drawn up and presented to each party, the responsibilities and separate contributions can be assigned. At this point, it is sometimes useful for all parties to agree to exclude certain costs from the calculation. Prime candidates for exclusion are costs that are relatively equal in value and costs that present potentially controversial points. For example, where staff effort will be contributed in roughly equal amounts by both agencies, the cost of staff time is often excluded from the direct cost base for the purposes of coming to an agreement, although it certainly should not be ignored in the independent calculation the programmer must make to determine the financial viability of the course. Overhead elements, because of the built-in inequities previously mentioned and because of a lack of comparable cost pools and allocation bases, are also often eliminated from the financial agreement. When this happens, the programmer should make sure that the respective organizations are sharing the cost of functions used by the program but which, under normal circumstances, would be included under the over-head allocation. The cost of enrolling students is an example.

Cosponsorship often involves extensive negotiations. Many of the negotia-tion strategies and considerations described in our discussion of instructor compensation are also applicable to cosponsored programs. Certainly reward/risk ratios are involved. Which agency puts up what and when is crucial. To equalize the risk and avoid inequities caused by incorrect estimates of costs, agencies will often agree to bear the risk equally or in fixed proportions, regardless of which agency actually pays the cost, and settle up at the comple-tion of the course when all cost figures are in. If this kind of arrangement is not in place, great care should be paid to the distribution of sunk, fixed, and variable costs and their effect on the possible outcomes of the course.

The concept of relative contribution is also important in these negotiations. Although hard dollars-and-cents contributions can be easily specified, the value of the name and reputation of the agencies involved or of access to a particular mailing list or newsletter are much harder to describe in monetary terms. As a rule of thumb, continuing education enterprises, especially those associated with institutions, tend to sell themselves too cheaply, undervaluing the marketing advantages that a cosponsored program will enjoy by being associated with the name and reputation of their institution.

Deciding in advance how the final decision about holding the course will be reached is most important. Cosponsoring agencies are likely to have unequal stakes in the success of the program. In addition to differences in financial investment and in the share of financial risks, the risks of embarrassment and loss of reputation that the organizations run may be different.

The final financial question to be resolved concerns the division of the residual loss or margin on the conference. We have already discussed most of the factors to be considered in deciding upon an equitable split. Usually division formulae require that each agency be compensated for costs incurred on behalf of the program and that the residual (either plus or minus) be allocated on a percentage basis. This scheme obviously requires a clear definition of costs and careful bookkeeping. Whatever division method is used—percentage of gross income, per student amount, percentage of expense contribution, or others—a meeting of the minds between the two agencies is required. A programmer informed by our previous discussions and the deci-sion/process model will be able to sort out the issues quickly and see clearly where institutional self-interest lies.

DEVELOPING AN OVERALL STRATEGY

Part 2 has so far dealt primarily with the economics and decision-making processes related to single courses. However, most programmers are involved with the development of many courses throughout the year and will be held financially accountable on an annual basis. Although most decisions made in dealing with a block of courses involve the same sort of reasoning needed for handling a single course, some additional considerations are worth noting.

Faced with an appropriately negotiated budgetary goal, one set high enough to stretch performance but low enough to be realistically attainable, the programmer must make some hard choices about how to invest the available resources, particularly his or her own time and effort. In many situations, making these choices requires a complex balancing act.

The first balance that must be struck is between adventure and safety. In any group of potential programs, some are tried and true, attract 30 enrollments term after term, and take almost no time to set up. These are like money in the bank—for awhile. Every experienced programmer knows how quickly and suddenly the market for a particular course or group of courses can turn down. For example, single-day management training seminars showed a sharp decline in the 1980-82 recession as corporate training budgets dried up. As the dollar strengthened in early 1983, the bottom dropped out of most domestic English as a Second Language programs. As they view these market vicissitudes, wise programmers learn constantly to look for new markets and programs. Entering any new area involves higher risk in the short run, but the riskiest strategy of all is to depend on traditional winners to keep on being winners. Thus, the best strategy is to spend part of the available resources on the new and untried while relying on the more tested courses to provide the short-run floor of stability necessary for confident adventuring.

The programmer should have an overall plan into which opportunities can be fit. Part of that plan should be an internal allocation of "venture capital" or "risk capital" for new programs or ideas. This allocation may be expressed in terms of person-hours or number of programs rather than dollars. The size of the proportion devoted to these new schemes will vary from programmer to programmer, but if it grows so large that failure of the new programs would seriously jeopardize the position of the programmer or imperil the financial position of the enterprise, then the programmer had better gain the consent of superiors before proceeding. Most enlightened organizations recognize the need for risk taking and will provide the latitude for it, but, the organization must consider overall risk with care just as individual programmers must balance risk and stability within a specific program group.

A balance must also be struck between long-term and short-term goals. For example, the programmer's personal involvement in the promotional effort for a course is normally a short-term project, but in the process the programmer may be making contacts or running across ideas that will aid future programming efforts. The allocation of time between current operations and long-term planning and research and development is done most effectively as a result of a conscious plan.

SUMMARY

Some programmers may feel that the discussion in this chapter contained more description and detail than was necessary or even useful. If a programmer is to calculate the fee, negotiate instructor compensation, evaluate promotion effectiveness, consider the pros and cons of making each cost element either fixed or variable, and determine the effects of overhead allocation methods for every course, little time is left for the other parts of the development process. In real life, institutions and their CE units usually work out policies and practices to make financial decisions about courses relatively easy and uniform, so many of these decisions do not have to be made by the programmer. Similarly, the evaluation of promotion effectiveness is usually dependent on an organization-wide accumulation of tracking data and information on promotion costs, and overhead allocation schemes are generally planned by management to meet organization goals. Nonetheless, programmers, particularly in smaller establishments, do sometimes have to make some of these decisions, and doing so competently requires not only an understanding of a particular course, but also a broader knowledge of the possible, of practices in other institutions, and of the theoretical background behind locally prescribed options. Special situations such as cosponsorship may also call on this deeper understanding.

The preceding three chapters sought to present programmers with a comprehensive understanding of the economics involved in budgeting and accounting for individual courses of instruction. Such an understanding cannot be complete, however, without the additional understanding of the principles and considerations that go into the development of an overall budgeting system for the entire CE organization. Such an understanding allows the programmer to place necessary decisions in an appropriate context. Part 3 of this book takes up these broader considerations.

PART THREE

• • • • • • • • • • •

Financial Management for Continuing Education Administrators

P art 3 will provide deans, instructors, budget and finance managers, and all who have responsibility for the leadership of CE organizations with an understanding of the theory and practice of CE financial management. (In this discussion, the term director refers to all people in charge of CE organizations.) Part 3 will also interest those in higher authority to whom the head of continuing education reports, particularly the appropriate budget or fiscal officer of the larger institution. Policy makers are increasingly interested in continuing education as it grows in importance as a possible source of both funds and problems. Because this part builds upon the foundation laid in Parts 1 and 2, it assumes a knowledge of the concepts previously covered, particularly the decision/process model, multidimensional budgeting, and activity-based costing.

After reading Part 3, readers will be able to

- plan a comprehensive financial management system for a continuing education organization;
- establish an effective budgeting process in their organization;
- understand how multidimensional budgeting can be implemented throughout the unit;
- understand how activity-based costing can be used in a CE organization;
- establish an effective system of meaningful financial reporting; and
- understand the effects of the financial management process on the organization.

CHAPTER 9

Understanding and Setting the Context for the CE Financial Management System

F inancial management and planning for a CE organization is much more difficult and less precise than financial planning for programs because it involves more complex issues, particularly issues of human behavior. Part 2 focused on the behavior of costs; Part 3 views organizational financial planning as a process designed to influence the behavior of people.

The financial plan or budget of the CE organization serves an important integrating function in effective organizations. It links the managerial concerns of planning, organizing, controlling, and motivating in a way visible to everyone in the organization. The budget is not only involved in the reward system but (at its best) is an important communication tool, helping both supervisors and subordinates sharpen goals and objectives, lay out plans and implementation strategies, and evaluate success or failure.

The pervasiveness of the financial planning process in organizational life means that the establishment of a new management information system or changes in an existing system must be planned carefully by the organization's leaders. They must consider environmental factors that affect the process and then make basic decisions about the system's structure and roles in the organization.

Sooner or later, all organizations face the need to establish or change their financial management system. The change agent may be a new organizational arrangement brought about by management awareness of new audiences, demographic change or other external factors, new financial requirements, a decrease in subsidy, poor financial results, or, frequently, a change in leadership in the CE organization or its parent institution. This chapter is written for directors facing such change, and for directors who need to understand factors that affect their present systems.

The first step in introducing a new financial management system is understanding the environmental factors that influence the structure and effectiveness of that system. Once these elements are clear, basic decisions about the process can be made.

Three categories of environmental factors can affect budgets: external, institutional, and internal. Exhibit 9.1 is a representation of these factors. In this chapter, we will examine these environmental factors and the impact they can have on the development of a CE financial management system. We will also review the basic decisions CE managers face as they develop and use the system.

EXTERNAL ENVIRONMENTAL FACTORS

External factors lie outside both the organization and any parent institution. These factors are usually beyond the control of the organization and must be accepted as givens (although adjustments, accommodations, and counterattacks may be made).

The Economy

For both self-supporting enterprises and those with subsidies, the state of the economy, both national and local, strongly affects decision making in CE, including decisions having to do with systems. In good times, when public revenues and resources are more available and many students are willing to pay for an education, CE enterprises may adopt flexible systems with relatively loose controls. In hard times, where cost control is emphasized and decisions affecting even relatively small amounts of money are important, a more rigid system may be necessary. (However, a bad economy may sometimes mean an increase in students, even for a self-supporting enterprise, because more people have more time and are willing to spend money to make themselves more attractive in the job market.)

Political Environment

The external political environment can also be an important influence on the CE budget, especially for subsidized organizations drawing all or part of their subsidy directly from public funds. Tax revolts, the vagaries of state and local

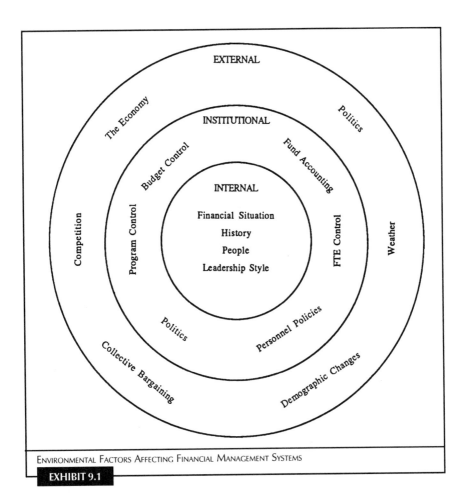

ENVIRONMENTAL FACTORS AFFECTING FINANCIAL MANAGEMENT SYSTEMS

EXHIBIT 9.1

governments, and the public attitude toward education, particularly toward continuing education, all have powerful effects. Self-supporting organizations may also be profoundly influenced by the political climate. On the one hand, budget cuts in subsidized continuing education can improve the market for self-supporting units. On the other hand, CE organizations are frequently asked by parent institutions to help make up the institution's budget shortfalls.

The form of the CE financial system may also be significantly affected by the external political climate. Where education budgets are subject to public scrutiny and debate, the budget process may be rigid and formal, with much attention paid to detailed costs and charges and great time and effort spent on budget defense and justification. In a more favorable political environment, the budgeting process may be more open and venturesome.

Competition

The nature and extent of the competition facing a particular continuing education organization is also important. Effective organizations analyze their competition and adjust their goals and objectives, their marketing strategies, and their budget systems with competition in mind. For instance, an organization may decide not to compete in an area, geographical or professional, where the competition is well established and strong. On the other hand, where the competition is assailable, the organization may establish market share goals. For instance, it may set itself the goal of achieving a 20 percent share of the business and management courses given in its geographical area within a year. Meeting this goal may require extraordinary expenditures for promotion and marketing for the year and result in the hiring of highly paid professionals to develop and teach the courses. Thus, competition has exercised a powerful (and not necessarily negative) effect on the organization's budget and financial management process.

Other External Factors

Other factors influence the character of the financial management process, some directly and some indirectly. Collective bargaining comes into play when budgets and financial performance are part of the wage administration policy. Even weather may influence budgeting—courses may be attended heavily in the fall and spring terms and more lightly in the winter, a fact that has obvious financial implications. Less obviously, the winter may be seen as a relatively slack period during which the annual budget may be prepared; thus, the weather can influence the timing of the budgeting process. Demographic changes might also have an effect on the process as programs and marketing efforts are adjusted to recognize changes in the age and nature of the local continuing education audience.

INSTITUTIONAL ENVIRONMENTAL FACTORS

Institutional factors have a more immediate effect on the CE financial management system. Continuing education organizations, as part of larger institutions, must operate within a framework of rules, regulations, and goals set by those institutions. In higher education institutions, continuing education is usually organized either as a separate entity (centralized) or as a part of a department or school that is responsible for continuing education in its particular subject area (decentralized). The choice of a centralized or decentralized structure has obvious financial impact, and sound budgeting may well reveal which choice is the more economical and efficient for a particular institution. Continuing education is also part of a larger whole in many other institutions—museums, community centers, religious institutions, service organizations, and professional societies—and thus is influenced by institutional factors.

Budget Control

Direct budget control is the most immediate influence an institution can exert on the CE organization. Usually the parent institution can exercise absolute control over budget line items and can impose spending limitations as it wishes. In practice, this control is rarely exercised to the limit; the director of CE usually has some flexibility in making budgetary adjustments and in developing systems suited to the needs of the organization. The relationship between responsibility and authority is important here. If the director is ordered to "make money," to make the CE organization fully self-supporting, or even to serve a specified number of students per term, then the parent institution should invest that director with enough authority, including budgetary authority, to carry out the assigned responsibility.

In some organizations, an expense budget is given to the CE unit, and the director of that unit has the responsibility of limiting spending to the amount allocated. (Sometimes restrictions are even more severe; the director must not only keep within the budget but actually go below it by meeting a "savings target," often in the form of "salary savings.") In these situations, the director's main job is to allocate resources among programs and services. Organizations falling into this pattern are called fixed resource organizations.

This restrictive case can be contrasted with the opposite end of the spectrum—the variable resource (usually self-supporting) organization. Such an organization typically has two sides to its budget—income and expense—and the amount available for expenses varies with income. Again, the resources of the organization must be allocated among programs, but here CE managers have the additional task of generating the resources required. Variable resource organizations and their budgets have to be flexible so that they can adjust to market conditions, contracting when the market shrinks and expanding when market opportunities arise. Thus, directors of variable resource CE organizations usually have more autonomy and more opportunity to make budget adjustments.

In reality, pure examples of either type of organization probably do not exist. Most CE organizations are funded from a number of different sources, and these sources often have different budgetary restrictions attached to them. For example, student fees may be relatively free of expenditure restrictions, but subsidies from the parent institution and monies received from contracts and grants, gifts, endowments, and tax revenues may be tightly controlled.

Another form of budget control by parent institutions, more subtle than direct financial control, is the imposition of charges (sometimes quite ingenious) for services provided, or the more candid requirement that the CE organization return money directly to the parent institution. The assessment of indirect costs (overhead) is a further example of "parental" control. Such charges may be for personnel services, administrative space, library use, or other aspects of the institution used by the CE organization. However expressed, these charges burden the CE budget, removing funds from the control of the CE director and, in bad times, contributing to budget deficits and thereby giving higher authority an excuse to impose even greater budgetary restrictions. On the other hand, as CE organizations become more important in the financing of parent institutions' operations, meeting recharge payments or a targeted budget surplus often means greater autonomy, freedom, power, and influence for continuing education. The ideal is a relationship between the CE organization and the parent that is based on a full understanding of the underlying economics of the CE market.

Before a budget system is introduced or changed, the degree and nature of budget control by a parent institution should be understood and taken into account.

Fund Accounting

Closely related to the question of institutional control is the matter of fund accounting, to which most CE enterprises must adhere for at least part of their support. Fund accounting calls for money to be segregated and separately accounted for when special restrictions or conditions attach to its transfer. With fund accounting, a separate accounting entity must be established on the books of the organization and each expenditure of funds must be examined to make sure it accords with the terms and conditions under which the organization was given the funds. Fund accounting therefore has a profound effect on the form and process of the budget system.

Obviously, the requirements of fund accounting can severely reduce the ability of CE management to act. For instance, money given under government contract to train medical technologists may not be used to train medical librarians, even if the latter are more urgently needed.

Fund accounting falls into several categories. Restricted funds must be dedicated to a particular purpose. Unrestricted or discretionary funds may usually be expended as management wishes. A general operating fund is usually an unrestricted fund used to support the overall operations of the organization.

Lapsing funds terminate either at the end of the organization's fiscal year or at the end of a special term provided for in the funding agreement. All money unspent at the end of the term must be returned to the funding source. Nonlapsing funds may be carried over and spent in subsequent periods. Lapsing funds present management with severe restrictions and often dictate decisions about courses. Lapsing funds require an organization's budget and accounting systems to be comprehensive, accurate, and timely.

FTE Control

A specialized form of budget control, called here FTE (for "full-time equivalent" employees) control, is sometimes imposed upon CE organizations, especially those associated with higher education institutions. In colleges and universities, both dollars, including payroll dollars, and number of employee positions are subject to strict budget control. Standard budget allocation formulae used by institutions of higher education are based on proportionate FTE; by formula, each FTE brings with him or her an increment in the supplies budget, the photocopying budget, the telephone budget, and the secretarial support budget. Elaborate budget controls and much paperwork surround the addition or transfer of FTE from one budgetary unit to another. This system may be acceptable in the larger institution, where the primary budget task is to allocate a fixed amount of resources among budget units, but it can devastate a CE organization expected to be fully or partially self-supporting. To be successful, such an organization must be flexible and able to respond to market opportunities. The necessity of responding to institutional requirements of FTE control can have a far reaching impact on the CE budgeting process.

Personnel Policies

The personnel policies of the parent institution are also important in shaping the CE organization's budgeting process. Where unions or civil service traditions rule, any attempt to change the budget system may change what are considered "conditions of employment" and may fall under the "meet and confer" category of issues, which are subject to negotiation. This is particularly true where the budget system is (as it should be) tied to the employee reward system. Pay raises for employees, both performance related and cost-of-living related, are often part of official policy. For example, cost-of-living adjustments for many state-supported institutions are often determined by the legislature well after the beginning of the fiscal year, resulting in retroactive payments to employees. Such adjustments typically apply to all employees of the institution, no matter from what source they are paid; thus, self-supporting CE organizations are often burdened with large increases in payroll costs without a budget allocation to fund them.

Thus, the director of a CE organization is responsible for paying employees at rates consistent with those in other parts of the parent institution, but often has no say in what those rates should be. The director is often granted no additional funds to pay salary increases, other than those funds generated by the CE organization itself. Furthermore, the director is almost always constrained by policy in matters of firing or disciplining unproductive workers, establishing limits on job authority, or changing work assignments. These limitations can have a considerable effect on establishing or changing a budget system.

Programming Restrictions

Beyond direct budget control, the most common and powerfully restrictive institutional factor affecting CE financial management is the ability of the parent institution to exercise programmatic control over the CE organization—that is, control over the nature and subject matter of instruction. Such control can take a number of forms. Most direct is an explicit order not to do certain types of programs. For instance, a major research university may not allow its CE division to set up courses in automobile repair, deeming such courses inappropriate to the mission and image of an institution of higher education. In another case, a museum may not allow its continuing education unit to present programs not directly related to a current or upcoming exhibit.

Sometimes agreements between institutions prevent a particular institution from programming in certain fields. For instance, a community college in a given city will offer all the courses in woodworking, and the YMCA will offer photography courses. Such agreements, especially when they require considerable investment in capital items and facilities, can serve the public interest by concentrating community resources and thereby providing better services. This same kind of agreement can exist within an institution. For example, the CE arm of a major university may be prohibited from offering courses in business and management because courses in this subject area are given by an institute attached to the school of business administration.

As a less direct form of programming control, an institution may insist that only regular faculty teach courses in CE, or it may establish implausible requirements for the hiring of faculty. In a field such as computer education, institutional policy may require instructors to have a degree that is actually irrelevant to the field. Institutional policy may also influence decisions about whether to hold some courses. For example, summer session faculty contracts must often be honored no matter how few students enroll in a course.

Institutional control over programming can clearly have far-reaching indirect effects on financial management. It may require careful and costly program reviews by both the parent institution and the CE organization. Sometimes potentially profitable courses may not be attempted, or a course may become too costly for financial success. Bitter wrangling about educational quality may sidetrack budget hearings. Academic authority may call the quality of the CE program into question, while the CE director asks for more money to assure and maintain quality.

Politics

CE is often seen as being outside the central mission of a parent institution. Thus, the CE organization is usually politically weak and vulnerable to attack from "mainstream" units. When resources become scarce, CE is often one of the first units to have funding reductions (in subsidized situations) or to have additional charges assessed against it (in full or partial self-support situations). Of course, the more the parent becomes dependent on the stepchild for dollar support, the more influential the stepchild may become; but this progression is hardly assured, especially when the parent's financial expectations are not met.

The budgeting process is both profoundly affected by institutional politics and a powerful instrument of such politics. Political considerations may dictate that the director keep the CE budget a little obscure—"What they don't know won't hurt them" or, more often to the point, "What they don't know about my operation can't be used to hurt me." On the other hand, the political situation may require a comprehensive and detailed financial management system. Knowing that the budget will be inspected carefully by the officers of the parent institution, a CE director will want to be "squeaky clean" in the budget presentation. He or she should have sufficient backup information to support all requests represented in the budget and fend off anticipated attacks. Often, the form of the budget presentation, complete with neat schedules and fully explained requests, will prove more important than the budget's substance. Chapter 10 will consider some strategies the CE director might employ in presenting a budget to supervisors.

INTERNAL ENVIRONMENTAL FACTORS

Assessing the internal or intra-organizational factors that can influence the shape of the financial management process requires detailed knowledge of the organization and the personalities involved. Such assessment is often difficult, but it must be made if the process is to be effective.

Financial Situation

Recent events, including a fluctuating economy, have placed financial strains on higher education; most CE organizations are currently experiencing a financial crisis or will face one shortly. Often CE financial systems are born of financial crisis, and the alert manager can use concern about a possible crisis to institute tighter budget controls or to change an existing system. Unfortunately, the crisis is often at hand before the organization sees the need for a more comprehensive and accurate system.

It is better to plan and gain employee support for budget reforms while the organization is still on a firm footing. For one thing, the footing may not be as firm as it seems. Not all successful organizations are well managed, just as not all unsuccessful organizations are poorly managed. An organization may be successful because of a happy accident of geography and lack of competition—external factors not under the control of the management—and gross management errors may be hidden behind the mask of success. If an incident suggests a reason for increasing financial control that will make sense to the rank and file, the astute manager will take advantage of the occasion to prevent trouble later on.

History

The history of the organization, particularly with regard to budgeting and financial control, is an important variable when a new situation arises. Many academics view budgeting or anything having to do with money as distasteful. Furthermore, many people have grown up with the idea that education ought to be free to those who wish it and that educational institutions should provide their services at nominal cost to the individual. In a CE organization, this attitude can be a significant barrier to acceptance of a financial system.

Another kind of problem arises if the organization has a long history of failed budgetary control. When budgets are not compared with actual results or used to evaluate performance, they become empty forms that many employees see (perhaps correctly) as a waste of time and energy.

Even when an organization has had a positive history of budgetary control, it may need a change in its system. It may have become accustomed to a system that is really an empty form but is so much a part of organizational life that it is no longer resented. In these cases, changes in the system, even if obviously desirable, often will be resented and resisted. The changes must be introduced slowly and their differences from the old system de-emphasized.

People and Leadership Style

The people in an organization are critical to the success or failure of a financial management system, but the many effects this "variable" can have are difficult to describe. Certainly the ages of the members of an organization, their length of employment, and their attitudes toward the organization and toward budgeting and financial control will all be important. When introducing budgetary (or any other) change, a manager must be sensitive both to the needs of the organization and the needs and perceptions of the people who make up that organization. Meeting both can be most difficult in matters of budgeting and financial control.

Leadership style has an important effect on the form and texture of the financial management process. The budget system chosen by an organization is usually very much an extension of the style and philosophy of the organization's managers. Directors of CE organizations should be self-aware enough to identify their own leadership styles and figure out how those styles can be carried through in the budget system.

Like administrative officers, financial management systems can be authoritarian or democratic, rigid or flexible. They can concentrate on small details or on overall objectives. These categories can be used punitively or as part of a reward system. They can support the leadership style of the director, or they can decrease leadership effectiveness by sending mixed messages to the organization. For these reasons, leadership style is an important influence on the budget system.

SETTING THE CONTEXT

While the external and institutional environments may be beyond the influence of CE managers, the internal context can be adjusted through careful managerial action. In fact, a change in the financial information system frequently both signals and effects a change in organizational culture. A new financial system can validate a change that has already occurred and can create the conditions for further change. As they contemplate or are compelled to develop new CE financial information management systems or alter existing systems, CE managers face a number of decisions. They have to decide what the mission, goals, and strategic direction of the CE organization will be and communicate these to the stakeholders in the organization. They must also determine or define the responsibility structure of the CE organization, a logical organizational segmentation scheme, the categories of income and expenses (line items) that will be kept track of, methods of cost allocation or assignment, and the degree of flexibility and control that the financial system will incorporate.

Strategic Planning

The most important (but not the only) purpose of a CE financial management information system is to help CE management achieve the mission and goals of the organization by providing timely information for management decisions. It is logical then, that before new systems are developed, the key elements of a strategic planning process should be in place. These elements are usually a mission statement, a "vision" of what the organization should be at some time in the future, a set of values to guide the institution, and some statement of the strategic goals and objectives of the organization. The CE financial management information system provides some of the "metrics" or means of measurement by which the organization can evaluate its progress in achieving its goals.

Strategic directions, organizational goals, and objectives have a direct and important impact on financial management systems. If we follow the logic of activity-based costing described in Chapter 13, the strategic planning process will define strategic directions (serving the health care field), markets (for public enrollments and contract training), customers (individual health care practitioners and institutions providing care), and management goals (growth and institutional relationships). Thus, the strategic planning process provides a beginning template for the financial management system.

Responsibility Structure

CE managers also have to decide who is going to be responsible for what. No organization can function without a general statement of its responsibility. Responsibility may reside in individuals or, increasingly, in teams of individuals, but it must be defined and clearly assigned. In traditional CE organizations the vertical or "stovepipe" responsibility structure is common. In this model, programming responsibility is assigned to individuals according to some portfolio definition scheme, such as subject matter (engineering), course format (evening courses), or credit classification (noncredit courses). Nonprogramming departments are defined by function: marketing, registration, business services, reprographics. Typically, each service department has a manager responsible for carrying out the functions of the department. We will examine the full range of possibilities below, in the section entitled "Organizational Segmentation."

New management philosophies are pushing the development of different models of responsibility assignment. In "matrix" organizations, individuals may be assigned responsibility in several ways, including through team membership. For instance, an individual programmer may be responsible for a particular subject matter portfolio (health care courses) but also for serving a particular client group within that area (contract training customers). These new responsibility structures require the application of ABC and MDB; traditional budgeting and cost accounting simply cannot supply the information necessary to administer these new structures effectively. Thus, the choice of responsibility structure has a significant impact on the kind of financial management information system chosen.

Organizational Segmentation

Closely associated with the responsibility structure is the organizational segmentation scheme. The responsibility structure requires that the CE organization be divided into parts to measure how well each part is doing. The choice of responsibility structure (traditional, nontraditional) influences the *choice and type* of the financial management information system (e.g., traditional with course as cost object or new using ABC and MDB); the organizational segmentation scheme influences the *form and content* of the system. In deciding how to parse the organization, CE managers exert a profound influence on the culture and behavior of the people in it.

Development of a useful and realistic organization segmentation plan should begin, like the choice of a responsibility structure, with the strategic plan of the organization and the natural service functions. Even with new management philosophies, CE organizations can usually be segmented initially into two general categories—service departments and programming departments.

Service departments, such as those listed below, provide the support services necessary to carry out the presentation of continuing education programs but are not responsible for programming courses.

- **Director's Office** provides overall administration of the CE organization but is usually not directly involved in programming; necessary information includes director's salary and salary of immediate support staff.
- **Cashier's Office** handles cash receipts and depositing.
- **Personnel Services** provides services, including recruitment counseling, training, and dispute resolution, to staff and academic employees and sometimes to instructional staff.
- **Business Office** processes paperwork involved in ordering and paying for goods and services.
- **Financial (Accounting) Services** prepares periodic financial statements, financial analyses, and budgets.
- **Registration Office** enrolls and provides information to students.
- **Student Records** maintains and issues student records (transcripts).
- **Program Processing** handles room assignments, processes course and teacher approvals, orders books, and maintains files of course outlines and examinations.
- **Reprographics (Print Shop)** handles production of course and promotion materials.
- **Promotion (Marketing) Department** provides or administers outside contractors in promotion and marketing services.
- **Computer Center or Laboratory** provides support for computer-based instructional and administrative functions.
- **Conference Facility** operates and maintains a conference center.

Most CE organizations will need all the service functions in this list, but may arrange them in different ways. Some may be provided free by a parent organization or through a fee-for-service arrangement. Personnel services and registration functions may be handled under administrative auspices not controlled by the CE director.

When designing a new financial management system, the CE director can rearrange the segmentation of service functions to provide the organization with more or different information or to allow the realignment of service departments with strategic goals. For instance, the director may decide to budget the marketing department as a single department or to handle it at a greater level of detail, with separate budgets for the art department or the editorial department. More detailed budgeting provides an opportunity for more precise evaluation of individual segments, but at a cost. Multiple budget units require more attention from the whole administrative apparatus—more budgetary review, more accounting and bookkeeping services, more statement presentation and analysis. Thus, detailed segmentation may not be necessary or desirable for service units that are relatively stable and present few managerial problems, but may be worth the expense for units that are likely to develop problems or be subjected to periodic cost scrutiny.

Although the most common segmentation scheme for service departments is by functions, a logical alignment might be along strategic or market dimensions. For instance, the registration of international students might be handled by an organizational segment defined by the international market it serves rather than by the registration function. The international programming, marketing, registration, and student services functions might more sensibly be combined in one unit than split apart by functions. Coordination and communication might be improved and result in better service for the students.

Segmentation of programming departments presents a different set of complexities, especially in regard to information gathering. Determining current and forecasting future information requirements is more crucial for programming departments than for service departments because decisions made in programming departments are usually more important to the overall health of the organization. Financial information, including that generated through the budget process, helps programmers and management stay in touch with changing market conditions as well as monitor the effectiveness of decision making.

Careful segmentation can greatly aid information gathering. For example, budgeting and accounting for a departmental segment labeled "Business and Management" will provide only general information to management because the group of courses covered is so large. If "Business and Management" were divided into defined portfolios such as "Real Estate," "Accounting," "MBA Prerequisites," and "Personal Financial Planning," however, the results from all these segments could be tracked, and opportunities and downturns in the markets served by the individual segments could be discerned. Again, the trade-off is the increased cost of maintaining and analyzing the additional information.

Many other bases of programming department segmentation are possible. The traditional or functional approach reflects the difference in the organizing tasks involved in mounting credit courses and those of noncredit conferences and institutes (C&I). This segmentation by credit classification might be valuable where the parent institution is interested in these categories or where they seem to reflect market structure.

Another basis for segmentation is curriculum groupings. The "MBA prerequisites" category in our earlier example, or multi-course certificate or degree programs might be curriculum groupings. Such a basis for segmentation makes sense primarily where student motivation for taking the courses is homogeneous. If, for instance, an accounting course in the MBA prerequisites category regularly enrolls students with no interest in the MBA degree, the category carries less value as a segmentation basis.

A variation of this method might relate to the parent institution. Where individual courses can be related to a specific department of the parent, say, the School of Business Administration, and where there are other good reasons for it, this segmentation scheme may be called for.

So far, we have talked about program segment categories that reflect the attributes of the programs being presented. These categories can be contrasted with responsibility categories, which reflect the responsibility structure of the organization. The individual programmer and associated clerical support staff make up an obvious responsibility center. This kind of segmentation makes sense when programmer performance evaluation is based, at least in part, on financial results.

Responsibility center segmentation by geographical location is often desirable to track separately the budgets and finances of programs located in different geographical parts of the CE service area. A downtown location may serve a market segment distinctly different from that served by a suburban or campus location, even when both offer the same courses. When this is true, a geographical segmentation scheme could provide valuable information.

Many other possible segmentation schemes are possible, and the methods described here are not mutually exclusive, particularly when multidimensional budgeting will be used. The director should choose the segmentation plans that provide the most useful financial information and are most responsive to the organization's style of control. For instance, where an individual programmer has the exclusive right to program in a specific subject matter area and that subject matter area is the only one with which the programmer is involved, the individual responsibility segment and the program or subject matter segment will coincide. On the other hand, if two programmers representing two separate responsibility centers both decide to program, say, computer courses, the director has three choices 1) stop one of the programmers from programming computer courses thereby maintaining the coincidence in responsibility center and subject matter assignment; 2) abandon subject matter as an organizing principle; or 3) adopt MDB.

Several other issues associated with organization segmentation should be mentioned here. The first is the cost-benefit ratio. Even with the most efficient computer system in the world, more segmentation schemes and greater segmentation detail means the resulting analysis will cost more because more work must be done to prepare budgets, code income and expenses, define segments, and classify budget objects. This work must be done carefully; unless someone places budget objects into consistent categories, the organization will incur the cost of poor decisions based on imprecise, meaningless information. The cost of maintaining an excessively elaborate information structure thus may well exceed the information's value to the organization. Information from a budgeting and accounting system must be both interesting and useful in shaping decisions or performing other tasks that pay a real return to the organization. Too much information can be as hard to interpret as too little.

Another problem related to information systems and organization segmentation can be described as the "unquenchable thirst for information." All financial information, no matter how detailed and precise, gives rise to a need for additional information. This is because all financial information requires some form of interpretation, and each successive iteration of interpretation in turn requires further objective verification.

For instance, let us suppose that a self-supporting CE organization is experiencing a decline in income. Segment analysis determines successively that the general decline is due primarily to a decline in the Business and Management Department, that Programmer A (a responsibility center) is not doing as well as last year, and that the Real Estate program is the primary reason for Programmer A's poor showing. This information certainly narrows and defines the problem, but the director might still feel the need to know more. Part of that need might be satisfied by the existing accounting and budgeting system, but part might require information that must be obtained outside the system. For instance, the decline might be isolated to one-day programs directed at practicing professionals. This information could be obtained easily if the organization was segmented according to course format, but if not, further analysis would be necessary. Alternatively, it might turn out that downtown one-day programs were thriving but courses on campus were in trouble. In this case, further analysis would be needed only if the segmentation scheme did not include geographical location. And even with the most comprehensive and detailed segmentation plan, management is still likely to be left asking: Why the decline? Is the programmer at fault for failing to design exciting new courses able to attract sophisticated urban professionals? Has competition moved in with a slick promotional campaign? Has something occurred in the urban real estate market that the programmer has not yet incorporated into course offerings? Whatever the reason, outside investigation will probably be needed to uncover it.

After each successive analysis of a financial problem, the pressure to provide further information becomes more intense because the final answer seems ever closer at hand. The "unquenchable thirst for information" cannot be avoided. All a director can do is try to strike a balance between the lower cost and lesser precision of a lower level of segmentation and the higher cost, but greater discriminatory power, of a higher order of segmentation.

One other factor to keep in mind when developing a segmentation plan is the value of historical data. Budgetary and financial data become most useful when they are compared both with future actual results and with the results of a prior period. When new systems are being planned, the tendency is to emphasize the inadequacies of the predecessor process, sometimes to the extent of complete abandonment of the former structure of financial and budget analysis. If this happens, the organization has at least temporarily lost the use of its history.

Line Items

Line items (see Chapter 3) list kinds of expenses by "natural classification" and are generally displayed running down the left side of financial statements (sometimes called the "stub"). For instance, a payment to an instructor might be an expense associated with a real estate program. The program (columnar) classification of this expense would be "real estate," and its line item classification would be "teacher compensation."

Establishing or changing line item classifications is usually easier than establishing or changing organization segments, but the selection of line items is nevertheless important. They should be chosen with present and anticipated information needs in mind. What kinds of expenses must be tracked? What kinds of decisions regarding expenses must be made? Should, for example, the travel budget be cut by 50 percent during the next budget crisis, or a 10 percent salary saving be effected in the last half of the year? If so, we will need to know what our budget for travel is, and how much we have spent to date, and who is being paid how much. Of course, the usual trade-off must be kept in mind; greater detail in the line item classification scheme means more information as well as greater cost and difficulty in maintaining and monitoring the scheme.

A detailed and categorized listing of possible line items appears in Exhibit 9.2. Rarely would an organization use every item listed, but the list can be adapted and rearranged to suit a variety of institutional settings and managerial purposes. It incorporates all the line items listed in the course budget worksheets in Part 1 and adds a number of others.

Volume measures
   Number of programs
   Number of enrollments
   Number of student credit hours

Income
   Student fee income
   (Less) pass through costs
   Net student fee income
   Transcript fee income
   Conference accommodation fee income
   Subsidy income
         Federal contract and grants
         State contracts and grants
         Private contracts and grants
         Endowment fund transfers
         Institutional support payments
   Other income
         Conference facility rental income
         Book sales
         Parking fee income
         Royalties

Expense
   Expenses associated directly with courses
         Promotion expenses
               Advertising costs
               Categorized by media
                     Radio
                     Television
                     Newspapers
                     Magazines
                     News releases
                     Internet, WWW
               Categorized by natural classification
                     Space costs, spot costs
                     Production costs
                         Writing
                         Printing
                     Distribution costs
                     Actor's fees
                     Audiovisual equipment rental
                     Other

TYPICAL ORGANIZATION BUDGET LINE ITEMS

EXHIBIT 9.2

Production costs categorized by type of piece
    Catalog
    Brochure
    Flyer
    Poster
    Newsletter
    Letters
Production costs categorized by natural classification
    Editing
    Layout
    Paste up, computer composition
    Illustration
    Cover design
    Author fees
    Copyright fees
    Typesetting
    Printing
    Paper
    Envelopes
    Staff time
Mailing costs
    Postage (perhaps by class of mail)
    Mailing label purchase
    Mailing label extraction
    Mail house (handling charges)
        Folding
        Binding
        Stuffing
        Sorting
        Affixing labels
        Pickup and delivery
        Warehouse storage
        Administrative costs and profit
Other promotion costs
    Displays/exhibits
        Fees
        Production costs
        Setup costs
        Staff time
    Press kits
    Hospitality, entertaining
    Telephone selling
Teacher compensation
    Instructor compensation
    Reader and teaching assistant compensation

Typical Organization Budget Line Items

EXHIBIT 9.2 (CONTINUED)

Course development compensation
Instructor travel
    Local
    National
    International
Other direct course costs
    Audiovisual equipment and related
        Film, videotape rental, purchase
        Equipment rental, use charges
        Delivery, mailing charges
        Transmission charges (satellite time, phone lines)
    Course materials
        Text books, other books
        Reproduction costs
            Copyright and license fees
            Printing
        Lab fees
        Room rental
        Security service
        Janitorial service
        Ushers, crowd, traffic control
        Coffee, refreshments
        Lunches, meals
        Staff expenses
            Courier
            Cashiers
            Programmer on-site time
            Travel, per diem
            Meals
            Incidentals
        Entertainment
        Registration costs
            Registration package
            Hotel charges
            Name tags
Expenses associated directly with responsibility centers
    Payroll costs
        Programmer salary and benefits
        Clerical support salary and benefits
        Occasional assistance wage and benefits
    Unallocated promotion
    Travel
    Telephone

TYPICAL ORGANIZATION BUDGET LINE ITEMS
EXHIBIT 9.2 (CONTINUED)

Office supplies
Office machine maintenance, rental
Computer charges
Entertainment
Reproduction costs
Space rental
Incidentals
Other costs

TYPICAL ORGANIZATION BUDGET LINE ITEMS

EXHIBIT 9.2 (CONTINUED)

Indirect Cost Allocation and Cost Assignments

CE directors using traditional methods must decide how indirect costs will be allocated to cost objects, usually operating departments or individual courses. They must decide on a method and a basis for allocating overhead costs to courses or departments. In organizations using ABC activity centers, cost pools and cost drivers must be defined so that costs can be assigned to appropriate product, customer, or managerial initiative cost objects. Chapter 14 thoroughly discusses the issues associated with direct cost allocations.

Chapter 11 discusses the application of ABC to the CE organization, including to the process of defining and assigning costs. This chapter explains the rationale for allocating indirect costs, allocation methods, and the sources of "distorted behavior" that can result from the misunderstanding of cost allocation schemes. The distinction between *allocating* costs in traditional methods and *assigning* costs is sometimes subtle, but the implications are far reaching. Because ABC admits a much wider variety of cost objects it avoids much of the arbitrariness that characterizes overhead allocations in traditional methods.

Flexibility

Although flexibility is a desired quality in any financial management system, it is often difficult to define and achieve. In broad terms, a financial management information system is flexible if it can be added to and manipulated easily and if it tolerates changes or deviations from expected outcomes without distorting decision making. The need for the first type of flexibility occurs whenever strategic plans change or when new information is needed. For instance, a CE organization may adopt a new strategic initiative for distance education using satellite technology, or might incur a new category of marketing expense in dealing with the Internet and "electronic commerce." The ease in which these new features of organizational life can be incorporated into and reflected by the financial management system is a test of the system's flexibility.

The second kind of flexibility usually arises in the context of the budgetary process. One problem with preparing budgets is that they are obsolete as soon as they are prepared. An event occurs or some condition changes, and the carefully prepared budget plan that presumed to project the future suddenly becomes an historical document. The change may be internal to the organization, as when a budget is based on the continued services of a programmer who subsequently decides to leave the organization. The "hole" left in the budget is unlikely to be filled in exactly the same way by another programmer. Or the change is external, as when a change in tax laws creates an opportunity for a large program on taxation that had not been anticipated in the budget; or, conversely, a weakening dollar causes a drop in overseas travel program enrollments. A third kind of change results from a simple deviation from the budget plan. For instance, a programmer might have planned in the budget to present 30 courses during the fall term but ended up offering only 20, or enrollment projections may be off.

Whatever the reason for actual or potential deviations from the budget, management, especially the director, must decide what to do when they occur. The budget can always be recast, and it is sometimes desirable to do so; but frequent revision of a budget can be time-consuming and expensive and can decrease the value of the budget as a standard against which performance is judged. Deviations from budgets are facts, and facts should not be hidden. The alternative to frequent budget recasts is to allow the deviations to occur and record reasons for them as they become apparent.

As the preceding discussion suggests, the budget's roles as a standard of comparison for actual results and as a forecasting and planning instrument can come into conflict. Before establishing a budget system, management should define the kinds of circumstances that will require a budget revision and the sorts of budget deviations for which managers will be held accountable. The ability of a budget to maintain its usefulness as both a standard and a planning document in the face of changing conditions is another form of budgetary flexibility. This form of flexibility is established through custom, personality, stated policy, or experimentation. Management's attitude toward revisions and deviations suffuses the budget process, especially the part involving feedback or monitoring.

Control

A CE director must also determine the level and degree of managerial control that the financial management system will represent. "Control" here means, first, control over setting the organization objectives themselves. Who will set those objectives, and with what specifications and restrictions? In a large CE organization, with several departments composed of several programmers each, the budget targets may be set for the department chairs, who are then left to implement the targets, distributing the load among their subordinates; or targets may be set individually by the director for each programmer. Centralized organizations tend to have more detail in goals; decentralized organizations usually establish general goals and leave their implementation to a lower level of management. For instance, a director in a centralized structure might set a target for a programmer of a year-end "available for overhead" figure of $20,000, but might also place a limit of $15,000 on promotion expenditures and require that at least 100 courses be offered in the year. In a decentralized organization, the same end result ($20,000 available for overhead) might be specified, but no restrictions would be placed on how that goal should be achieved. Theoretically, if the programmer were to meet the goal by presenting only one extremely successful course, the director would be satisfied.

A second form of control represented by the financial management system has to do with its monitoring or feedback function. In order to be effective, the process must compare actual results against the budget and reinforce performance that meets or exceeds budget standards. But who is to make the comparison—the programmer, the programmer and the department chair, the director and the programmer? When is the comparison made—every month, every term, twice a year?

The control represented by the budget can be exercised either before or after basic program decisions are made. For instance, programmers may be required to prepare course budgets before spending any significant amounts on proposed courses. If these budgets are subjected to a rigorous review before the programmer can proceed, control is exercised before the fact, and the reviewer is participating in decisions about the course. On the other hand, if course budgets are either not required or not carefully reviewed before a program is attempted, control is exercised after the fact when results are examined and compared with the budget. Rewards or sanctions can be meted out on the basis of performance, and the certainty that accounts will be compared is usually enough to influence behavior in the desired direction. Predecision control is tighter but generally uses a lot of expensive administrative time and effort. Such tight control may well be necessary, however, in organizations where the record shows consistently unsound financial decisions either across the board, or by one programmer or another.

Other Issues

CE managers need to take many other issues into account as they change or introduce new financial management information systems. Managers need to determine the degree to which the staff reward system is predicated on financial results as set, monitored, and reported by the system. In many CE organizations, management's ability to formally reward desirable behavior or favorable operating results is rather restricted. There may be budgetary restrictions on employee compensation, or the salary and wage administration policies of the parent institution may not recognize the criteria for reward established in the CE organization. When formal reward is not possible or is limited, informal symbols of recognition—the figurative "pat on the back"—are called for. Even where the director can reward employees with raises or promotions, such rewards are unlikely to be granted solely on the basis of financial or budgetary performance. Scholarship, teaching ability, community service, and the educational quality of courses offered are often accorded equal or superior status in performance evaluations, especially of programming staff.

Nonetheless, achieving or failing to achieve budgetary goals should be related to the reward system. Such a relationship can go a long way toward establishing the legitimacy of the budget system and assuring its success. The mechanisms of interaction between the two systems should be carefully worked out in advance and clearly communicated to those who will assume budget responsibility.

Another issue has to do with the treatment of hidden subsidies or program or project funding that comes from several fund sources. For instance, in many CE organizations the salary of the director is paid through a funding source not associated with the CE cost center, or the fringe benefits of employees are paid from fund sources outside the CE budget. Because these items are not part of the CE budget, they tend to be ignored by the financial management system.

The existence of these hidden subsidies makes inter-institutional cost comparisons difficult and obscures the true cost of the CE organization from the management of the parent institution and even from the management of the CE enterprise itself. Hidden subsidies often lead to distorted financial statements and ultimately to poor management decisions. There are often good practical and political reasons for not recognizing these hidden subsidies in the formal budget; for example, bringing attention to such subsidies during a period of tightening resources may lead to their disappearance. But, at least in the informal financial planning that accompanies the formal process, these subsidies should be taken into account. Somebody, somewhere, should know what is really going on.

The CE director should consider at least two other issues before launching a new or revised financial management system. The first is the question of openness versus secrecy. How open should the process be? Are budget targets for each responsibility center going to be universally known? Are comparisons of actual results to budgets going to be available to everyone in the organization? Are rewards and sanctions going to be known? How will decisions regarding financial issues be made and communicated? Who should know "how things are going," when, and from whom?

The second issue is the question of who does what, when. The introduction and maintenance of a financial management system are time-consuming and difficult tasks requiring careful coordination of the efforts of a large number of people. Clear assignment of tasks and establishment of deadlines are essential ingredients for success.

Once these preliminary decisions are made, the financial management information system itself can be established. A key element of such a system is the budget or plan for financial results. Chapters 10 and 11 explain in detail the stages in developing and implementing a budget for a CE organization.

SUMMARY

The revision or introduction of a financial management information system represents a significant change for an organization, and change never takes place in a vacuum. A new or revised organizational system must be consistent with the environment it is supposed to serve and compatible with the goals and objectives of the organization's management. Narrowly conceived systems, directed at correcting a transitory problem or merely increasing managerial control, are unlikely to succeed. The planning of a financial management system must involve examination of the organization's history, its place vis-a-vis the parent or other organizations, its external environment, and, above all, its people and their attitudes.

This examination of the organizational environment must guide important preliminary decisions about the way the system will be structured. Perhaps the most important decision concerns the way the organization will be segmented or divided so that responsibility for the performance of the parts will be clearly defined. The relationship of the financial management system to the employee evaluation and reward system is also important. The system will not be effective unless it means something—unless budgets are compared with actual results and used as a basis for decisions and employee evaluation.

Another vital decision concerns control. Financial systems are unquestionably part of the control structure of an organization, and the control aspect of any potential system should be carefully considered by management. A system that is too heavy-handed in its control will create resentment and fear in employees, while a system that is too flexible and easily altered may not be sufficiently effective as a standard.

Before instituting or revising a financial management system, a CE organization's management should be clear on these issues and incorporate them in a clearly articulated implementation plan. Such a system can be controversial, especially in its early and fragile stage when it is likely to be looked upon with suspicion and apprehension. Early errors—those of tone and style as well as those of substance—can severely damage the future effectiveness of a financial system. Only a broad view of the process, one that includes its effect on people and their perceptions of their jobs and the organization they work for can lead to successful budget system design.

CHAPTER 10

The Budget Process

The budget process is central to every CE financial information management system, no matter what managerial philosophy guides the organization or what methods are used to control resources and measure financial results. A budget represents a plan for the allocation of resources for the achievement of organizational goals and usually becomes a standard by which financial results are measured. Although the application of ABC and MDB add some complexity to the budgeting process, the basic steps remain the same. Chapters 11 and 12 examine those steps, noting where budgeting under the newer paradigms differs from traditional budgeting. Chapters 11 and 12 also illustrate how ABC and MDB can be applied to the budget and related financial management processes.

Although budgeting varies greatly from organization to organization, certain steps in the process are universal.

1. Establishing budget guidelines
2. Setting sales/volume targets
3. Budget call and initial preparation
4. Negotiation
5. Coordination and review
6. Final approval
7. Distribution
8. Feedback and monitoring

Steps 3, 4, and 5 represent the bulk of the work in the budgeting process and may be repeated several times as the budget takes shape. Although important, step 8, feedback and monitoring, is often not recognized as part of the process because it is carried out after the original budget is prepared.

We will examine these steps in detail in this chapter, using as an example a sizable CE organization that is largely self-supporting, has many service and programming departments, and has segmented the latter into a number of responsibility (profit) centers. We will assume that the organization uses traditional accounting and budgeting methods and that the smallest budget object is the individual course. This model will not exactly describe all, or even perhaps most, CE organizations, but it represents a comprehensive and complex organization structure and is therefore useful for expository purposes. The explanations presented in connection with it can be applied to a large variety of CE organizational forms, including subsidized organizations.

ESTABLISHING BUDGET GUIDELINES

The first step in the budgeting process proper is to establish planning guidelines. This task follows the preliminary steps, described in the last chapter, of adopting an organization segmentation plan, choosing appropriate budget line items, and setting a basis and method for indirect cost allocation.

Deadlines

Deadlines are an important element in budget guidelines. Usually the budget for a CE organization must be presented to its parent institution for approval and inclusion in the institutional budget, and the deadline for this submission is often used as a date by which other deadlines can be determined. Exhibit 10.1 is a Gantt chart showing a typical budget preparation schedule with deadlines. (Because they are so interrelated, all the exhibits for Chapter 10 have been grouped together at the end of the chapter for easier comparison.) The chart indicates that the parent institution has established a May 1 deadline (item 7 on the chart) for budget submission, presumably in preparation for a July 1 fiscal year. Backing up from that date, we can establish deadlines and time periods for each stage of the budgeting process. Where deadlines set by parent institutions are not a factor, the budgeting process should be timed to fit in with the workload of those who will take part in it. If timing is poor, budgeting will seem more burdensome than it would otherwise be. Because the budget is a planning instrument, often a long-range planning instrument, it is most usefully prepared when time and reflection can be spent in developing a well-thought-out look at the future. It should be prepared early enough to be able to influence the future, but not so early that implementation is at too far a remove from the development of the plan. In some organizations, a budget prepared in March and April for a fiscal year beginning in July would have to include a summer program that had already been prepared. This is obviously unwise, since the value of the budget as a plan is lost if it includes a portion that, in effect, has already been implemented.

Basic Assumptions

Those asked to prepare budgets must be given assumptions upon which to base their estimates of activity. These assumptions may involve some of the environmental factors described in the last chapter, including the economy and market conditions. Such assumptions may be broadly and simply stated, or they may relate to specific markets and anticipate complex relationships. (Exhibit 10.3 on page 194 gives examples of basic assumptions.) They may be general assumptions about the state of the economy (an inflation rate of 5 percent), assumptions about specific costs (a postage rate increase of three cents for second class postage or a general cost of living adjustment for all staff of 4 percent), notification of funding reductions from the parent institution, or management-mandated conditions such as across the board fee increases or the addition or discontinuance of specific programs or services. In addition, communications from CE management should establish what might be called the "level of optimism" or "level of reality." Ideally, budgets should set goals that are difficult but not impossible to achieve, and they should be realistic about the future. Too optimistic or too pessimistic a forecast may lead to poor management decisions and damage the budget's usefulness as a planning tool. CE management can help set the appropriate level with such requirements as "projected enrollment in excess of 10 percent lower or higher than last year's must be supported with a narrative justification."

Estimates of Indirect Costs

A starting point for many CE budgets is estimation of the total amount of indirect or overhead costs that must be covered from operations. Obviously of great importance to self-supporting units, such an estimation is of equal importance to subsidized units, where the distinction between their overhead or service and their programming or operating departments seems, on the surface, to be less. Indirect cost charges from the parent institution should be built into the budget guidelines for the organization's subunits. For instance, the subunits could be instructed to budget 10 percent of total expense as institutional overhead.

Another level of indirect cost arises from the CE organization itself. In the last chapter we listed a number of service departments that might be associated with a CE organization. Funds for these services have to come from somewhere. In self-supporting units, that "somewhere" is obviously the programming departments. The first step in calculating what the organization needs to generate in "available for overhead" is to estimate what that overhead will be—i.e., how much will each service department cost in the next budget period.

To aid in this task, preliminary budgets for the service departments should be prepared. Fortunately, costs in service departments (with the possible exception of the promotion or marketing department) are generally stable. Payroll costs usually constitute the bulk of their expenses, and, unless the number of employees is likely to change significantly, these costs (based on the payroll increase assumption of the budget) can easily be estimated. Unless the organization is rapidly expanding or contracting, other line item costs for service departments usually can be estimated from the actual results of either the current year or the last full fiscal year.

In preparing these preliminary budgets, planners have two options. First, they can do a "quick and dirty" cost estimate, hoping to arrive at a reasonably good approximation, and then request individual service center budgets along with the rest of the responsibility center budgets. Alternatively, they can ask service department managers to prepare relatively detailed budgets based on volume or use estimates that they either supply or allow the managers to specify. These budgets can then be added together to arrive at the total costs. Exhibit 10.2 shows a careful estimate of the costs for the service departments of a CE organization. The exhibit is consistent with the data presented in Exhibit 3.3 in Chapter 3.

Note the form of the worksheet in Exhibit 10.2; we will use it again and again. It shows the responsibility centers in columns across the top and the line item expenditures down the left side, thus allowing the expenditure budgets and the program budgets to be shown simultaneously. Note also that income associated with a particular service center, such as transcript fees for the Student Registration Department ($130,000) and outside rental income for Classroom Facilities ($340,840), is shown at the top and serves to reduce the total cost of the service center. The total of all expenses for all departments ($7,317,851) is shown on the "Total indirect costs" line. The next line shows total expense less total income, producing a total net indirect cost of $6,640,511.

This goal for adding to reserves might also be considered a contingency fund, or it might be increased to handle contingencies. The contingency amount provides a cushion against a shortfall anywhere in the budget, such as a cost overrun in a service department or the failure of an expected source of income. Prudent managers always provide a contingency factor, and putting it in at this stage of the budgeting process means that it will be built into the whole budget plan. The amount of the contingency is a matter of managerial judgment but should probably be at least 5 percent of the total budget. Of course, contingencies get tucked into all kinds of places in the budget as each manager provides a certain amount of "fat"; this overall contingency should be made explicit.

The addition of a contingency factor to the indirect cost calculation can also be used to build into the budget system an "excess" or "available for overhead" amount assessed by the parent institution. Exhibit 10.2 shows indirect costs from the parent institution ($386,051) in the last line under "other." We will assume that the CE organization is required to "break even," with a small surplus going into a reserve to prevent an overall deficit. However, surplus or excess targets can easily be incorporated into the budget planning process.

Estimating indirect costs near the beginning of the budgeting process can lead to a special problem (which is discussed more fully below in "Coordination and Review"). Service department budgets should be based on estimates of volume—e.g., number of enrollments or programs—which can only be supplied by the program departments. Since preliminary service department budgets are prepared before program department budgets, they must usually be adjusted after program departments have completed their plans. Indirect promotion costs are particularly subject to this kind of adjustment, which must take place later in the budgeting process.

SETTING TARGETS

Having estimated what the service departments will cost for the budget period, budget planners can now go about setting preliminary targets for the programming departments. This process can be either simple or complex, depending on the situation.

The simplest tactic is for management to set no targets at all, allowing each programming department to come up with what it believes to be a reasonable financial goal for the next year. If the departments are conscientious and honest, and it is relatively easy for the organization to meet financial expectations, this tactic can be effective. However, if extensive revisions later become necessary to "balance the budget," this managerial failure to set targets can lead to much wasted time and effort.

Another relatively simple tactic is to set "available for overhead" targets based on the service department costs. For instance, the $6,640,511 calculated as the total service department costs in Exhibit 10.2 might be allocated to programming departments on some basis, say, a proportional allocation based on the actual contribution to overhead made by each programming department in the prior year. In the CE organization, several programming departments have more than one programmer. Each of these departments has the responsibility to develop a budget that, after all costs associated with the department have been covered, provides an excess of income over expense of at least the amount specified. This "available for overhead" tactic is simple to calculate, concentrates directly on the "bottom line," and does not involve much subsequent reconciliation. It may also be too simple, ignoring important factors and resulting in poorly established goals. It also does not relate the volumes upon which the service department costs were based to the volumes anticipated in the programming department budgets. For instance, Arts and Sciences may plan to achieve its budget by offering 20 percent more courses for the next budget period than for the last, which would mean that those service departments whose costs are related to enrollments (Registration, Cashier, Student Records) and number of programs (Program Processing) might be underbudgeted.

So far we have been discussing the setting of targets based upon covering the cost of service departments and any contingency or surplus requirements. However, targets may be set on many other bases. For example, total revenue or enrollment levels may define targets, particularly where they bear consistent relationships to such other financial elements as costs. They might even be based on (apparent) nonfinancial aspects such as student retention rates or student satisfaction or graduation rates.

ISSUING THE BUDGET CALL

Having established guidelines and targets, we can now issue the call for the budget and request managers of successively lower levels of the organization to prepare their budgets. Managers of the Arts and Sciences, Business and Management, and other departments of our example CE organization are assigned targets for the "bottom line"—the amount "available for overhead." The department managers in turn are responsible for assigning "available for overhead" targets to the programmers who report to them. Assigning indirect costs this way keeps our example simple. However, the budgets for the service departments will still have to be reconciled with the volume assumptions from the program departments.

The manager of each department is also given certain other information: the salary for each employee in the department, the total departmental supplies and expense figure as projected for the current year, and the amount of promotion overhead that the department will have to bear. In our example, most promotion costs are charged directly to the programming departments on a per job basis, according to a rate schedule established at the beginning of every year. The programmers estimate their promotion costs by using this rate sheet. The amount of unrecharged costs is also estimated for budget purposes and assigned to departments. Promotion costs are carefully reconciled between the programmers' anticipated use and the promotion service department budget.

In contrast to promotion costs, the amounts charged to the programming departments by the reprographics department are not closely reconciled. The costs of reproducing materials are not controlled as a budget line item; rather, they are built into the programming department budgets in a number of places and cannot be pulled out. However, since the reprographics department has a strict cost control system and since prices for the department's services can be compared with those of outside vendors, the reconciliation is not as crucial as with promotion.

The budget call serves three purposes. First, it communicates budget assumptions and targets. Second, it provides the preparers with some of the information they need to prepare their own budgets. Third, it gives them worksheets in formats which, when completed and returned, will facilitate consolidation, coordination, and review. These worksheets are useful both in conveying information (such as projected payroll) and in structuring requested information.

The budget call is the issuance of the worksheets and instructions for preparing the budget. Instructions to department managers in our example organization are given in Exhibit 10.3, and instructions to the programmers are given in Exhibit 10.4. Read these instructions carefully; they establish the premises of the example. The worksheets provided to department heads and programmers illustrate the successive levels of detail on which the budget summaries are based. Each schedule "ties in" to the schedules above and below it, as shown in Exhibit 10.5. We will use Arts and Sciences for our sample department and Cindy for our example programmer (responsibility center) within the department.

Once the budget call has been issued, preparation can begin. Each manager makes the required computations and assigns targets to the programmers. The programmers then begin preparing the detailed estimations upon which the whole budget rests. In our example, the programmers will compute individual estimated course budgets for each term; in reality, this method is often impractical—there are too many unknowns, especially in the most distant term. Groups of courses or "average" courses can be estimated, or programmers may be able to predict their results for the term more accurately without going to course detail estimates. Exhibit 10.6 shows the worksheet as it was filled in by the department manager. The schedule has been compressed for display purposes with a row and a column for "programmers 3-N" as indicated. The department manager has distributed total payroll costs to the various responsibility centers identified by the name of the responsible programmer.

Exhibit 10.7, the Arts and Sciences Budget Summary Worksheet, represents the next level of detail. The responsibility centers for the Arts and Sciences Department, which in this case are programmers, are listed across the top of the page and totaled in the last column. This total will be carried forward to a worksheet summarizing all programming departments (Exhibit 10.10).

The "adjustments" column enables the department manager to adjust the totals turned in by the programmers. In this instance, the manager felt the totals were too optimistic. As the budget target was exceeded and the manager did not want to interfere with the self-imposed program targets, the manager used the adjustment column to pull down income by $120,000, increase instructor compensation by $33,000, and increase fringe benefits and supplies and expense by $20,000. This left Arts and Sciences with a budgeted "available for overhead" of $2,340,080, very close to the targeted amount.

Exhibit 10.8 shows the projected activity, by term, for one of the Arts and Sciences programmers, Cindy. Again the total column will be carried forward to the next worksheet, and each column is supported, in turn, by a separate worksheet (Exhibit 10.9) that shows the detailed calculations made by Cindy in estimating her fall term activity down to the "gross margin" point. Her course planning for the fall term has apparently progressed far enough that she can be specific in estimating the costs of the 24 courses she plans for the fall. Such specificity of detail is desirable, but is rarely possible for distant terms.

The programmer budget gives the programmer an opportunity to forecast and plan the future. This process involves an understanding of the time and resource allocations it will take to achieve the budget goal. To be useful, these allocations should be based on reasonable calculations expressed in written form so they can later be compared to actual events and results.

Approved budgets, even though based on estimates, represent quasi-contracts. Programmers, department managers, and directors are bound to fulfill them to the best of their abilities or to explain why they were not fulfilled. This contractual characteristic gives rise to the next step in the budgeting process—negotiation.

The preparation of the budget ideally proceeds in building-block fashion, with programmers first thinking carefully about the programming they will do in the next budget period. If they can plan each term course by course (as assumed here), estimated course budgets will become the lowest accounting entity upon which the whole budget is based. If the details of future courses cannot be estimated, as is often the case, more global estimates must be made.

All course budgets for one programmer for one term will be added together, and the total will be combined successively with totals for other terms and other programmers within the department to arrive at a departmental budget, a process repeated in each department until the whole budget is developed. The budget call must establish uniform worksheets so that this summation can be done easily and quickly. As the budgets pass from one level of the organization to another—in our example, from programmer to department manager and then from manager to director—the budgeting process proceeds to the next steps: negotiation, review, and coordination.

So far, the various parties involved in the budgeting process have not had much interaction. Management has gone about the tasks of setting guidelines and targets and making indirect cost estimates with little formal contact with those who are primarily responsible for budget preparation. Of course, there should be a great deal of interaction between management and the programmers and department heads, but, in our example, such interaction has not been named as a part of the process. The next three steps in the budget process—negotiation, coordination and review, and final approval—explicitly involve the interplay between budget preparers and budget approvers, which is the essence of budgeting as a form of communication for both organizational and individual goals and expectations.

NEGOTIATION

In many ways, negotiation is the most crucial aspect of the budgeting process. Negotiation can—and does—take place at many stages of the process, but I have chosen to discuss it here because in most CE organizations the most important negotiation takes place between the programmer and the department manager.

The manager must be able to establish realistic targets that motivate programmers and provide a standard against which performance can be measured. Too ambitious a goal can lead to frustration and bitterness, and too easy a goal can undermine the budget and the managerial control system. The quality of the negotiation between manager and programmer is also important. Programmers should be able to present reasonable arguments for target reductions if their calculations and expectations indicate that they cannot attain their targets, but "game playing" and irresponsible ploys should be discouraged. The manager can establish a healthy negotiating atmosphere by supporting the chosen targets with calculations and documentation. Financial results from the recent past can usually be used as a standard upon which to base targets for the upcoming period, with appropriate adjustments made to reflect anticipated changes.

The departmental target-setting process is particularly difficult when differential targets must be established. Just as it was unreasonable for the director in our example to expect the Education Department to produce as much available for overhead as the Business and Management Department, it is often unfair to expect all programmers to produce the same bottom line. Thus the manager must often defend not only the targets themselves but also the differences between them. Supporting calculations and a clear rationale are crucial in this situation.

In addition to the actual level of the targets, negotiations must also address the methods that will be used to reach the goals. Here managers should look for a balancing of risks and rewards. For instance, a programmer may propose to reach her target by producing just three blockbuster programs during the year. The manager may decide that reliance on only three programs represents too great a risk of failure and thus will ask the programmer to schedule more programs. Alternatively, a programmer may not be venturesome enough, relying on tried and true programs that are declining. The manager in this situation may require the programmer to add new programs to bolster the old.

Finally, the timing of the financial results may come under discussion. The programmer who expects to do poorly for the first two quarters of the budget year and then make it all up in the last two puts the organization at risk, since no adjustments can be made if the last two quarters also fizzle out. Thus, the manager is likely to ask for reasonably even distribution of results.

The desired outcome of the negotiating process is a commitment by the programmer to achieving the goals set by agreement between programmer and manager. Ideally, the manager, in approving the programmer (responsibility center) budget, has agreed that the programmer will have done a "good job" if the budget goal is met, and the programmer has agreed that the goal is achievable.

Upon reaching agreement with each of the programmers in the Arts and Sciences Department, the department manager in our example adds up all the budget goals for the programmers on the Arts and Sciences Summary Worksheet (Exhibit 10.7). Finding that the programmer targets add up to more than the target for the department as assigned by the director, the Arts and Sciences manager, unwilling to reduce the targets the programmers have agreed to, builds a contingency by adjusting income, instructor compensation, and direct supplies and expense—areas where experience indicates that the budget has not provided enough. If the department budget had come up short of the target set for it, the manager would have the choice of going back to the programmers and asking for more or negotiating in turn with the director for a lower target.

COORDINATION AND REVIEW

Having collected all the department budgets, the director or budget officer is now ready to put the institution budget together. In our example, this is done with the summary worksheet shown in Exhibit 3.3, on page 35. This worksheet adds all the programming departments, then adds the total of the service department calculations from the Service Department Budget Summary Worksheet (Exhibit 10.2) to get the total budget for the CE organization. Each line item of expense has been calculated as a percentage of adjusted income to facilitate both comparisons between departments and of a single department's performance over several years.

With the entire budget in view, the managers can begin the coordination and review process, which has the following goals:

- To determine, to the extent possible, whether assigned targets will be met
- To determine whether the total budget now represents a realistic estimation of the future
- To reconcile the interrelated parts of the budget
- To "balance the budget," making sure it represents a plan acceptable to, or at least worthy of presentation to, those who must approve it at a higher level

Adjustment of Targets

The first and easiest task in reviewing the budget is to determine whether all the assigned targets have been met. The review of each department's budget may require a hearing in which the manager of the department has an opportunity to voice opinions about the chances of attaining the goal. If the overall goal cannot be met, a realistic goal must be negotiated. If an earlier hearing has not been held, departments that have not met their assigned targets must be questioned. In each case, the director or the budget officer should examine the process by which the department manager arrived at conclusions to determine whether it was thorough and whether the conclusions are justified. Assuming that they are, the director and the manager must decide what to do next: revise the goal downward or take additional action to make possible the achievement of the goal.

Reality Tests

Once the director has determined that all the assigned targets have been met or equitably adjusted, the entire budget can be reviewed to determine whether it presents a realistic forecast of the future. This review is done by comparing against a given set of standards both the actual figures and the relationship between figures for departments and for line items. One fairly common procedure involves comparing the details of departments and line items in the budget with the actual results for prior periods and then comparing appropriate segments of the organization with others in budget terms. When, as in our example, the budget is prepared by adding parts together, a particular line item is likely to be systematically under or overstated, and such an error should show up when comparisons are made with prior periods. For instance, many programmers budget too little for promotion. If total promotion costs in the budget are considerably lower than the total for the prior year, promotion is probably underbudgeted and some adjustment will have to be made. Not only should the totals for line items be compared, but each department's budget should also be compared with a prior period, line by line, to make sure that the budget appears reasonable.

Ratio analysis can also be used to compare present to prior periods and to make comparisons between departments. The worksheet in Exhibit 3.3 on page 35 shows each item of expense expressed as a percentage of income. The high ratio of direct expenses to total income for Arts and Sciences would probably require explanation.

Internal Reconciliation

In our example, the budgets for the service departments were developed first, based on estimates of the volume of activity to be generated by the programming departments. The coordination and review process must make sure those volume estimates are sound. For instance, the registration office budget was based on an estimate of the total number of enrollments for the budget period. If the total enrollments derived by adding all the programmer budgets together is significantly higher than the initial estimate, the budget may need to be revised. This revision, especially if it is upward, might send the whole budget out of balance and require increasing targets or reducing costs in other places. If targets have to be revised, the total enrollment figures might change again, so the registration office budget would need further revision. A certain amount of this back-and-forth process is usually unavoidable whenever the budget is put together in interrelated parts. However, revisions that take place after difficult negotiations have resulted in realistic targets for all responsibility centers can be demoralizing and time-consuming for everyone concerned. If such interactions are anticipated, extensive revisions may sometimes be avoided by building more into the contingency or providing some flexibility in the service department budgets.

Balancing the Budget

Using the phrase "balancing the budget" to describe the process that concludes the coordination and review function can be misleading because a budget in which income and expenses match exactly is not its goal. The desired end product of the budget review process is a budget that presents the organization with an attainable goal and is acceptable to the higher authority to whom it is presented. Effective budgets must provide room for contingencies—unexpected events or conditions that could cause one or several parts of the organization to fall short of their budget goals. The size of this cushion, or margin of safety, may vary, but it must be present. The budget that is carefully "balanced" between income and expense is in balance only on paper and for a short time. Determining the appropriate size for the contingency reserve, and having the nerve—sometimes under great pressure—to resist decreasing that reserve, is an important test of the director's ability to understand and control the organization.

Having put together the budgets from all the programming departments and performed the internal reconciliations, management can now review the organization budget to see whether it represents a realistic plan, using something like the Budget Summary Worksheet in Exhibit 3.3 (page 35). All our example organization's departments met, or came close to meeting, their targets, so further action in this case is unnecessary. In reality, however, the budget rarely comes so close to what was originally planned. Targets may have been renegotiated, the internal reconciliation process may have disclosed factors that change the budgets of the service departments, or events may require a change of assumptions. Circumstances may have made the contingency larger or, more likely, smaller than was planned.

If the budget produces a figure higher than target, management is in happy circumstances. But let us look at the more common experience. Suppose that instead of the $6.9 million that was anticipated, the final figure is $6.8 million, and the reconciliation process indicates that the promotion department budget must be increased by $150,000. There is a budget shortfall of $250,000. In the absence of an effective activity-based costing system, the director has several choices.

Reduce Overhead Costs

It may be possible, given projected reductions in volume, to reduce either the costs in the service departments or the contingency. If, however, the service department budgets were prepared carefully and a reduction in the contingency is not justified, reducing overhead will be difficult.

Increase Targets

Another possibility is to ask the programming departments to come up with more available for overhead. This alternative can be destructive, however, especially if the preceding steps were done with care. Such a request will appear to be evidence of bad faith, or at least bad planning, by management. However, where there is a large difference between income and expense, it may be necessary to redo the budget in all its steps.

Eliminate Deficit Prone Programs

This step may have many serious affects, especially on staff morale. It may be precipitated by a sudden turn of events, but it is more likely to become necessary because of a cumulative weakness. In effect, where a segment shows a deficit or a relatively minor contribution to the available for overhead, it may be desirable to eliminate the unit or reorganize it to effect a saving in service department costs. If, by eliminating unproductive programming departments, management can reduce service department costs by more than the amount the unproductive departments are scheduled to contribute, the budget deficit would be lessened. However, many other factors have to be considered before making such a serious policy decision. The morale of the employees throughout the organization might be damaged by a decision to close down departments (although carrying losing programs can also be damaging to morale). Political considerations may make program elimination difficult, and it may hurt the public's perception of the CE organization to see its "product mix" become less extensive and varied.

In a case like this, management must also consider whether eliminating any large segment of the organization will change the economies of scale for the service departments, making the per unit costs increase to a point where some departments can no longer operate efficiently. For instance, an unproductive department may be scheduled to pay a portion of the cost of the catalogs. If this department is eliminated, the overhead costs included in the catalog costs will have to be spread over a smaller pool, increasing the price of catalogs to other users. Similarly, "embedded" overhead costs may have to be considered. Unproductive departments may be paying overhead amounts that are not easy to see and, thus, the gain from the department elimination would not be as great as it might at first appear.

Another consideration is that in eliminating a program or department management is eliminating the possibility for a return that may exceed budget expectations, either in the long or the short run. Experienced CE professionals are well aware of the cyclical nature of the popularity of certain subject matter areas. Education and teacher training, which had been the mainstay of many continuing education organizations from the 1930s to the early 1970s, fell off drastically after 1975 throughout the country, but such programs will probably regain some strength in the mid- and late 1990s. External conditions change so rapidly that it is difficult to predict where the next market opportunity may spring up.

Of course, only a particular segment of a department may be unprofitable. A detailed enough budget and accounting system can provide the information necessary to determine if the segment should be eliminated. Finally, the cost of closing a department and phasing out its operations has to be considered. Severance pay or extensive paid but unproductive time may be necessary, students currently in structured programs may have to be served by programs and courses that are not economically viable, and much time and managerial effort may have to be spent in carrying out the reductions. Despite all these possible drawbacks, it may still be necessary, after a hard look at all the factors, to eliminate a deficit prone department.

Reduce Line Items

A traditional way of dealing with prospective budget deficits is to attempt to reduce line items in "across-the-board" budget cuts. In examining line items for potential savings, it usually makes sense to look first to the largest items as having the most potential for savings—barring known inefficiencies in the smaller items, of course. For instance, it is tempting to try to reduce departmental supplies and expense, since these expenditures all take place inside the organization. However, they amount to only 5.61 percent of the example budget (Exhibit 3.3). To save 1 percent of the budget ($240,000), management would have to reduce departmental supplies and expense expenditures by 18 percent, which might be extremely difficult, especially if the expense budgets were developed in good faith by the managers. On the other hand, to save the same amount the instructor compensation budget would have to be decreased by only about 3.6 percent, perhaps by eliminating the payment for local travel or by not paying instructors for meeting the first class in courses that cancel. Of course, reducing any aspect of instructor compensation is likely to be a visible and widely challenged decision.

Payroll costs are also likely to constitute a high percentage of a CE organization's budget. Some reductions in staff and payroll costs are usually possible through attrition and "salary savings" (i.e., savings effected by unpaid leaves of absence, by gaps in the time between the leaving of one employee and the arrival of a replacement, or by replacement of a highly paid employee with a new employee paid at a lower rate). If the amount of the budget deficit is great, real staff cuts that actually eliminate performance of certain tasks may be necessary. Such losses should not cut into the "muscle" of the organization or sap morale too badly, and the cost savings effected by the cuts must not be offset by a decrease in the organization's ability to generate income.

Reductions in line items are often delegated to the department managers, who are asked to effect a percentage reduction either in particular line items or anywhere in their budget. In some departments, for instance, reducing staff may be easier than reducing instructor compensation, or fees may be raised in some courses to provide the targeted available for overhead. Again, these steps are difficult after negotiations have been held. Certainly the director should know exactly where the savings or additional income will come from to evaluate the validity of the proposal and should establish a monitoring system to see that the cuts or additional income sources are effective.

Combine Approaches

Most directors facing prospective budget deficits will use some combination of the approaches described. Whatever approaches are chosen, care must be taken that the interrelated parts of the organization remain in balance and an objective view of the possible is maintained. Managers and programmers, driven to an extreme, are likely to be less conservative than in their initial calculations and less inclined to take the hard steps they are being asked to take. They are more likely simply to revise their estimates of income or class size upward to accommodate the difference.

Reorganize and Negotiate for an Acceptable Deficit

In cases where the prospective budget deficit is large, the budget system may be indicating that the organization is seriously off track and that no simple reduction method is going to be enough. In this situation, a complete reshaping and probably an adjustment of the scale or size of the organization may be necessary. A director of an organization in this position needs time to rethink and reshape the organization and time to see the results of that reshaping in financial returns. Usually a deficit is unavoidable in the interim period, and certainly a new budget reflecting the phase-out, phase-in period and the eventual desired organizational structure is required. In most organizational settings, such reorganization must be sanctioned by higher authority, and that authority will have to recognize that a budget deficit is unavoidable on the way to what will hopefully be a brighter future.

FINAL APPROVAL

In most cases, the CE director does not have the authority to approve the final budget. Such authority usually resides with the administration of the parent institution or the board of directors of the CE organization. Having worked hard to produce a budget that meets all appropriate criteria, the director must now defend that budget and the methods used to produce it. The CE director must have confidence in the completed budget, and this confidence can come only from thorough prior review. Directors with extensive budgeting experience develop a "feel" for the process and can sense when a budget is realistic and when it is not.

Often the form in which the budget must be presented to higher authority does not coincide with the form in which it was developed. Indeed, when the presentation form is dictated by the parent institution, it may create an inaccurate picture of the CE organization because it ignores factors important in self-support undertakings. If this happens, the CE director should try to structure the presentation in a way that follows institutional practices when possible but also points out where following such practices may lead to faulty decision making.

In this section, we will look at several standard budget presentation formats and then discuss some strategies that may be used by those who review the CE organization budget. Knowledge of these strategies can help the CE director prepare the budget, including special schedules, for presentation and defense.

Standard Budget Presentation Formats

Of the two standard budget formats, the line item format is more familiar to most institutional budget officers because it is the same as the format usually used in colleges and universities for reviewing subsidized programs and departments. An illustration of the line item format, using information from the example we have been following, appears in Exhibit 10.10.

The exhibit compares the proposed budget (which is taken from the last column of Exhibit 3.3 on page 35) compared with the projected results of the current fiscal year and the actual results of the previous fiscal year. The comparison is carried out in actual dollars and also through ratio analysis by computing the percentage that each category of expense bears to total income.

The other commonly used presentation format is the program or departmental format. This format (see Exhibit 10.11) shows the financial results for each segment of the organization. The advantage of the departmental format is that the rise and fall of departments (at least over the three years presented here) can be seen easily, and the financial results of the same department can be compared over a number of periods. For instance, Programs 1 and 2 in our example organization are growing steadily.

The worksheet format used in Exhibit 3.3 on page 35 can also be used to present a budget because it combines both of these formats by showing programming departments in the columns and line items down the side of the worksheet. However, it does not show historical comparisons clearly, and it presents so much data in such a compact form that reviewers unfamiliar with the organization may not be able to interpret it readily.

Summary schedules in any format can be supported by more detailed schedules, some being the same worksheets we have already seen, and some being developed separately to answer anticipated questions. For instance, a question is likely to come up about Program 1 in Exhibit 10.11. Why do expenses stay essentially the same between the prior year and the budget year ($4,371-$4,343) with an increase of income in the budgeted year of $362,000? The director might want to prepare supplementary schedules that isolate the cost problems and indicate some of the interrelationships of income and expenses in this department, which may be different from those in other departments.

So far we have followed an example of a self-supporting CE organization. The budget process for subsidized organizations is often considered to require a different approach and to be governed by different considerations, but such an assumption shows a lack of understanding of the real purposes of budgeting. For instance, in a fully self-supporting organization, the acceptance or rejection of the budget by higher authority is likely to be based upon the degree of realism of the budget's assessment of market conditions and the soundness of CE management's implementation strategies. In fact, some version of the "market test" should also be employed in evaluating subsidized budgets. In a self-support situation, the question might be: Has the manager correctly evaluated the market potential for CE courses? In a subsidized situation, the question would be: Has the CE organization provided the target clientele with what they want or need? Self-supporting organizations have automatic feed-back on this question—a program either makes or loses money. In a subsidized situation, other evidence must be gathered, such as number of enrollments, number of completions, client evaluations, external evaluations, or client learning outcomes.

Similarly, the budget review process in subsidized organizations often uses the incremental approach. Under this approach, the budget of the current year is considered the base, and budget review concentrates primarily on changes (or increments) to this base. A budget presentation in an organization that uses this approach usually calls for a defense of the base and a plea for funds to be added to it, both supported by appropriate arguments and evidence. A version of the incremental approach can also be usefully employed in the budgeting of self-supporting or "variable resource" organizations. Portions of the self-support budget can be identified as being stable and dependable producers of income and margin, and the total of these programs can be considered the base. The budget review can then concentrate on the less stable, more risky programs—the "increment."

Budget Review

Just as programmers negotiate with the department chair over responsibility center budgets, the CE director will probably have to negotiate with those to whom the organization budget is presented. In such negotiations, the director has the advantage of knowing the organization and its budgeting process far better than the reviewers. However, reviewers have the power to ask a broad range of questions and demand changes in the budget without warning. If the CE director is not prepared to answer these questions or counter these suggested changes, the advantage of superior knowledge is lost. The CE director must, therefore, anticipate the behavior of the budget reviewers. Reviewers' questions and challenges are likely to fall into the following categories.

Questions About Budget Schedules

In preparation for any budget review, each schedule to be presented should be carefully scrutinized so that questions can be anticipated and answers prepared. It is a good practice to allow someone unfamiliar with the organization to review the budget schedules and raise questions that are likely to occur to outsiders but may be neglected by those who deal with budgetary matters every day. All possible or likely questions should be written down, and answers, including supplementary schedules where appropriate, should be prepared. The surest way to "sell" a budget is to demonstrate an obvious grasp of all its aspects, and diligent preparation is absolutely necessary to achieve this mastery.

Across-the-Board Cuts

One strategy traditionally used by reviewers in institutional settings is to require that proposed budgets be reduced by a stated percentage, say, 5 percent. This method suggests a certain desperation or an unwillingness in reviewers to make tough budget decisions personally. In subsidized organizations, the CE director who anticipates such a demand should prepare in advance an alternative budget, indicating how and where the cuts will be carried out. The consequences of cutting should also be clearly spelled out. One slightly Machiavellian counter strategy is to propose to cut a program that the reviewers regard as important in the hope that the cut will be restored. Of course, this strategy can backfire and create greater problems.

Across-the-board cuts can be particularly troublesome for self-supporting organizations. Income and expense are interrelated, and a reduction in expense may also mean a reduction in income. Directors of such organizations should be prepared to remind reviewers of this fact and to show that cuts anywhere will ultimately directly affect income. Across-the-board cuts mean that the organization reduces its ability to serve its students and thus also reduces its ability to generate income. The best strategy for countering across-the-board cuts is to choose the least harmful element for reduction and then outline the consequences of the reduction as clearly as possible to the reviewers.

Discontinuation of Programs or Departments

Another possibility is for the reviewers to request or suggest that a particular program or department be discontinued just as a director faced by an unbalanced budget might do. For instance, in our example, the reviewers might suggest that the Conferences and Institutes Department be discontinued in light of the small available-for-overhead amount it generates in relation to its size. We have already discussed some of the problems associated with removing a segment of an organization. If such a suggestion is likely to arise, the director should have made in advance careful calculations indicating the effect of the reduction on indirect costs and should have estimated the cost of the phaseout (e.g., severance pay and redistribution of service to present students). It may also be important to discuss the effect that the discontinuance will have on the organization's product mix and the public image of the institution.

Alternative Scenarios

Sometimes the reviewers require several budgets to be presented, each prepared under a different assumption. For instance, they may require one budget that assumes a 10 percent increase, another that assumes no change from the previous year, and a third that assumes a 10 percent decrease. This approach requires the director to identify new targets of opportunity that might be pursued if the budget were increased and cuts that might be made if the budget had to be reduced. This is probably something the director should do anyway, and it can lead to productive discussions with budget reviewers; in fact, the CE director might be the one to suggest it. If this approach is planned or expected, three separate budgets might be built from the ground up, or the director might develop a budget according to one set of assumptions and then adjust it to reflect others. Sometimes this strategy simply attempts to hide the reviewers' intention to reduce a budget, but it can represent a real opportunity to inform those in higher authority about the CE organization, and the wise director will exploit it as such.

Line Item Attacks

Another frequently encountered set of questions, likely to come particularly from reviewers accustomed to analyzing subsidized budgets, concerns the appropriateness of individual line items. For instance, a reviewer examining Exhibit 10.10 might ask why less is budgeted for departmental supplies and expense in the current year than was spent in the previous year. Another reviewer might require that budgeted instructor compensation expense, which shows an increase, be reduced. In some cases, an attack on line items may require such extensive revision that the whole budget must be redone. Line item defense, like defense of budget schedules as a whole, requires careful preparation and anticipation of possible attacks.

Increases in Fees

Especially in colleges and universities, the CE organization budget is often reviewed by people who are not familiar with the market aspects of continuing education. Such reviewers often propose a seemingly quick and simple answer to any budget difficulty—raising fees. Assuming that the fee structure has been carefully considered in the budgeting process, the best way to counter this suggestion is to provide the reviewers with a schedule of the fees of competitors in the area. The reviewers should be reminded that the CE structure cannot be adjusted without careful consideration.

In presenting the organization budget to higher authority, the CE director must be able to articulate clearly the consequences of changes in that budget, either positive or negative. In subsidized organizations, the director should have a clear idea of the levels of service that the budget represents and the effect on those levels of increases or decreases in funding. In self-supporting organizations, the director should have a clear understanding of the broader aspects of the markets being served and the relationship of various items of expense to the production of income. The wise director views the budget hearing as an opportunity to gain the approval not only of the budget but of the management decisions that are revealed through it. It is a chance to educate those who are in charge of continuing education and to include them in the decision-making process.

DISTRIBUTION

Distribution of the approved budget is an important element in the budgeting process. The director who does not formally express approval to those who worked so hard to achieve a reasonable budget by giving them copies of the final product has missed an opportunity to validate the whole process and to bring the budget preparation phase to an official completion. He or she has also missed the chance to make clear the nature of the contract that the budget for each responsibility center represents. Finally, the distribution step is useful for providing each person involved in the process with an understanding of the whole that might not have been apparent during budget generation. Each responsibility center must see itself and must be seen as a part of the organization.

Although distribution is the last step in the preparation of the budget, it is not the last step in the budgeting process. The budget should provide decision makers with a framework in which the interrelationships of all the organization's parts have been considered and a standard against which actual results can be judged. If the budget is to have this kind of continuing importance, an effective way of monitoring progress toward the budget goal and evaluating results as they occur is needed. Thus, the last "step" in the budgeting process is really a walk—a continuing series of steps throughout the budget period that provide those responsible for performance with the feedback they need to understand whether they are fulfilling, exceeding, or falling short of their "contract." Let's now examine how multidimensional budgeting fits into this picture.

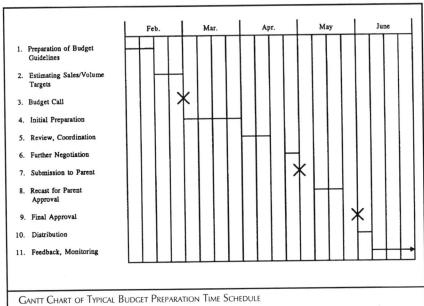

GANTT CHART OF TYPICAL BUDGET PREPARATION TIME SCHEDULE

EXHIBIT 10.1

	Director's Office and Personnel	Business Office and MIS	Registration	Classroom Maint. & Rent	Marketing (Unrecharged)	Other	Total
Revenue			$130,000	$340,840		$206,500	$677,340
CE Org. Indirect Costs							
Payroll	$617,574	$1,048,708	$899,812	$754,269	$824,290	$207,959	$4,352,612
Supplies and expense	258,140	343,389	248,227	1,677,928	1,144,877	791,187	4,463,748
Equipment	3,086	89,847	18,377	36,299	12,440	37,125	197,174
Internal recharges		(20,000)	(10,000)	(493,824)	(1,166,481)	(391,429)	(2,081,734)
Other						386,051	386,051
Total indirect costs	$878,800	$1,461,944	$1,156,416	$1,974,672	$815,126	$1,030,893	$7,317,851
Net indirect costs	($878,800)	($1,461,944)	($1,026,416)	($1,633,832)	($815,126)	($824,393)	($6,640,511)

ANNUAL BUDGET: SERVICE DEPARTMENT SUMMARY

EXHIBIT 10.2

To: Department Managers

From: Budget Officer

Re: 19A-B Annual Budget

Here is the call for the 19A-B budget computation for your department. It should be completed and returned to me by April 1, 19A. The budget should be prepared in accordance with the following assumptions and instructions.

Budget Assumptions. For the purposes of this budget, you should assume that economic conditions will remain the same as last year, except that there will be a 5 percent inflation rate. Market conditions will remain the same except where you have information to the contrary. Fees are to be increased by 10 percent, and instructor compensation rates are to be increased by 15 percent. Promotion costs should be computed by using the present promotion cost guide increased by 10 percent. The budget for each responsibility center should reflect a goal that, if achieved, represents more than satisfactory performance.

Budget Targets. The costs for the service departments have been calculated as follows:

Director's Office and Personnel	$ 880,000
Business Office and MIS	1,462,000
Registration	1,028,000
Classroom Maintenance and Rent	1,640,000
Marketing (Unrecharged)	815,000
Other	825,000
Addition to Reserves	250,000
Total	$6,900,000

The Director has allocated these costs, based on projections for the current year on market conditions, as follows:

Arts and Sciences (Program 1)	$2,400,000
Business and Management (Program 2)	550,000
Other (Programs 3-N)	3,950,000
Total	$6,900,000

You should allocate the target for your department to your responsibility centers, setting appropriate goals for them and adding whatever contingency you feel is appropriate.

Responsibility Center Allocations. Before issuing the budget call to your responsibility centers, you should compute the payroll costs for each center based on the enclosed worksheet (Exhibit 10.6). Make adjustments

BUDGET INSTRUCTIONS TO DEPARTMENT MANAGERS

EXHIBIT 10.3

to these calculations based on your own information or plans and allocate the salary of each person to the appropriate responsibility center. Then post the salary figure to the Programmer Term Summary Worksheets (Exhibit 10.8). Fringe benefits should be calculated as 20 percent of total salaries.

Several other allocations should also be made. First, you should calculate the amount of "departmental" promotion—promotion costs that cannot be allocated to any one responsibility center. Unrecharged promotion department costs, which should be included in departmental promotion, have been calculated to be $50,000 and have been allocated as follows:

Arts and Sciences	$13,000
Business and Management	15,000
Other (Programs 3-N)	22,000
Total	$50,000

Departmental supplies and expenses should also be allocated to the Programmer Term Summary Worksheets. As a guide, the actual supplies and expense figures for last year are given below:

Arts and Sciences	$ 32,000
Business and Management	$ 30,000
Other Programs (3-N)	$102,000

Please make these calculations and allocations and distribute the programmer worksheets as soon as possible. If you or your programmer need assistance in filling out these worksheets, let me know.

BUDGET INSTRUCTIONS TO DEPARTMENT MANAGERS

EXHIBIT 10.3 (CONTINUED)

To: Programmers

From: Budget Officer

Re: 19A-B Annual Budget Preparation

Here is the call for the 19A-B budget computation for your responsibility center. The Director, after reviewing the projected costs of the service departments, has set the margin target for each department. The department chair, in turn, has set the available for overhead target for each responsibility center. This target appears on the last line of the Programmer Term Summary Worksheet (Exhibit 10.8). After you have completed your calculations, you may wish to discuss your target with your department chair. Also allocated to you is your share of payroll costs, departmental promotion, and departmental supplies and expense. Unless there is a compelling reason to do otherwise, you should allocate these costs equally to the four terms. Although we expect some balance in programming volume among terms, it is not necessary to break even or exceed break-even every term as long as the total available for overhead target is attained.

You should complete a Programmer Course Summary Worksheet (Exhibit 10.9) in as much detail as possible for each term, then post the totals of each worksheet to the top part of the Programmer Term Summary Worksheet (columns a-d). This year we are paying particular attention to promotion costs. You should calculate promotion costs according to the latest promotion cost guide, increasing all rates by 10 percent.

The deadline for submission of these worksheets to your department chair is March 20, 19A. If you have questions or need assistance in filling out these worksheets, please let me know.

BUDGET INSTRUCTIONS TO PROGRAMMERS

EXHIBIT 10.4

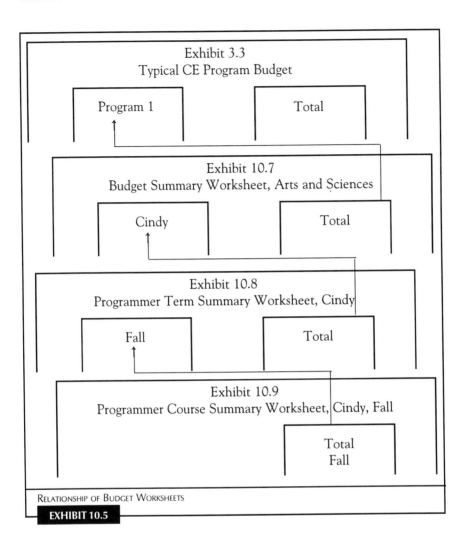

Exhibit 3.3
Typical CE Program Budget

| Program 1 | Total |

Exhibit 10.7
Budget Summary Worksheet, Arts and Sciences

| Cindy | Total |

Exhibit 10.8
Programmer Term Summary Worksheet, Cindy

| Fall | Total |

Exhibit 10.9
Programmer Course Summary Worksheet, Cindy, Fall

Total
Fall

RELATIONSHIP OF BUDGET WORKSHEETS

EXHIBIT 10.5

	Current Salary and Benefits	Expected Increases	Estimated New Salary	Cindy	Debbie	Programmers 3 - n
Programmers						
Cindy	$63,500	$3,175	$66,675	$66,675		
Debbie	54,700	2,735	57,435		$57,435	
Programmers 3-n	420,000	21,000	441,000			441,000
Total	**$538,200**	**$26,910**	**$565,110**	**$66,675**	**$57,435**	**$441,000**
Staff salaries						
John	$32,000	$1,600	$33,600	$33,600		
Mark	44,000	2,200	46,200	4,938		$41,262
Carole	39,000	1,950	40,950			40,950
Pete	42,000	2,100	44,100			44,100
Judy	49,000	2,450	51,450		$25,725	25,725
Connie	37,000	1,850	39,055			39,055
Open positions	200,000		200,000			200,000
Total	**$443,000**	**$12,150**	**$455,355**	**$38,538**	**$25,725**	**$391,092**
Total	**$981,200**	**$39,060**	**$1,020,465**	**$105,213**	**$83,160**	**$832,092**

PROGRAMMING DEPARTMENT PAYROLL WORKSHEETS, ARTS AND SCIENCES (UNCOMPLETED)

EXHIBIT 10.6

	Total	Adjustments	Cindy	Debbie	Programmers
Number of programs planned	925		95	120	710
Number of programs cancelled	87		10	13	64
Cancellation rate	9%		11%	11%	9%
Programs carried	838		85	107	646
Enrollment (Carried programs)	21,375		2,351	2,568	16,456
Average Class Size	25.5		27.7	24	25.5
Fee Income	**$6,682,698**	**($120,000)**	**$1,120,675**	**$1,098,500**	**$4,583,523**
Direct expense					
Promotion	$638,039		$47,750	$55,600	$534,689
Teacher compensation	1,825,397	$33,000	218,460	259,654	1,314,283
Direct supplies and expense	615,634	20,000	222,025	175,000	198,609
Total direct	**$3,079,070**	**$53,000**	**$488,235**	**$490,254**	**$2,047,581**
Course margin	**$3,603,628**	**($173,000)**	**$632,440**	**$608,246**	**$2,535,942**
Departmental expense:					
Payroll	$1,020,465		$105,213	$83,160	$832,092
Supplies and expense	131,000		17,030	15,900	98,070
Departmental promotion	91,000		10,920	9,850	70,230
Equipment	21,083				21,083
Total departmental	**$1,263,548**		**$133,163**	**$108,910**	**$1,021,475**
Total expenses	**$4,342,618**	**$53,000**	**$621,398**	**$599,164**	**$3,069,056**
Available for indirect cost	**$2,340,080**	**($173,000)**	**$499,277**	**$499,336**	**$1,514,467**

BUDGET SUMMARY WORKSHEET, ARTS AND SCIENCES

EXHIBIT 10.7

	Fall	Winter	Spring	Summer		
Number of programs planned	24	28	30	13	95	
Number of programs cancelled	2	3	4	1	10	
Cancellation rate	8%	11%	13%	8%	11%	
Programs carried	22	25	26	12	85	
Enrollment (Carried programs)	594	650	754	353	2,351	
Average Class Size	27.00	26.00	29.00	29.42	27.66	
Fee Income	**$282,744**	**$309,400**	**$358,904**	**$169,627**	**$1,120,675**	**100.0%**
Direct expense						
Promotion	$12,158	$13,304	$15,433	$6,855	$47,750	4.3%
Teacher compensation	55,135	60,333	69,986	33,006	218,460	19.5%
Direct supplies and expense	55,983	61,261	71,063	33,717	222,025	19.8%
Total direct	**$123,276**	**$134,898**	**$156,482**	**$73,578**	**$488,235**	**43.6%**
Course margin	**$159,468**	**$174,502**	**$202,422**	**$96,049**	**$632,440**	**56.4%**
Departmental expense:						
Payroll	$26,303	$26,303	$26,303	$26,303	$105,213	9.4%
Supplies and expense	4,258	4,258	4,258	4,258	17,030	1.5%
Departmental promotion	2,730	2,730	2,730	2,730	10,920	1.0%
Total departmental	**$33,291**	**$33,291**	**$33,291**	**$33,291**	**$133,163**	**11.9%**
Total expenses	**$156,567**	**$168,189**	**$189,773**	**$106,869**	**$621,398**	**55.4%**
Available for indirect cost	**$126,177**	**$141,211**	**$169,131**	**$62,758**	**$499,277**	**44.6%**

PROGRAMMER TERM SUMMARY WORKSHEET, CINDY

EXHIBIT 10.8

	Course 1	Course 2	Course 3	Courses 4-24	Cancelled	Fall
Number of programs planned						24
Number of programs cancelled						2
Cancellation rate						8%
Programs carried						22
Enrollment (Carried programs)	25	30	45	434	-60	594
Average Class Size						27.00
Fee Income	**$7,500**	**$13,500**	**$12,825**	**$230,919**	**($18,000)**	**$282,744**
Direct expense						
Promotion	$800	$250	$1,000	$10,108		$12,158
Teacher compensation	1,200	3,200	4,000	40,735	($6,000)	55,135
Direct supplies and expense	600	1,500	3,000	46,883	(4,000)	55,983
Total direct	**$2,600**	**$4,950**	**$8,000**	**$97,726**	**($10,000)**	**$123,276**
Course margin	**$4,900**	**$8,550**	**$4,825**	**$133,193**	**($8,000)**	**$159,468**

PROGRAMMER COURSE SUMMARY WORKSHEET, CINDY, FALL

EXHIBIT 10.9

	Budget 199A-B (Exhibit 1.3.3)	%	Projected Current Year	%	Better (Worse)	%	Actual Last Year	%	Better (Worse)
Number of programs	2,435		2,266		169		2,125		310
Number of enrollments	60,125		55,819		4,306		52,771		7,354
Fee Income/revenue	$23,981,079	100%	$22,800,000	100%	($1,181,079)	100%	$21,700,890	100%	$2,280,189
Direct expenses									
Promotion	$2,205,793	9%	$2,150,000	9%	(55,793)	9%	1,987,345	9%	($218,448)
Instructor compensation	6,380,682	27%	5,988,000	26%	(392,682)	26%	5,920,987	27%	(459,695)
Supplies and expense	1,864,386	8%	1,902,500	8%	38,114	8%	1,953,080	9%	88,694
Total direct	$10,450,861	44%	$10,040,500	44%	($410,361)	44%	$9,861,412	45%	($589,449)
Gross margin	$13,530,218	56%	$12,759,500	56%	770,718	56%	$11,839,478	55%	$1,690,740
Departmental expense									
Payroll	$4,047,135	17%	$3,950,000	17%	(97,135)	17%	3,906,160	18%	($140,975)
Supplies and expense	1,345,268	6%	1,300,000	6%	(45,268)	6%	1,736,071	8%	390,803
Promotion	480,585	2%	378,000	2%	(102,585)	2%	420,945	2%	(59,640)
Equipment	94,479	0%	53,000	0%	(41,479)	0%	5,800	0%	(88,679)
Other	(5,000)	-0%			5,000	0%			5,000
Total departmental expense	$5,962,467	25%	$5,681,000	25%	(281,467)	25%	$6,068,976	28%	$106,509.40
Available for indirect costs	$7,567,751	32%	$7,078,500	31%	489,251	31%	$5,770,502	27%	$1,797,250
CE organization indirect costs									
Payroll	$4,352,612	18%	$4,043,000	18%	(309,612)	18%	3,896,903	18%	($455,709)
Supplies and expense	4,849,699	20%	4,768,000	21%	(81,699)	21%	4,576,890	21%	(272,809)
Equipment	197,174	1%	154,700	1%	(42,474)	1%	123,876	1%	(73,298)
Internal recharges	(2,081,734)	-9%	(1,988,000)	-9%	93,734	-9%	(1,902,674)	-9%	179,060
Total indirect costs	$7,317,751	31%	$6,977,700	31%	(340,051)	31%	$6,694,995	31%	($622,756)
Addition to CE reserves	$250,000	1%	$100,800	0%	149,200	0%	($924,494)	-4%	$1,174,494

CE Organization Budget, Line Item Format

EXHIBIT 10.10

	Budget 199A-B	Projected Current Year	Better (Worse)	Actual Prior Year	Better (Worse)
Income					
Department 1 (Arts & Sci.)	$6,683	$6,453	$230	$6,321	$362
Department 2	1,693	1,656	37	1,594	99
Departments 3-N	15,605	14,691	914	13,786	1,819
Total	**$23,981**	**$22,800**	**$1,181**	**$21,701**	**$2,280**
Expense-Program Depts.					
Department 1	$4,343	$4,163	($180)	$4,371	$28
Department 2	1,196	1,168	(28)	1,192	(4)
Departments 3 - N	10,874	10,390	(484)	10,367	(507)
Total	**$16,413**	**$15,721**	**($692)**	**$15,930**	**($483)**
Available for Indirect Costs					
Department 1	$2,340	$2,290	$50	$1,950	$390
Department 2	497	488	9	402	95
Departments 3-n	4,731	4,301	430	3,419	1,312
Total	**$7,568**	**$7,079**	**$489**	**$5,771**	**$1,797**
Less Service Departments					
Director's and Personnel	$879	$820	($59)	$799	($80)
Business and MIS	1,462	1,402	(60)	1,380	(82)
Registration	1,156	1,124	(32)	1,100	(56)
Classroom	1,975	1,899	(76)	1,677	(298)
Marketing	815	794	(21)	756	(59)
Other	1,031	939	(92)	983	(48)
Total	**$7,318**	**$6,978**	**($340)**	**$6,695**	**($623)**
Increase (Decrease) in Reserves	**$250**	**$101**	**$149**	**($924)**	**$1,174**

ANNUAL BUDGET, DEPARTMENTAL FORMAT (IN THOUSANDS).

EXHIBIT 10.11

CHAPTER 11

Multidimensional Budgeting for the CE Organization

As we have seen in Chapters 3 and 7, MDB is a powerful new method CE managers can use to align the use of resources with customer (student) needs and organizational strategies. This chapter will complete our discussion of the budget process up to the feedback or management information stage. Budgets are primarily plans and the feedback stage provides CE managers with information needed to make decisions and to assess the degree of plan attainment. MDB provides CE managers with a wider range of options and information, and this chapter will show them the kinds of choices available.

ORGANIZATIONAL MDB USING COURSE AS COST OBJECT

In Chapter 7, we prepared an ABC-based budget for a programmer named Cindy (see Exhibits 7.2, 7.3, and 7.4 on pages 112, 113, and 114). Using the build-up method, we could combine selected elements from all programmer worksheets prepared by programmers in Cindy's organization to develop an overall organizational budget for contract programs, which is shown in Exhibit 11.1. (All exhibits for Chapter 11 are grouped together at the end of the chapter.) Then we could do the same thing for the other initiatives and derive a summary organizational budget with costs assigned down to the departmental level, as illustrated in Exhibit 11.2.

The budget in Exhibit 11.2 is "strategic" because it seems to define some strategic directions for the CE organization. It is not intended to supplant the traditional budget based upon the responsibility structure. This traditional budget, which shows how Cindy expects to do each term, remains in force and will be an important standard for her to meet and a useful source of information to management. The "strategic budget" supplements the traditional one, and provides management with additional information.

These examples illustrate the range and structure of choice available to CE managers. We chose to classify our strategic initiatives into three categories, but we could have chosen more. For instance, we could have further broken "international programs" into those programs that serve people overseas and those that serve foreign students who come to the U.S. We could also add more dimensions to our analysis; for instance, we could prepare additional separate budgets categorized by geographical location, course credit classification, or course format. However, the more dimensions and categories we add, the greater the effort and complexity required to complete the budget process and keep track of things later. Much of this effort will fall upon programmers who will be forced to set down the same information according to several separate schemes. Fortunately, when the course remains the primary cost or budget object, much of the potential cost of producing financial reports based on actual data can be avoided by adding attributes to a course database file. Again, the integrity of the budget or accounting process depends upon adherence to the exhaustive, exclusive rule. For instance, no single course in our example could be both an international and a contract course. If we wanted to keep track of international contract courses, we would have to develop a separate category for such courses. However, if we wanted to set up a new dimension, say, credit classification, a course could be both an international course (on the strategic dimension) and a noncredit course (on the credit classification dimension).

Exhibits 11.1 and 11.2 assign only the direct and departmental costs to the initiatives on the basis of ABC; the managerial initiatives (happy workforce and efficient operation) are line items. CE organization indirect costs remain unassigned. They could have been allocated to the four categories on one or another basis, much as such costs are allocated as overhead in traditional budgeting, but such allocation schemes would be arbitrary and have the potential for error. Again, ABC, this time applied to the service departments, provides the answer.

ORGANIZATIONAL MDB USING ABC

As the number of possible budget objects expands to include first activities and then a combination of product (course), customer (student group), and strategic/managerial objects, both the complexity of the system and its potential value as a source of information increase. The fullest expression of MDB calls for the production of five separate budgets—the traditional (responsibility structure) budget, the activity budget, the product budget, the customer budget, and the strategic/managerial budget. The relationships among these budgets appears in Exhibit 3.5 on p. 41. At first, producing them all may seem a complex and arduous task. However, the work can be reduced without damaging accuracy. We will employ one simplifying technique in our example by making the product (course) categorization scheme coincident with the customer (student) scheme—both will have the three elements of public, contract, and international. This simplifying process is valid in CE when the same product (course) serves no more than one customer group. The MDB and ABC combination can be used selectively in the organization to concentrate on the areas of greatest concern. Again, this is where managerial choice is crucial to success.

To illustrate the full use of MDB, let's extend our example by supposing our CE organization has the following strategic goals:

1. To expand the enrollment of public courses offered in our service area
2. To expand the number of contract courses
3. To expand the international program
4. To improve employee morale and motivation
5. To improve operational efficiency

These goals are purposely kept simple to aid in presenting a coherent example; each might be specified in more detail. Goal number 5 is a kind of catch-all category to provide that exhaustive aspect necessary to maintain integrity. The structure of the ultimate, strategic budget is now established, and we want to trace all our resources to these objectives or identify those resources not supporting at least one of these objectives.

To do this, we need to apply ABC to the service departments in the same manner as we did with the program departments. Exhibit 10.2 in the pevious chapter shows the total net cost of our Registration Office as $1,026,416. Exhibit 11.3 shows the Registration Office segmented into four activity centers, one of which is Program Processing. Program Processing has four cost drivers, calculated as follows:

Number of new credit courses	400
Number of new noncredit courses	200
Number of credit courses	50
Number of noncredit courses	25

Using these calculations, we can assign the cost of program processing to our strategic initiatives by determining or estimating the credit classification of courses presented in each category. Exhibit 11.4 shows this calculation. When we do this for each activity center in Registration, we obtain the summary presented in Exhibit 11.5.

Exhibit 11.5 first shows how Registration Office costs, including Program Processing unit costs, are assigned, and then continues with the other service departments. The results of these assignment worksheets can now be plugged into our strategic budget Exhibit 11.2. Exhibit 11.6 expands the previous strategic budget. We can now see that both public and contract programs contribute significantly to the financial health of the organization, but the international program will actually cost the organization about $150,000. The managerial catch-all called "efficient operations" is a significant $2,307,600. This figure bears further analysis and represents an unexplained cost. On the other hand, the organization can now put a price tag on efforts to create and maintain a happy workforce—over $600,000.

This illustration underscores the importance of choosing strategic objectives that are exhaustive of the full organization, which requires some form of "catch-all" category to take up all the miscellaneous items. As long as these items are reasonably well identified as not falling into the "non-value added" category, such a category should not detract from the usefulness of MDB. The illustration also shows the importance of aligning product and customer definitions. Of course, the same product can serve two customers and assignments can be based upon estimates of the proportional use of the product by the customer groups. These and other complications will crop up as real life situations are encountered. Such complications can usually be handled by adding detail or making intelligent assumptions. It is also possible to use ABC-based MDB selectively, purposefully leaving certain activities unanalyzed and either showing the cost of such activities as a line item or allocating or assigning the cost on some basis much like overhead is allocated in traditional budgeting. In other words, MDB does not have to be implemented in the comprehensive version used in this illustration.

In the next chapter, we will examine the methods used to provide feedback to the budget process and to provide CE managers with the information they need to make decisions. Because MDB places unusual demands upon the underlying financial information system, we will also discuss the role ABC can play in the development of a comprehensive financial information and budgeting system.

| | Programmers | | | |
	Cindy	Debbie	3-N	Total
Number of programs planned	10	12	65	87
Number of programs cancelled	0	0	0	0
Cancellation rate				
Programs carried	10	12	65	87
Enrollment (Carried programs)	450	350	2,450	3,250
Average Class Size	45.0	29.2	37.7	37.4
Fee Income	**$148,500**	**$250,000**	**$1,785,000**	**$2,183,500**
Direct expense				
Promotion	$10,000	$15,000	$200,000	$225,000
Teacher compensation	44,550	75,000	624,750	744,300
Direct supplies and expense	16,335	24,000	124,950	165,285
Total direct	$70,885	$114,000	$949,700	$1,134,585
Course margin	**$77,615**	**$136,000**	**$835,300**	**$1,048,915**
Percent margin	**52%**	**54%**	**47%**	**48%**
Departmental expense:				
Product related	$21,905	$25,400	$186,000	$233,305
Customer related	19,308	17,800	85,000	122,108
Managerial related				
Total departmental	**$41,213**	**$43,200**	**$271,000**	**$355,413**
Total expenses	**$112,098**	**$157,200**	**$1,220,700**	**$1,489,998**
Available for indirect cost	**$36,402**	**$92,800**	**$564,300**	**$693,502**
Percentage of income	**25%**	**37%**	**32%**	**32%**

CE ORGANIZATION BUDGET FOR CONTRACT PROGRAMS

EXHIBIT 11.1

	Public	%	Contract	%	International	%	Managerial	%	Total	%
Number of programs	2,425		87		56				2,568	
Number of cancelled programs	131		0		2				133	
Cancellation rate	5.4%		0.0%		3.6%				5.2%	
Programs carried	2,294		87		54				2,435	
Number of enrollments	54,375		3,250		2,500				60,125	
Average class size	23.7		37.4		46.3				24.7	
Fee Income	**$20,218,779**	**100.0%**	**$2,183,500**	**100.0%**	**$1,578,800**	**100.0%**			**$23,981,079**	**100.00%**
Direct expenses										
Promotion	$1,782,793	8.8%	$225,000	10.3%	$198,000	12.5%			$2,205,793	9.20%
Instructor compensation	4,956,382	24.5%	744,300	34.1%	680,000	43.1%			6,380,682	26.61%
Supplies and expense	1,499,101	7.4%	165,285	7.6%	200,000	12.7%			1,864,386	7.77%
Total direct	**$8,238,276**	**40.7%**	**$1,134,585**	**52.0%**	**$1,078,000**	**68.3%**			**$10,450,861**	**43.58%**
Gross margin	**$11,980,503**	**59.3%**	**$1,048,915**	**48.0%**	**$500,800**	**31.7%**			**$13,530,218**	**56.42%**
Departmental expense										
Product related	$3,168,175	15.7%	$233,305	10.7%	$176,000	11.1%			$3,577,480	14.92%
Customer related	823,685	4.1%	122,108	5.6%	246,700	15.6%			1,192,493	4.97%
Managerial related							$1,132,869		1,132,869	4.72%
Other							59,625		59,625	0.25%
Total departmental expense	**$3,991,860**	**19.7%**	**$355,413**	**16.3%**	**$422,700**	**26.8%**	**$1,192,494**		**$5,962,467**	**24.86%**
Available for indirect costs	**$7,988,643**	**39.5%**	**$693,502**	**31.8%**	**$78,100**	**4.9%**	**($1,192,494)**		**$7,567,751**	**31.56%**
CE organization indirect costs										
Payroll									$4,352,612	18.15%
Supplies and expense									4,849,699	20.22%
Equipment									197,174	0.82%
Internal recharges									(2,081,734)	-8.68%
Total indirect costs									**$7,317,751**	**30.51%**
Addition to CE reserves									**$250,000**	**1.04%**

CE ORGANIZATION STRATEGIC BUDGET

EXHIBIT 11.2

	Total	Program Processing	Information Service	Records & Transcripts	Room Scheduling
Revenue	$130,000			$130,000	
Payroll	$899,812	$198,000	$327,012	$278,000	$96,800
Supplies and expense	248,227	75,800	99,627	50,500	22,300
Equipment	18,377	1,000	11,377	4,500	1,500
Internal recharges	(10,000)			(10,000)	
Total expense	$1,156,416	$274,800	$438,016	$323,000	$120,600
Net expense	$1,026,416	$274,800	$438,016	$193,000	$120,600
Payroll allocation					
Employee 1	$34,500	$34,500			
Employee 2	28,900		$28,900		
Employee 3	46,900		23,450	$23,450	
Employee 4	25,700				$25,700
Employees 5-N	763,812	163,500	274,662	254,550	71,100
Total	$899,812	$198,000	$327,012	$278,000	$96,800
Supplies and expense Allocation					
Telephone	$87,900	$32,600	$45,200	$4,500	$5,600
Office supplies	76,430	15,600	35,630	21,900	3,300
Equipment maintenance	7,800	3,100	2,200	2,000	500
Expenses 4 - N	76,097	24,500	16,597	22,100	12,900
Total	$248,227	$75,800	$99,627	$50,500	$22,300

REGISTRATION OFFICE ACTIVITY CENTERS

EXHIBIT 11.3

	Cost Driver Amount	Total Number of Courses	Total Cost	Public No.	Public Cost	Contract No.	Contract Cost	International No.	International Cost
New Credit Programs	$400	325	$130,000	310	$124,000	5	$2,000	10	$4,000
New Non-credit programs	200	189	37,800	69	13,800	80	16,000	40	8,000
Credit courses	50	1,712	85,600	1,677	83,850	20	1,000	15	750
Non-credit courses	25	856	21,400	748	18,700	67	1,675	41	1,025
			$274,800		$240,350		$20,675		$13,775

ASSIGNMENT OF PROGRAM PROCESSING COSTS

EXHIBIT 11.4

	Total	Public	Contract	International	Managerial Happy Workers	Managerial Efficient Ops.
Program Processing	$274,800	$240,350	$20,675	$13,775	$15,000	$56,000
Information Services	438,016	292,916	40,650	33,450	2,000	7,000
Records and Transc.	193,000	145,600	12,700	25,700		
Room Scheduling	120,600	115,600			2,000	3,000
Total Registration	**$1,026,416**	**$794,466**	**$74,025**	**$72,925**	**$19,000**	**$66,000**
Director's Office	$878,800	$263,640	$43,940	$87,880	$131,820	$351,520
Business Office & MIS	1,461,944	1,111,077	14,619	43,858	73,097	219,292
Classroom costs	1,633,832	1,572,882	2,500	13,450	5,000	40,000
Marketing (Unrechgd)	815,126	793,726	4,000	6,500	4,000	6,900
Other	824,393	24,048				800,345
Total	**$6,640,511**	**$4,559,839**	**$139,084**	**$224,613**	**$232,917**	**$1,484,057**

REGISTRATION OFFICE AND CE ORGANIZATION INDIRECT COST ASSIGNMENT

EXHIBIT 11.5

	Public	%	Contract	%	International	%	Managerial Happy Wrkfrce	Managerial Efficient Ops.	Total	%
Number of programs	2,425		87		56				2,568	
Number of cancelled programs	131		0		2				133	
Cancellation rate	5.4%		0.0%		3.6%				5.2%	
Programs carried	2,294		87		54				2,435	
Number of enrollments	54,375		3,250		2,500				60,125	
Average class size	23.7		37.4		46.3				24.70	
Fee Income	$19,541,439	100.0%	$2,183,500	100.0%	$1,578,800	100.0%			$23,303,739	100.00%
Direct expenses										
Promotion	$1,782,793	9.1%	$225,000	10.3%	$198,000	12.5%			$2,205,793	9.47%
Instructor compensation	4,956,380	25.4%	744,300	34.1%	680,000	43.1%			6,380,681	27.38%
Supplies and expense	1,499,101	7.7%	165,285	7.6%	200,000	12.7%			1,864,386	8.00%
Total direct	$8,238,274	42.2%	$1,134,585	52.0%	$1,078,000	68.3%			$10,450,860	44.85%
Gross margin	$11,303,164	57.8%	$1,048,915	48.0%	$500,800	31.7%			$12,852,879	55.15%
Departmental expense										
Product related	$3,168,175	16.2%	$233,305	10.7%	$176,000	11.1%			$3,577,480	15.35%
Customer related	823,685	4.2%	122,108	5.6%	246,700	15.6%			1,192,493	5.12%
Managerial related										
Happy workforce							$368,950		368,950	1.58%
Efficient operations								$763,918	763,918	3.28%
Other								59,625	59,625	0.26%
Total departmental expense	$3,991,861	20.4%	$355,413	16.3%	$422,700	26.8%	$368,950	$823,543	$5,962,467	25.59%
Available for indirect costs	$7,311,303	37.4%	$693,502	31.8%	$78,100	4.9%	($368,950)	($823,543)	$6,890,412	29.57%
CE organization indirect costs	$4,559,839	23.3%	$139,084	6.4%	$224,613	14.2%	$232,917	$1,484,057	$6,640,510	28.50%
Contribution margin (net cost)	$2,751,464	14.1%	$554,418	25.4%	($146,513)	-9.3%	($601,867)	($2,307,600)	$249,902	1.07%

CE ORGANIZATION STRATEGIC BUDGET—FULL COST ASSIGNMENT

EXHIBIT 11.6

CHAPTER 12

Developing a Management Information System for the CE Organization

Having a budget system is the first step in developing a management information system (MIS) for a CE organization; the budget defines the information managers want and the elements of the operation they want to control. In organizations limited to traditional methods of accounting and control, the defining decisions relate to the segmentation of the CE organization into responsibility centers. With MDB, such defining decisions are considerably more numerous; to determine responsibility means considering the added dimensions of activity, product, customer, and strategic initiatives, each of which may have many components. In this chapter, we will discuss considerations basic to developing an MIS for any CE organization and, using the traditional model, illustrate some basic management reports required by most systems.

The purpose of any management information system is to provide managers with the information they need to make decisions. Although we usually think of computers and numbers when we think of an MIS, such systems may contain qualitative as well as quantitative elements and have both formal and informal aspects. The qualitative or informal aspects are hard to describe because they are composed of individual and group interaction patterns. The extent to which an individual or a small group (e.g., a department) reflect the ideals of educational quality and appropriateness is within the "informal" sphere. The budget system, by contrast, is part of the "formal" system of control, composed largely of quantitative standards and measures. An unfavorable variance from the budget standard is a signal to management for corrective action, while a favorable variance is a signal for reward and recognition.

A good MIS accumulates income and expenses in meaningful categories and a timely fashion. Categories are "meaningful" when they correspond to the plan upon which the budget was based, clearly assign responsibility for results to individuals or defined groups, match or bracket income and expense in defined time periods, and, most importantly, provide management with the information needed to make decisions.

PRELIMINARY CONSIDERATIONS IN DEVELOPING AN MIS

MIS systems should produce useful information, avoid information overload, and be cost-effective, timely, and readily interpreted with accuracy.

Production of Useful Information

Too many accounting or management information systems generate useless information. An example in CE might be enrollment information. A programmer might decide that if the enrollment in a particular course is less than 35 one week before the course begins, the course will be canceled. The programmer might be interested in enrollment figures two weeks before the beginning of the course, but, since no decision will be based on the earlier enrollment figure, that information is not truly useful or meaningful. Knowing how much telephone costs have increased over the last 10 years, assuming that everything reasonable has already been done to keep phone costs to a minimum, is not really useful because the information will not lead to any decision. Of course, either piece of information might lead to a decision in certain situations, but it is usually not desirable to develop a financial accounting system that produces information useful only in special and limited circumstances.

Avoidance of Information Overload

Computers can inexpensively generate information. Unfortunately, managers have limited ability and time to interpret data. More information means more time and effort are required to consider and interpret it. Irrelevant data tend to cloud management decision making, at times hiding what is relevant. For instance, a large CE organization installed a comprehensive promotion tracking system that produced each month for each course a complete profile of the source of enrollments, broken down by individual mailing list, promotion piece, and categorized by home and work zip code, with optional resorting by interest code. Each month's report was several inches thick. It was soon obvious that only a small portion of this monstrous document was ever used to make decisions. Even where the report could have been useful, it was not used because extracting relevant data from it was too time-consuming. Inevitably, the old "seat of the pants" methods for evaluating promotion effectiveness was being used instead.

The most obvious way to avoid information overload is simply to limit the amount of information produced to what is relevant to decision making. Just as most closets contain some clothes that will never be worn, most systems, no matter how carefully conceived, produce some information that is never used.

Another common way to avoid overload is to construct a database from which relevant information can be extracted as needed for decision making. However, this method requires a careful definition of each decision and the kind of information relevant to it. Such a degree of preplanning is uncharacteristic of many managers, who prefer to "browse" in the data, shopping for relevance as they walk along the aisles of the database. They often lack a clear understanding of how the database is structured and how data can be extracted from it.

Another way of avoiding information overload is to aggregate data at different levels of detail for different levels of management. For instance, members of upper management probably need to know only that, say, promotion costs are increasing as a percentage of income and that most of the increase appears to be in the cost of mailing lists. On the other hand, operating personnel—the mailing list coordinator, for instance—would need to have more specific information (on the relative response rate to specific mailing lists, perhaps) so that the least cost-effective lists could be discontinued. This detailed information would be irrelevant to upper management personnel because they would not be involved in the individual decisions that go into correcting the cost increases. The more detailed the information, the less subject to interpretation and the more clearly presented the information must be.

Cost-Benefit Ratio

Information has both a value and a cost, and its value lies primarily in the improved decision making it can produce. The "true" value of relevant and accurate information can seldom be measured precisely, just as the correctness of a decision is difficult to measure. The cost of information is also difficult to determine. We may be able to tell how much it costs to physically produce a particular report from a database, but often we cannot properly attribute all the relevant costs of maintaining and inputting the data. An accounting system that requires the use of 100 expense classifications or codes is bound to be less expensive than one requiring 1,000 expense codes. The coding process will be more time-consuming in the larger system, and the chance of error will be greater; faulty conclusions caused by such errors can cost an organization dearly. On the other hand, the 1,000-code system will allow for more detail and precision, which might "pay" in some circumstances.

Decisions must be made about the level of complexity and detail an accounting system should incorporate. Too simple an aggregation of data—for instance, down only to the department level—may invalidate a budget system that requires detail down to the programmer (responsibility center) level; too complex an aggregation may cost more than it is worth. The cost-benefit calculation is an extremely important consideration in the design of a useful accounting system.

Timely Reports

Information delivered too late to affect a decision it could have informed is as useless as information never generated, and has probably cost the organization resources that cannot be recovered. An accounting/management information system must deliver accurate information on time. When this does not happen, the fault may lie either with the system or with decision makers who did not allow enough time for information to be delivered. An effective information system must have a consistent as well as a timely reporting schedule.

Accuracy of Interpretation

The level of complexity of the interpretation that any report requires must be matched with the ability of the readers of the report to make that interpretation. A financial report comparing the "available for overhead" produced by two programmers, one in the humanities and one in business and management, would defy interpretation by someone who did not understand both the programs involved and the organization that produced them. Inability to interpret data is one argument against widespread dissemination of financial results of responsibility centers in CE organizations, where wide variation between programs is often expected. Those unfamiliar with the markets addressed and the costs and difficulties of presenting particular programs are likely to make straightforward but invalid comparisons.

CHARACTERISTICS OF CE ACCOUNTING

Several common characteristics of the accounting environment of CE organizations affect their information needs.

Lack of a Balance Sheet and Double-Entry System

Those unfamiliar with the principles of accounting often use accounting terms rather loosely, and the terms "balance sheet" and "double entry" are often misunderstood. A balance sheet is a listing of the assets, liabilities, and owners' share of a particular accounting entity. It reflects what is known as a basic accounting equation: Assets = Liabilities + Owners' Equity. This equation is simply a way of saying that whatever things of value currently exist in a business (assets) were put there either by creditors (which "putting" is recorded as a liability) or by owners. Unfortunately, most CE organizations do not have control or even knowledge of their own balance sheets. They are limited to the single dimension of the income statement. A complete description of the issues involved in accounting for balance sheets is provided in Chapter 15.

This lack of a balance sheet and double-entry bookkeeping is perhaps the largest single barrier to the adoption of "business-like" practices by CE organizations. It prevents the use of management systems that have evolved over the years to serve private businesses.

Antiquated or Misdirected Parent Systems

Because CE organizations usually exist within larger institutions, they must often conform to reporting and accounting practices not useful to the purposes of a CE administration. The principles of fund accounting, designed to assure that the fiduciary duty of the parent institution is carried out, are not well suited to the information needs of CE management, particularly where the CE organization is self-supporting. Where CE is part of a college or university, the supporting accounting systems are usually geared to a slower pace and a longer periodicity than the CE organization is comfortable with, since the parent does not need information as crucially or as quickly for decision making. Where the CE organization may need monthly or quarterly reports and may need enrollment information daily, the parent may be satisfied with reports on a semester or bi-yearly basis and may pay real attention to financial matters only near the year's end. All these factors usually mean that the CE organization must develop a separate management information system to meet both institutional requirements and its own needs.

Lack of Information

Another characteristic of the control structure of CE organizations, albeit not unique to them, is the continuous need for management to make decisions without adequate information. No matter how detailed and responsive a management information system is, it can never describe the external world so completely that decision making becomes automatic. The CE director who does not recognize this will become frustrated with any information system. A good MIS can provide relevant information, but it can never substitute for wisdom and seasoned judgment.

STANDARD MANAGEMENT REPORTS IN TRADITIONAL SYSTEMS

Management reports generally take the form of comparisons of actual results with either the budget or with past periods. Comparison with the budget allows managers to see how well the plan represented by the budget is working and comparison with past periods allows management to spot trends. Such reports are interpreted through an analysis of the variance between the actual results and the results to which they are being compared. Such an analysis then leads to a set of questions and decisions. For example, suppose a report indicates that a particular program portfolio did not produce the budgeted available-for-overhead figure set for it and that the main cause of that failure was a dramatic difference between budgeted and actual promotion costs. This analysis would lead to more investigation to determine the reason that promotion costs were so high for the program. High promotion costs may result from a high cancellation rate—programs were promoted and then cancelled. The management decision would then be focused on how to reduce the cancellation rate rather than on reducing printing costs.

Traditional MIS systems apply to two general kinds of CE organizations, fixed resource organizations and variable resource organizations. Fixed resource organizations are generally subsidized; the amount of resources available to the organization in any period is fixed and known at the beginning of the period. Budgets in such organizations concentrate on expenses (outflows) since the main objective is not to overspend the allocated funds. In variable resource CE organizations, the amount of resources available in any period is more or less unknown at the beginning of the period and is usually dependent upon the performance of the organization. Variable resource organizations usually incorporate both the income (source) and expense (outflow) sides into their budgeting and planning process.

MIS in Fixed Resource Organizations

There are few purely fixed resource CE organizations any more—most charge some kind of fee for the courses they offer. However, CE organizations commonly have some element of their operations or program subsidized under fixed funding arrangements.

The objective of most fixed resource organizations is to spend exactly what is provided for in the budget. To exceed the budget is to fail to live up to one's financial responsibility and is the cardinal sin in organizations of truly fixed resources. Overspending in one area must be made up by underspending in another whenever possible. Paradoxically, underspending also carries sanctions. If the amount provided is not completely spent by the end of the period, it will often lapse and not be available for future periods. Further, underspending may signal to authorizing bodies that budgeted amounts should be reduced in the next fiscal period. This failure to provide incentive for economy and efficiency is the greatest failure of fixed resource budgeting.

Fixed resource organizations generally employ pure fund accounting methods. The objective of spending no more and no less than is budgeted shapes the feedback and control structure. The main problem is keeping track of "discretionary" funds—the amount of uncommitted money that remains in the accounting period. This means that commitments for future expenditure of funds, as well as for present, actual expenditures, must be accounted for.

Keeping track of future commitments can be difficult because documentation is rarely generated automatically to support them. It is also difficult to match actual expenditures with related estimates of future commitments so that the encumbrances and commitments can be relieved (reduced) when payment is made. Failure to reduce the encumbrances and commitments will incorrectly reduce the discretionary funds available to the organization. Futher, since commitments are often estimates and may differ substantially from the amount that is finally paid out, differences will exist between encumbrances and expenditures. A method must be devised to relate all the stages of a particular transaction so that the amount of funds remaining available is always known.

In order to properly manage fixed resource organizations, directors must be provided with up-to-date reports that clearly show the amount of funding remaining available and also indicate where commitment balances must be adjusted. This need usually requires a budget that establishes a rate-of-expenditure plan. Such a plan divides the budget for a particular period (such as a year) into smaller periods (say, 12 months) so that expenditure rates throughout the larger period could be monitored.

MIS in Variable Resource Organizations

Although self-supporting CE organizations can be budgeted like fixed resource organizations, such organizations are usually in the variable resource categories. Their financial objectives may range from spending no more than is taken in to making as much surplus as possible.

Unlike the fixed resource organization, in which the purpose of the feedback and monitoring system is keeping track only of outflows—expenditures, the rate of expenditure, commitments, and the ultimate effect on discretionary funds—the variable resource organization must track both inflows and outflows. In addition, variable resource organizations require their MIS to consider their cost structure and the timing of transactions; they also need a progression of reports based on available information in the light of necesssary decisions.

Cost Structure

The establishment of the control or responsibility structure of a CE unit, of which the financial reporting process is an important instrument, requires understanding several concepts: controllable costs, noncontrollable costs, discretionary costs, and committed costs. As has been noted, people cannot fairly be held responsible for costs they cannot control, such as organization overhead in the case of individual responsibility center managers in a CE organization. Other costs, however, are controllable by managers to various degrees. Costs controllable entirely by the manager, such as many promotion costs, are called discretionary costs. The ability of a manager to balance such costs with the income they are supposed to produce should be a significant factor in evaluation of the manager's performance.

Some costs that seem, in a strict sense, to be controllable, may not be entirely discretionary. Take, for example, when instructor compensation per course is fixed. In this case, the amount of instructor compensation is a function of the number of courses offered and is not directly discretionary. The manager may be able to vary the number of courses offered and determine minimum enrollments and maximum class sizes, but these parameters only indirectly influence instructor compensation totals. If the manager or the programmers determined the rate of compensation for each instructor individually, instructor compensation would become discretionary.

Feedback and control structures also must comprehend the nature of committed or sunk costs. Like courses, individual responsibility centers and entire CE organizations have sunk costs—either costs already paid for or future costs for which the organization is obligated. Promotion costs are common examples; once it has been determined how a course or group of courses will be promoted, the costs associated with the promotion campaign become committed. Payroll costs also are usually committed costs, since only under unusual circumstances will the number of employees be reduced during a budget period. The distinction between committed and uncommitted costs is important because decisions about the incurring of these costs are made at different times. For example, decisions about staffing levels and the amount to be spent on promotion are usually made earlier than decisions about expenses involving the actual presentation of courses, such as room rental, course material costs, or entertainment costs. Because such committents are givens, they often have more impact on the overall level of operation and the financial success of the organization than do other kinds of costs. Decisions to commit costs, therefore, are important.

Timing

All feedback systems must account for the time financial results take to become clear, and managers (and programmers) are constantly pressed to make decisions before these results are available. For instance, because of long preparation and promotional lead times, planning for the winter term must usually be complete before the results of the fall term are known. Thus, a course that proves to be an utter failure in the fall might be included in the winter catalog because of an early promotion deadline. (Of course, if the spring course is a roaring success, the programmer can take credit for persever-

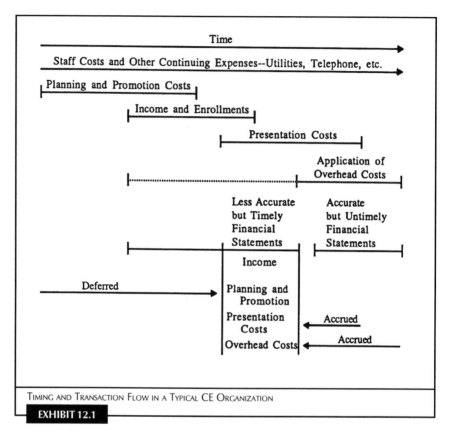

TIMING AND TRANSACTION FLOW IN A TYPICAL CE ORGANIZATION

EXHIBIT 12.1

ance.) Feedback systems must incorporate the "natural" timing of financial transactions and the trade-offs that are necessary between comprehensiveness and precision, on the one hand, and timeliness and relevance to decision making on the other.

Exhibit 12.1 is a graphic representation of the timing and transaction flow of a typical CE organization.

The major categories of transactions pictured in this exhibit are as follows:

- **Staff costs and other continuing expenses.** These costs tend to be expended uniformly over time, with little variation from one period to the next. They are often indirect (overhead) costs and are allocated in some way to the appropriate income-producing segment and time period.
- **Planning and promotion costs.** The costs of planning a course or group of courses precede all other transactions related to those courses, and although the bills for promotion costs may come in later, promotion costs are committed during this early period.

- **Income and enrollments.** Income and enrollments are received during periods immediately preceding the start of the courses. Because they are the first real indications of the success or failure of a program, levels of income and enrollment are usually watched closely.
- **Presentation costs.** Once it has been determined that the course or courses should be held, the costs of actually presenting the course(s) are committed.
- **Application of overhead costs.** The timing of the application or "billing" of overhead costs to the responsibility centers can vary greatly from organization to organization. The allocation may be a function of income or expense in some way and thus may be applied when all other transactions are completed, or it may be applied as transactions occur. For instance, overhead might be allocated on a per student basis, in which case it would be possible to apply the overhead as each student enrolls. If overhead were allocated on the basis of expense, however, it could not be applied until all expenses were known.

The most accurate picture of financial results can be obtained late in a budget period, when all the transactions related to it are complete and most or all the bills and invoices are received and paid. However, management may need a good sense of the results considerably earlier than this. Thus, the financial picture must be put together in pieces, using best estimates of some transactions. The earliest practical time for this piecing together is close to the end of the enrollment period, when total enrollment and income figures are fairly complete and accurate. A financial statement prepared this early will require an estimate of future presentation costs and any overhead costs that would normally be applied in the future. To properly match income and the expense related to it in the same period, it will also be necessary to carry over from previous periods any planning and promotion costs and any income related to this period's courses that had been received or spent in prior periods. Because estimation is involved in this method, error is possible, and one of the problems in rendering financial statements that involve accruals is the necessity of reconciling the estimates with actual results when they are finally available.

Reports

Standard reports for variable resource organizations using traditional methods are based upon comparisons of actual results with the budget and, sometimes, with a prior period, usually the previous year. Exhibits 12.2 through 12.6 show successively larger aggregations of data corresponding to the progression from the individual course budget all the way to the budget for the whole organization. The exhibits also indicate, by the order in which they are presented, the timing of the availability of the information. For instance, Exhibit 12.2, called the "inventory" report, compares the sum of the course budgets for the fall term with the numbers on the annual budget for fall on the crucial measures of number of programs, number of projected enrollments, income, and available for overhead. Because course budgets are prepared before any actual results are available, this report provides CE managers with the earliest information they can get about the financial health of the organization. This report allows them to compare the size of the "inventory" of courses to be offered with what the programmers projected when they prepared their annual budgets. An inventory lower than the annual budget is usually an early warning that a program portfolio is in trouble.

In the last column of this report, and in most other reports that show comparisons, a judgement is made about whether a number is better or worse, and the "worse" condition is always shown in brackets. When, as in the example, income per the course budgets exceeds the annual budget, it is shown as "better," and when course budget expense exceeds the annual budget, it is shown as "worse." Using this convention consistently aids inter-pretation of the report.

This report deals with the income part of the budget and with course margins; it does not deal with expenses at all. The report could be expanded to include expenses at this point, since annual budgeted expenses are known and the sum of the expenses in the course budgets could be obtained. However, the details of the expenses probably would not add much to the information that managers need to make decisions.

Exhibit 12.3 compares the next available information about the financial results of the term. This report is prepared as soon after the term begins as is possible, at the time when most of the income has been collected and the courses are being presented. Again, the important elements of number of programs, number of enrollees, and income, this time on an actual basis, are compared with the annual budget. In addition, actual income is compared with the sum of income from the course budgets (shown on Exhibit 12.2); this comparison provides feedback on how well individual programmers are able to estimate course income. While this report does not show the important bottom line component, available for overhead, it will indicate areas of strength and weakness.

Exhibits 12.4 through 12.5 show the beginning of a progression of reports that are possible once expense information is available. Exhibit 12.4 shows the results for a single course, and Exhibit 12.5 shows the results for a programmer for the term; such a report could be summarized for the other programmers in Cindy's department to get the departmental results for the term. At the end of the year, these term figures could be added to get the total results for the year for the department. The departments could then be added together to derive a statement for the entire organization. At each successive level, actual results can be compared with the annual budget.

Exhibit 12.6 shows the culminating report and compares actual results with the annual budget of the CE organization as shown in Exhibit 3.3 on page 35. It also compares the actual figures with the results from the prior year. Examining these figures will bring many questions to mind. Why are promotion costs so much higher than budget and instructor compensation so much lower? Why are payroll costs so close to costs last year when everyone received a raise this year? Raising these questions is the purpose of any financial statement. The answers may lie in the subsidiary reports where issues might be isolated by department or term, or may require special analysis.

Report Analysis

Analyzing and interpreting the information displayed in reports is an art requiring quantitative skills combined with an intimate knowledge of the organization and its parts. Aids to analysis may be embedded in the reports. For instance, Exhibit 12.6 shows some useful ratios to aid comparisons. Other ratios can be derived from the data presented in these reports. For example, we could derive an average "productivity index" for programmers by dividing the total departmental payroll ($3,988,127) into the available for overhead produced by programmers.

$$\frac{7,470,815}{3,988,127} = 1.87$$

Every dollar spent on programming payroll produces $1.87 for covering indirect costs. This figure might then be compared with similar calculations for individual programmers to determine relative productivity. As with any financial data, however, these calculations must be interpreted with great care. Cindy's index, for instance, might exceed the index set for her in the budget. Another programmer might have an index higher than Cindy's but lower than budgeted. In such a case, a simple comparison between the two programmers might be misleading and thus might have to be extended to include a comparison with budgets or other factors.

Another method of analysis is called analysis of variance, in which the source of the variations between budget and actual results is identified. Three kinds of budget variances are price, volume, and mix variances. Price variances occur in expenses when the price we expected to pay for some item of expense proves to be different from what we actually have to pay. When applied to income, which is done less frequently, "price variance" refers to a difference between the fee an organization expected to charge and what was actually charged. Volume variances occur because the actual volume of

	Per Course Budgets	Per Annual Budget	Better (Worse)
	Number of Programs		
Cindy	25	24	1
Debbie	30	29	1
Programmers 3 - N	208	197	11
Total	**263**	**250**	**13**
	Number of Students		
Cindy	602	594	8
Debbie	650	675	(25)
Programmers 3 - N	4,973	4,756	217
Total	**6,225**	**6,025**	**200**
	Income		
Cindy	$289,788	$282,744	$7,044
Debbie	295,590	264,654	30,936
Programmers 3 - N	1,294,522	1,092,202	202,320
Total	**$1,879,900**	**$1,639,600**	**$240,300**
	Course Margins		
Cindy	$168,900	$159,468	$9,432
Debbie	154,978	145,789	9,189
Programmers 3 - N	802,822	793,264	9,558
Total	**$1,126,700**	**$1,098,521**	**$28,179**

FALL COURSE INVENTORY COMPARED TO BUDGET, ARTS AND SCIENCES

EXHIBIT 12.2

	Actual	Per Annual Budget	Better (Worse)
Number of Programs			
Cindy	23	24	(1)
Debbie	29	29	0
Programmers 3 - N	200	197	3
Total	**252**	**250**	**2**
Number of Students			
Cindy	580	594	(14)
Debbie	659	675	(16)
Programmers 3 - N	4,901	4,756	145
Total	**6,140**	**6,025**	**115**
Income			
Cindy	$275,689	$282,744	($7,055)
Debbie	290,145	264,654	25,491
Programmers 3 - N	1,299,887	1,092,202	207,685
Total	**$1,865,721**	**$1,639,600**	**$226,121**
Course Margins			
Cindy	$163,789	$159,468	$4,321
Debbie	150,578	145,789	4,789
Programmers 3 - N	809,159	793,264	15,895
Total	**$1,123,526**	**$1,098,521**	**$25,005**

FALL ACTUAL ACTIVITY COMPARED TO ANNUAL BUDGET, ARTS AND SCIENCES

EXHIBIT 12.3

Programmer: Cindy
Course : 1

	Actual	Budget	Better (Worse)
Enrollment	32	25	7
Fee income	**$8,000**	**$7,500**	**$500**
Direct Expense			
Promotion	$945	$800	($145)
Teacher Compensation	1,300	1,200	($100)
Direct supplies & expense	850	600	($250)
Total direct	**$3,095**	**$2,600**	**($495)**
Course margin	**$4,905**	**$4,900**	**$5**

COURSE ACTUAL COMPARED TO COURSE BUDGET

EXHIBIT 12.4

	Actual	Annual Budget	Better (Worse)
Number of programs planned	24	24	
Number of programs cancelled	1	2	1
Cancellation rate	4%	8%	
Programs carried	23	22	1
Enrollment (Carried programs)	580	594	(14)
Average Class Size	25.22	27.00	(2)
Fee Income	**$275,689**	**$282,744**	**($7,055)**
Direct expense			
Promotion	$11,567	$12,158	($591)
Teacher compenstion	56,780	55,135	1,645
Direct supplies and expense	43,553	55,983	(12,430)
Total direct	**$111,900**	**$123,276**	**($11,376)**
Course margin	**$163,789**	**$159,468**	**$4,321**

COMPARISON OF ACTUAL WITH BUDGET, CINDY, FALL

EXHIBIT 12.5

	Actual 199A-B	%	Budget 199A-B (Exhibit 1.3.3)	%	Better (Worse)	Actual Last Year	%	Better (Worse)
Number of programs	2,590		2,435		155	2,260		330
Number of enrollments	63,250		60,125		3,125	56,079		7,171
Fee Income/revenue	$24,231,900	100%	$23,981,079	100%	$250,821	$22,886,789	100.00%	$1,345,111
Direct expenses								
Promotion	$2,635,461	11%	$2,205,793	9%	($429,668)	$2,156,788	9.42%	($478,673)
Instructor compensation	6,033,743	25%	6,380,682	27%	346,939	5,980,634	26.13%	(53,109)
Supplies and expense	2,253,567	9%	1,864,386	8%	(389,181)	1,913,298	8.36%	(340,269)
Total direct	**$10,922,771**	**45%**	**$10,450,861**	**44%**	**($471,910)**	**$10,050,720**	**43.91%**	**($872,051)**
Gross margin	**$13,309,129**	**55%**	**$13,530,218**	**56%**	**($221,089)**	**$12,836,069**	**56.09%**	**$473,060**
Departmental expense								
Payroll	$3,988,127	16%	$4,047,135	17%	$59,008	$3,951,238	17.26%	($36,889)
Supplies and expense	1,305,677	5%	1,345,268	6%	39,591	1,302,865	5.69%	(2,812)
Promotion	440,755	2%	480,585	2%	39,830	385,093	1.68%	(55,662)
Equipment	102,455	0%	94,479	0%	(7,976)	56,422	0.25%	(46,033)
Other	1,300	0%	(5,000)	-0%	(6,300)	(4,997)	-0.02%	(6,297)
Total departmental expense	**$5,838,314**	**24%**	**$5,962,467**	**25%**	**$124,153**	**$5,690,621**	**24.86%**	**($147,693)**
Available for indirect costs	**$7,470,815**	**31%**	**$7,567,751**	**32%**	**($96,936)**	**$7,145,448**	**31.22%**	**$325,367**
CE organization indirect costs								
Payroll	$4,187,900	17%	$4,352,612	18%	$164,712	$4,041,899	17.66%	($146,001)
Supplies and expense	4,789,234	20%	4,849,699	20%	60,465	4,752,788	20.77%	(36,446)
Equipment	256,788	1%	197,174	1%	(59,614)	156,433	0.68%	(100,355)
Internal recharges	(2,083,655)	-9%	(2,081,734)	-9%	1,921	(1,986,445)	-8.68%	97,210
Total indirect costs	**$7,150,267**	**30%**	**$7,317,751**	**31%**	**$167,484**	**$6,964,675**	**30.43%**	**($185,592)**
Addition to CE reserves	**$320,548**	**1%**	**$250,000**	**1%**	**$70,548**	**$180,773**	**0.79%**	**$139,775**

ACTUAL RESULTS COMPARED TO BUDGET AND PRIOR YEAR

EXHIBIT 12.6

	Budget 199A-B	Actual 199A-B	Better (Worse)	Actual Prior Year	Better (Worse)
Income					
Department 1 (Arts & Sci.)	$6,683	$6,503	($180)	$6,321	$182
Department 2	1,693	1,666	(27)	1,594	$72
Departments 3-N	15,605	16,063	458	13,786	$2,277
Total	**$23,981**	**$24,232**	**$251**	**$21,701**	**$2,531**
Expense-Program Depts.					
Department 1	$4,343	$4,224	$119	$4,371	$147
Department 2	1,196	1,174	22	1,192	18
Departments 3 - N	10,874	11,363	(489)	10,367	(996)
Total	**$16,413**	**$16,761**	**($348)**	**$15,930**	**($831)**
Available for Indirect Costs					
Department 1	$2,340	$2,279	($61)	$1,950	$329
Department 2	497	492	(5)	402	90
Departments 3-n	4,731	4,700	(31)	3,419	1,281
Total	**$7,568**	**$7,471**	**($97)**	**$5,771**	**$1,700**
Less Service Departments					
Director's and Personnel	$879	$830	$49	$799	($31)
Business and MIS	1,462	1,412	50	1,380	(32)
Registration	1,156	1,123	33	1,100	(23)
Classroom	1,975	1,911	64	1,677	(234)
Marketing	815	800	15	756	(44)
Other	1,031	1,074	(43)	983	(91)
Total	**$7,318**	**$7,150**	**$168**	**$6,695**	**($455)**
Increase (Decrease) in Reserves	**$250**	**$321**	**$71**	**($924)**	**$1,245**

DEPARTMENTAL SUMMARY (IN THOUSANDS)

EXHIBIT 12.7

activity (usually the number of courses or enrollments) is different from what was budgeted. A mix variance occurs when the budget estimate of volume is based on a particular proportional combination of elements that is different from the proportion actually achieved. A mix variance can be considered a special combination of price and volume variances. The formulae for computing price and volume variances are as follows:

Price variance: (Actual price per unit – Budget price per unit) x Actual volume

Volume variance: (Actual volume – Budgeted volume) x budget price per unit

Exhibit 12.4 illustrates each of these variances. Adjusted income for this course was $500 more than what was budgeted. This is a favorable variance because it will produce a larger bottom line than was anticipated. However, this favorable variance is smaller than we might have expected because seven more students enrolled than was anticipated. The cause of this favorable variance was the larger than expected enrollment partly offset by the lower than expected fee. We can analyze this variance by using the following formulae for computing the variances (note that $300 was the original fee for the course but we actually charged $250):

Volume variance (32 – 25) x $300=$2,100

The increased number of enrollments created a favorable variance of $2,100. However, the fee charged was not as high as had been budgeted. We can also compute the price variance as follows:

($250–$300) x 32=$1,600

($90–$100) x 310=-$3,100

The unfavorable price variance of $1,600 combines with the favorable volume variance of $2,100 to produce the net favorable variance of $500.

These same techniques can be applied to expenses. For fixed expenses (that do not vary with the number of enrollments), the analysis is fairly straightforward. In Exhibit 12.4, instructor compensation shows an unfavorable total variance of $100. This variance could have been caused by paying one or more of the instructors at a rate higher than anticipated, which would be a price or cost variance. Alternatively, it could have been caused by adding one lecturer to the program and paying him or her $100; this would be a volume variance, where "volume" refers to the number of instructors. It could also have been a combination of factors, say, additional instructors but lower payments to each instructor.

For variable costs, the issue is more complex because the volume we are talking about is enrollments. Going back to our original example (Exhibit 12.4) and looking at "other direct expenses," we see a net unfavorable variance of $511. To analyze the variance, we first must determine its fixed and variable components. For our purposes, let's suppose that promotion and instructor compensation is fixed and that the supplies and expense category is completely variable. Our analysis would show the following:

	Actual	Budget	Variance
Fixed	$2,245	$2,000	($245)
Variable	850	600	(250)
Total	$3,095	$2,600	($495)

$245 of the total unfavorable variance of $495 relates to fixed expenses. This variance could be analyzed in the same way we analyzed instructor compensation. The budget estimate for variable costs was based on 25 enrollments at $24 per enrollment ($600), but the actual variable costs turned out to be $850 for 32 enrollments, or about $26.56 per enrollment. Again, the total variance consists of a volume variance and a price variance.

Volume variance: $(32 - 25)$ x $24=$268 (unfavorable)

Price variance: $($26.56 - $24)$ x $32=$82 (unfavorable)

These two variances, added together, equal the total unfavorable variance of $350. These variances are unfavorable even though they are mathematically positive values. This is because we are dealing here with expense, and an increase in expense over budget decreases the margin.

This last example illustrates one of the problems of analyzing variances. The "unfavorable" volume variance of $168 was caused by seven more enrollments than had been anticipated, and it was more than offset by the favorable volume variance in revenue of $2,100. When variable cost budgets are exceeded because there are more enrollments than were expected, it is usually a positive rather than negative sign. A budgeting system that does not take this into account and imposes negative sanctions on programmers for exceeding line items of variable expense without relating those excesses to the increases in revenue associated with them is too rigid and will subvert the goals of the organization.

SUMMARY

Developing an MIS for a CE organization provides the feedback and control that is an integral part of the budgetary process, even though the information gathering takes place after the budget has been prepared. For the budgeting process to be effective, it must operate all year, serving as both a standard and a planning tool.

Feedback and control systems in CE organizations must meet certain criteria and be devised with certain considerations in mind. First, they must coincide with the forms and categories that structured the budget so that actual results can be compared to the budget. Second, a feedback and control system must be developed with the needs of the users (programmers and managers) in mind. It should provide accurate and timely information in a form and at a level of detail sufficient for managers to make informed decisions. Too much information, an increasingly common phenomenon in our computer age, can lead to information overload and problems of interpretation. The trade-off between the cost and the benefits of a control system should be explored, and general guidelines for assessing the cost-benefit ratio of feedback systems should be developed.

In developing control systems, CE managers must take into account a number of characteristics common to CE organizations. Such organizations can rarely develop a system similar to those used in business because CE organizations are usually part of a larger institution and do not have a separate balance sheet. The practical consequences of this fact are far-reaching. The inability to deal with an operating period greater than one year severely inhibits the kind of long-range planning that is vital to the continuing financial health of an organization. Also, the self-checking aspects of the double-entry accounting system often are not available to CE organizations. In addition, CE organizations often have control systems ill suited to their particular needs imposed upon them by the parent institution. Finally, CE managers often have to make decisions without adequate and timely information.

CE organizations may be involved in either fixed resource or variable resource budget contexts (or some of both). The structure and methods of budgeting in these two contexts differ, although the differences are not as great as traditional literature on the subject suggests. Fixed resource organizations have their resources "given" to them at the beginning of the budget period, and their main budgetary goal is to neither underspend nor overspend this budget. Most service organizations and governmental or quasi-governmental agencies fit this pattern. Variable resource organizations must earn their resources as they go, much like a traditional business.

Budgets are either static, prepared for only one level of activity, or variable, prepared for a range of activity. Although variable budgets provide a greater range of detail for analysis, they are time-consuming and expensive to administer. Analysis of variance techniques, used to isolate price, volume, and mix variances, are important tools in helping managers discover the underlying reasons for exceptional (higher or lower than budget) performance.

CHAPTER 13

Designing and Implementing an ABC System

This chapter fills in the final part of the picture we have been drawing of the CE management information system of the future. No CE organization is now using an activity-based costing (ABC) system. ABC is new and not widely understood, even in manufacturing industries where it was first applied. Thus, the explanation here is not based upon the actual experience of CE organizations, but is an illustration and experimental application of the principles of ABC to the CE situation to help guide practical uses of ABC. The previous chapter described one possible application of MDB using ABC; this chapter offers a hypothetical application of ABC to two elements of a mid-sized CE unit—programmer activity and an element of a service activity.[1]

DESIGNING AN ABC SYSTEM

The design of an ABC system begins with a clear organizational strategic plan and an understanding of management objectives. The design process can be seen as a series of choices. "The challenge for designers of an ABC system is to choose resource categories, activity centers, and cost drivers that provide a level of detail that matches the needs that managers have for information."[2] An additional challenge is to assure that the design leads to an easy, correct, and "natural" interpretation. The objective is to trace all the uses of resources (costs) to their sources; the sources are categorized as products, customers, or strategic goals.

Designers will confront several characteristics of ABC systems early in the process. First, any defect or ambiguity in the strategic planning process or in the statement of managerial objectives will be revealed. As the early choices are made about how products and customers are defined and as costs are traced to strategic objectives, gaps in the planning process will appear. These gaps can be filled by either revisiting the planning process in light of what ABC has revealed, or the ABC system can simply work around these gaps by placing all untraceable costs into an "other" category. This latter category can then be analyzed as an indicator of where better planning or thinking needs to be done. A second characteristic revealed by ABC is that all organizations, even similar CE organizations, are different. They are differentiated by their purposes, plans, and managerial orientations, and these differences must be recognized in the ABC system. CE organizations also have different levels of product and volume diversity (terms defined below) and different relative costs of aggregating data. These differences make any discussion of ABC difficult.

A third and important characteristic of ABC systems is that they pull the designer and implementers into a comprehensive reconsideration of organizational processes. This characteristic has both positive and negative aspects. It is positive in that it has the potential for improving operations by identifying those processes that are either unnecessary or consume resources disproportionate to organizational goals. It is negative in that it can push designers into excessive levels of detail or into a reengineering process that can consume the organization for a long period of time, perhaps delaying the implementation of an ABC system. Most CE organizations have thousands of processes, many more than would be cost-effective to analyze. To counteract this negative aspect, designers should concentrate on significant costs and on the relevance rather than the precision of information. It is better to have the right detail than to have more detail. Greater detail adds complexity and cost, and can cloud interpretation. The goals of an ABC design should be simplicity, ease of access to cost data, timeliness of information, and ease of interpretation.

Design of an ABC system follows some defined steps that will be mirrored to some extent in the implementation steps described in the next section.

1. Determine resource categories and develop fully costed departmental system
2. Define activity centers and key activities
3. Choose and determine the number of cost drivers
4. Define reports and design reporting system

Determining Resource Categories and Developing a Fully Costed Departmental System

In most CE organizations, this step is already accomplished. Resource categories, sometimes called "first stage drivers," are usually defined by what we have called "line items." "Instructor compensation" and "promotion costs" are examples of resource categories. Most CE organizations will also have a departmental system that assigns costs to departments. This departmental grouping of costs combined with the resource grouping provides the framework and a starting point for further analysis.

Defining Activity Centers and Key Activities

The work of CE organizations could be broken down literally into thousands of activities. The purpose of the ABC system is not to develop cost data for each of these activities. Rather, ABC attempts to recognize and track the activities *that cost the most* or are most important to the organization. These activities are performed in units called activity centers—units in which costs are grouped. One first example of an activity center is our programmer Cindy. The activities she performs take place in her activity center in the department of Arts, Letters, and Sciences. These activities are listed in Exhibit 7.3 on page 113.

A second example of an activity center can be found in the activities of a service department, such as the Registrar's Office. In our CE organization, the Registrar's Office registers students over the telephone, provides information to students, keeps student records, issues transcripts, schedules rooms, and performs a number of activities called "program processing." Each of these functions might be considered an "activity center." Our example activity center is "program processing," in which several functions are performed. All courses are assigned unique numbers, and the information about the courses (time, location, special needs, and teacher) are checked for accuracy, consistency, and proper recording on the computer system. The course description, outline, and instructor information is checked and then sent to the appropriate place for approval. Once approved, the program processing unit signals everyone that the course is official and can be offered to students.

These two examples illustrate some of the principles important in selecting activity centers. First, both sample activity centers are *relatively consistent with the departmental system*. In both cases, the activity centers are within existing departments defined by the traditional responsibility structure. Creating activity centers out of more than one department is difficult. For instance, one of the activities of the Registrar's Office is "providing information to prospective students." This activity is performed in many places in the organization, including the marketing department and all the program departments. It would probably be impossible to add up all the costs of providing information to prospective students in any meaningful way. Thus, no activity center could be created for this activity.

Activity centers should have *relatively homogeneous processes*. For instance, suppose the same people who worked in program processing also prepared, audited, and submitted travel vouchers for reimbursement. Creating an activity center called "program and travel processing" would not make sense. The two activities are so different that grouping them makes interpretation difficult. A corollary of this principle is that activity centers should be *driven by different activities*—no two activity centers should contain similar activities.

Activity centers should have *sufficient magnitude* to be worth tracking. For instance, if program processing could be performed by a half-time employee, making it an activity center, or analyzing it into its separate key activities, would probably not be worth the effort. Rather, we would look for another activity with which it could be associated. For instance, we might combine it with room scheduling and treat them together as an activity center.

Where possible, activity centers should be defined so that the activities within them do not serve more than one of the three stages of cost accumulation—product, customer, or strategy. As we will see, our Cindy example violates this principle and complicates our analysis.

Defining activity centers and key activities is perhaps the most time-consuming and exacting step in the ABC design process. Identifying core business processes can be an extensive undertaking requiring "thinking outside the box." The best sources for help in defining key activities are the people who perform the activities. While a review of procedure manuals and job descriptions might be helpful, the definitive source for information about activities will come from interviews with employees. Again, this process can take time and tends to draw the interviewer/designer into operational audits verging on reengineering projects. The designer of an initial ABC system should resist the temptations that present themselves and get on with the project. Later, when the first iteration of the ABC system is in place, reengineering projects can be defined with greater efficiency by concentrating on those activities that will yield the most savings or better service.

Defining and Determining the Number of Cost Drivers

Cost drivers (sometimes called "second stage cost drivers") are the factors that increase costs. Conceptually, a cost driver causes a cost. For instance, in our program processing activity center, a key cost driver might be the number of courses offered because each course offered must be processed by the activity center. Cost drivers usually have a linear relationship to activity costs: The greater the number of units a cost driver contains, the greater the cost. Putting it another way, if the cost driver were to disappear, the cost could be eliminated.

The way in which cost drivers are defined and the number of cost drivers selected will have a major impact on the complexity of the ABC system. For instance, in program processing, we might start with one cost driver defined as "number of courses offered." However, an analysis of the activities performed by program processing might indicate that credit courses took substantially more time to process than noncredit courses. We might then decide to create two different cost drivers: "number of credit courses offered" and "number of noncredit courses offered." In making this distinction, we have perhaps improved our accuracy and generated some useful information about an important aspect of our resource allocation structure, but we have also increased the complexity and cost of maintaining our system. Similarly, in our Cindy example, we have decided to track "number of new courses" instead of simply "number of courses offered." Cost drivers may be simply volume of items or volume combined with attributes. Adding the attributes "credit" and "noncredit" to the pure volume of "courses" changed the character of the cost driver in the example above.

A number of considerations are required in the selection of cost drivers. The designer must consider *the availability of data versus the cost of obtaining data*. For instance, it may turn out that program processing will spend a significant amount of time on course and teacher packets sent to campus departments for approval. While it might be interesting and useful to know how much the activity cost and how many follow-ups had to be undertaken each year, keeping track of this time and the number of follow-ups might be difficult and costly to obtain. On the other hand, the number of courses offered, including the credit, noncredit breakdown, is relatively easy to come by.

Another consideration in choosing cost drivers is the *correlation of data with the resource consumption versus the cost of error due to poor correlation*. In the Cindy example, we know that some new courses take much more time and effort to develop than others. Thus, the cost driver "number of new courses" might not provide the accuracy of data we want. For instance, in one year, most of the new courses Cindy offered might have been developed by others and simply offered for the first time in Cindy's market area, requiring little time and effort on Cindy's part. The next year, Cindy might engage in a major development effort herself, spending a lot of time developing new courses. In this case, "new courses offered" does not provide the information we need and may lead to poor decisions. We might want to identify "already developed elsewhere" or "borrowed" courses as a cost driver.

A final difficult consideration has to do with the *effect of the cost driver on behavior* (the value of positive behavior versus the cost of negative behavior). A cost driver may influence behavior if individuals believe that their performance will be evaluated based upon the cost driver. For instance, while determining the cost of new program development is valuable information, charging the costs of development to a new program may discourage new program development. Similarly, charging more for the processing of a credit course may encourage the development of noncredit courses. Depending on the circumstances and the goals of management, both examples may be positive or negative. The undesirable effects of cost driver selection can be overcome through management practices outside the ABC system—the performance review and reward system and sound communication between management and the affected employees about the measurement system. The director of CE might communicate clearly that programmers will be rewarded in part according to the number of new programs they develop, thus counter-balancing the possible negative effects of choosing "number of new programs offered" as a cost driver. ABC shares this feature with traditional methods. While it can provide a rational explanation for cost and cost accountability, ABC requires constant reinforcement from management to be successful.

Tied to the decision about what cost drivers are selected is the decision about the number required. The largest single source of complexity in any ABC system is the number of (second stage) cost drivers. Therefore, the designer of an ABC system must answer the following question: How many cost drivers do I need? The answer depends primarily on the complexity of the organization. If an organization has many products, serves many markets, and has many channels of distribution, it will need a relatively complex system.

A significant portion of organizational complexity derives from three sources—product diversity, the relative cost of activities, and volume diversity. In the financial context, products are diverse when they consume activities in different proportions. In our example, we have assumed that new courses are much more expensive to produce than previously offered courses. Courses requiring complex audio-visual arrangements, multiple instructors, or off-campus locations are also generally more expensive to produce than courses without those requirements. If a CE organization has significant numbers of new and complex courses, it has high product diversity and may require more cost drivers.

The relative cost of an activity becomes a factor in the number of cost drivers when one activity consumes a significantly higher percentage of the costs of any activity center. For instance, if the cost of processing credit courses in our program processing unit consumed 55 percent of the total costs of processing activities, and processing noncredit courses consumed 45 percent, we might not need more than one cost driver ("number of courses offered") because the information we would get by differentiating the courses would not make much difference. However, if processing a credit course took twice as much time and effort, two cost drivers would be necessary.

Volume diversity describes the differences in the volume of products produced. This kind of diversity is highly relevant in manufacturing where lots of different batch sizes are associated with set-up costs. An example drawn from CE might refer to the differences in the number of courses produced by different programmers. Some programmers may be able to offer 120 courses per year and others only 60. The difference in activity of each programmer needs to be reflected in the choice of cost drivers. The lower number may be in a rapidly changing field needing relatively high and expensive new development activity, or the courses may be more complex to develop and produce, or the programmer may have fewer "borrowed" offerings. In any case, the difference in volume needs to be analyzed and the number of cost drivers adjusted to the reality of the situation.

Other relevant factors in determining the number of cost drivers are the intended use of the system, the availability of resources, and the desired accuracy. An ABC system can be adjusted to many levels of use; it does not have to be a monolithic system tracking every cost to its source. For instance, it may be restricted simply to the product level, seeking to assign to courses only those costs associated with courses and placing all other costs into an "other" category. Or it may be used to track only one of several strategic objectives. If such tracking is the intention of management, the number of cost drivers can be adjusted accordingly.

Resource availability is also important. Adding complexity through the increase in cost drivers increases the cost of the system. Computer systems may have to be expanded, and people will need to be trained in greater depth in more complex systems. On the other hand, greater accuracy *may* be gained by adding cost drivers as activities are analyzed more closely and assigned more appropriately. A balance must always be struck between the possibility for higher accuracy and the cost of obtaining that accuracy in resource output and clarity of interpretation.

Defining the Reports and Designing the Reporting System

Implicit in much of the discussion thus far has been the notion that management needs certain information on a timely basis and that this information will be reported in useful ways. Thus, the kinds of reports needed by management drive much of the design of the system, and the selection of reports and standard ways to query the data is an important design task. As with each step in the design process, significant differences may exist among CE organizations with regard to report format. Exhibits 11.1 through 11.6 in Chapter 11 are examples of some reporting formats that might be useful in many CE organizations.

IMPLEMENTING AN ABC SYSTEM

Separating the design from the implementation of an ABC system is somewhat artificial because the design usually involves an organized effort to collect data and examine processes and activities. Robin Cooper, who has done extensive studies of ABC systems in action, divides the implementation of ABC systems into two stages.[3] The first stage is the making of some "up front decisions." The second stage is a structured approach to designing and implementing a system proceeding in several steps.

Preliminary Considerations and Decisions

An ABC implementation plan can be successful only if a number of factors are present. The plan should have the support of top management, the methods and rationale for ABC should be understood by all who will use the system, and the system should be accessible to and "owned by" those who will use it. Because of this emphasis on users, implementation of an ABC system incorporates significant levels of training, consensus building, and team work. From her study, Cooper has identified six decisions that should be made prior to implementing an ABC system.

1. Should the new system be a "stand alone" system or should it be integrated into the existing system? In many CE organizations, the integrating option is simply not available—existing systems do not have the capacity to deal with ABC. However, it may be possible to use some parts of existing systems in an ABC model, particularly those parts dealing with accounting for individual courses as cost objects.

2. Should a formal design be approved before implementation? The implementation of an ABC system can be an extremely large project involving the "reengineering" of large segments of organizational processes or it can involve relatively restricted areas of activity. Implementing an ABC system usually involves thinking about current practices and policies and then refining the new approach as aspects of organizational processes reveal themselves. (In such a situation, developing a fully conceived design before ABC implementation begins may be impractical.)

3. Who should "own" the final system? An ABC system is a management system, not a financial system, and should be given high value by managers. The selection of people in the organization for training and for developing the design and carrying out the implementation of the plan is of key importance both in terms of staff function and morale.

4. How precise should the system be? Greater precision is gained at greater cost. For instance, we might allocate programmer time on the basis of time sheets prepared by each programmer setting forth how the day was spent in half-hour increments. This process might yield great precision but might be intolerably burdensome to programmers and costly to summarize and report. In contrast, programmer time might be allocated on the basis of an interview or a budget sheet filled in once a year with time estimates from the programmer. This would certainly be less precise, but it would cost much less and perhaps yield valid data for decisions.

5. Should the system be based on historical or future costs? The greatest benefit from ABC will derive from calculations based on estimates of future costs, but this may not be possible, particularly at the beginning.

Historical costs are usually available and easy to obtain and may be an acceptable surrogate for future costs, particularly in stable financial conditions.

6. Should the initial design be simple or complex? One approach to the introduction of ABC is to analyze processes and activities in great detail and then simplify the analysis by combining like processes in accordance with decision models. Another approach is to start with a less complex conception of the organization and refine it by adding detail as it appears desirable to do so. Deciding which approach to use depends heavily on the amount of resources available—the complex start approach will require much more time and effort.

Implementation Steps

Implementing an ABC system might be described as taking an organization apart and putting it back together again. Designing the ABC system is a step in implementation as well as a process dependent upon later steps; in effect, redesign is a constant need.

Step 1: The ABC Team Seminar. CE management must first identify a group of people to be responsible for implementing an ABC system. This group should understand the purpose and role of ABC in the organization and should become familiar with the design concepts listed above. The group should also be clear about the strategic objectives and the vision of the CE organization.

Step 2: Defining the Cost Universe. The design and implementation of an ABC system must have a starting point defined as a statement of the total revenue and costs of the CE organization. For our illustration, we are choosing the statement first provided in Exhibit 3.2 (on page 33) as our starting point and universe.

Step 3: Select Major Product, Customer, and Managerial/Strategic Cost Categories. Because the premise of ABC is that every use of resources in an organization can be traced to either producing a product, serving a customer, or furthering a goal of management, product and customer groups and strategic organizational initiatives must be defined. In our example, product (course) and customer costs are combined into three groups—regional public, international, and contract. We are also addressing two strategic initiatives—happy workforce and efficient operation. Ultimately, all the costs of the organization will be assigned to these five elements or to an "other" category that becomes a focus for management attention.

Step 4: Assign First Stage Product (Course) Costs. In our discussions and illustrations, we have assumed that the CE organization has used individual courses as cost objects and is able to assign at least promotion and classroom costs directly to individual courses. Most CE organizations have systems that do this kind of tracking of costs either to individual courses or to groups of courses. This method provides the needed data for the first assignment of product costs. Courses should be grouped or categorized in a way consistent with the customer groupings because course costs must ultimately be assigned to customers. This first cost assignment, illustrated in Exhibit 11.2 (on page 209) down to the gross margin line, does not require activity analysis and gets these costs immediately out of the way so that the team can concentrate on the remaining costs.

Step 5: Identify Core Processes/Activities. The remaining costs are associated with activities that either increase the value of the product, serve a customer, further management objectives, or add no value to the organization. These activities have to be defined and identified with their objectives. Activity centers and key activities within them need to be identified at this step. This identification can be accomplished through interviews or management studies of one kind or another. We have already seen examples of this defining process. In Cindy's activity center (and those of her programmer colleagues), the core processes were defined to include "new program development," "marketing," "professional development," and so on. In our program processing activity center, "course approvals" was a core activity.

Step 6: Determine Cost of Activities. Once activities have been defined, their full costs must be determined. Much of the answer can be found in the traditional cost accounting system. A notable exception is often the cost of employee time. Cindy's salary is a significant cost element in her cost center and must be allocated among the various activities she performs. She (and we) will probably have to estimate the amount of time she spends on each activity. In other cases, we might be able to observe how the time is being spent through sampling or other techniques.

Step 7: Identify Cost Drivers. Each activity has one or two cost drivers that need to be identified. We have already discussed this process at some length. Again, "number of courses offered" and "number of students enrolled" are examples of cost drivers.

Step 8: Determine Volume of Cost Drivers Associated with Each Activity and Compute Activity-Based Costs. Once cost drivers have been defined, we have to establish their volume so that we can determine the relationship between costs and cost drivers. This is usually accomplished by dividing the total estimated cost of the activity by the number of cost drivers associated with it. Thus, we might determine that the total cost of processing credit course approvals each year is $85,600 and that we process about 1,712 course approvals per year. Thus, it is costing us, on average, $50 for every course approval processed. Similarly, if Cindy expects to devote $46,607 of effort to produce 12 new courses next year, the cost of development per course is $3,888.

Step 9: Develop Product (Course) Service Costs and Assign Them to Products, Customers, or Strategic/Management Initiatives. Now it should be possible to assign all costs to a particular product, customer, or initiative. Each activity has been defined, costed, and associated with its appropriate cost object (course, customer, initiative). Worksheets can be completed to show how all costs are assigned and helpful schedules, such as the cost driver scoring table shown in Exhibit 7.7 on page 119, can be prepared to guide administrators and program planners.

Steps 2 through 9 are described in Exhibit 13.1. This exhibit shows the iterative nature of the process, which really does not proceed in orderly steps but rather develops a cost model that gets more refined and accurate as more data are examined.

Step 10. Develop Recharge Mechanism, Algorithms, and Reporting Mechanisms. Once the cost structure and assignment architecture have been determined, methods can be devised to report, control, and use the data generated. ABC is designed to provide information to managers as they make decisions. The cost driver scoring table for course budgeting is an example. Using this table in the course budgeting process provides programmers with a way to calculate the effect of their decisions on the entire organization. Accumulated cost data can point the direction toward improvements and opportunities.

Step 11: Test and Refine the System. Does the system work? Are all costs accounted for? How useful is it? How can it be made more useful? Can important elements be reconciled? Does it make sense? Will people use it willingly and actively? These questions need to be answered after the first period of implementation. Adjustments will undoubtedly have to be made. Often, as the logic of the ABC system becomes more apparent to people, and as problems and wasteful practices are revealed, the desire for further refinements and greater detail will increase so that testing becomes part of a continuous process of improvement.

Each of the steps listed above has been only briefly described. It is not the purpose here to model a full-scale project management process for implementing ABC complete with suggestions about how a project team might go about its business. Rather, these steps flow from the logic of making a transition from a traditional CE management information system to an ABC system.

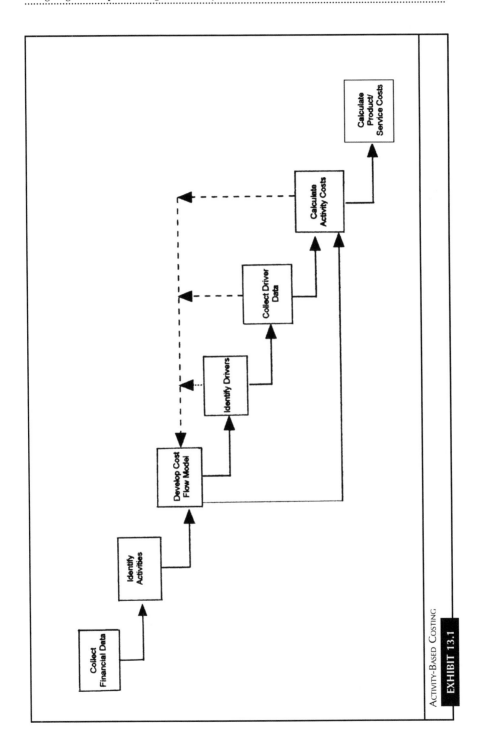

ABC COST ASSIGNMENT EXAMPLES

To illustrate the cost assignment process (steps 7 through 9 above), we will continue to use our two examples—the responsibility center designated as Cindy (programmer 1), and the program processing activity of the Registration activity center. We can build upon the analysis we have done of these two examples.

Exhibit 7.3 on page 113 shows the departmental (indirect) costs for Cindy's responsibility center assigned to activities. Cindy first estimated the time she would spend on each of the designated activities and assigned her payroll costs as well as other costs (e.g., supplies and expense, departmental promotion) to activities based on this estimate. This estimate is shown in the total column of the exhibit. Then cost drivers were defined for each of the activities and the costs were assigned to the strategic categories based on the volume of the cost drivers. For instance, Cindy estimates that she will develop 12 new courses next year, six new public courses and three new courses in both the contract and international categories. The total development cost of $46,607 is therefore distributed to the three categories based on the notion that, in general, each new course will take the same time and effort to develop—the cost of that effort will be $3,884 per course. Marketing costs might be assigned based on the number of special brochures or promotional pieces that are expected to be produced. Presentation and evaluation costs might be assigned based on the number of courses *presented* (85). The cost of presentation per course is about $157 ($13,316/85), so the cost of presentation assigned to public courses is $10,966 ($157 x 70). These assignments, made in the programmer's budget/responsibility center, can then be added together to create the strategic budget shown in Exhibits 11.2 (page 209) and 11.6 (page 213). From budgets prepared in this way for each programmer, activity budgets can be prepared by adding the costs of a particular activity together, using the same "build-up" method illustrated in traditional budgeting that used the course as the cost object. For instance, CE managers would be able to see how much has been budgeted for new program development and how many new courses are expected, and then be able to track actual results against the budget.

The assignment of program processing costs is illustrated in Exhibit 11.4 on page 211. First, the total costs of the activity were calculated ($274,800). Then it was determined that about 60 percent of the time and effort of the program processing unit ($167,800) was devoted to processing new programs and that it cost about twice as much to process new credit programs than new noncredit programs. The remaining costs of the unit ($107,000) were devoted to routine processing of all courses. Again, routine processing for credit courses called for about twice as much effort as processing noncredit courses. It was then determined that programmers expected to produce 514 new courses, of which 325 would be for credit, and expected to offer 2,568 courses in all, about two-thirds of which would be credit courses. When these volume estimates are applied to the costs, cost driver amounts can be calculated as shown in column one of the exhibit. These cost driver amounts are then published in a cost driver scoring table, such as the one shown in Exhibit 7.6 on page 118. This scoring table represents the algorithm to be used in assigning costs to courses (products).

ABC ON YOUR OWN

These two examples, one from a program department and one from a service department, are intended to illustrate the most basic applications of ABC, applications from which greater aggregations of detail may be built. I have indicated how such aggregations can be accomplished under the traditional model of budgeting, which uses the course, rather than an activity, as the cost object. This traditional treatment is a sound model for the way in which ABC-based budget and financial monitoring systems can be aggregated. A full-scale illustration of the application of ABC to a full CE organization is beyond the scale of this book, and probably beyond the capability or need of any CE organization. In several places in this book, the point has been made that ABC may be usefully applied in limited situations. However limited or expansive the application of ABC, the basic steps listed in this chapter should be followed. But ABC cannot be applied "by the numbers." Each situation is made different by the large number of possible variables. You may expect to encounter significant issues, particularly in the first, conceptual stages of implementation. You will soon discover that applying ABC to your CE organization is more art than science, a challenge that forces a reexamination of the kind of information you can best use because it expands the realm of the possible. Within that new realm is the competitive advantage CE organizations need to prosper in the future.

NOTES

[1]The material presented in this chapter is based upon a review of the literature of ABC as adapted to the CE situation. I have relied most heavily on Michael C. O'Guin's *Activity Based Costing* (Prentice Hall, 1991) and the writings of Robin Cooper and Robert Kaplan.

[2]George J. Beaujon and Vinod R. Singhal, "Understanding the Activity Costs in an Activity-Based Cost System," *Journal of Cost Management* 4, no. 1, (Spring 1990): 71.

[3]Robin Cooper, "Implementing an Activity-based Cost System," *Journal of Cost Management* 4, no. 1, (Spring 1990): 33.

PART FOUR

• • • • • • • • • • •

Special Issues in Continuing Education Information Management

P art 4 applies the theories and practices described earlier to several issues of concern to CE professionals, particularly CE managers. Chapter 14 addresses such issues as allocating overhead in traditional systems and evaluating the cost-effectiveness of promotion expenditures. Chapter 15 discusses accounting for and managing investments in such long-term projects as special facilities (computer labs) or educational products using new instructional technology that are expected to span more than one operating cycle. After reading Part 4, you should be able to

- know and evaluate the several methods of allocating indirect costs to cost objects in the traditional systems of budgeting and financial control;
- understand how to determine the cost-effectiveness of promotion efforts;
- know how to manage and account for long-term investments in facilities and programs; and
- understand the management information issues associated with investments in new instructional technology and distance learning.

CHAPTER 14

Indirect Costs and the Cost-Effectiveness of Promotion Expenditures

ndirect cost allocation methods and promotion expenditures have such significance in CE organizations using traditional methods of budgeting and financial control that they deserve a full discussion. With regard to indirect costs, activity-based costing is largely an effort to eliminate the need for indirect cost allocation schemes. ABC seeks to assign all costs on the basis of their ultimate purpose, thus eliminating indirect costs. However, until ABC becomes much more generally applied, how to determine and allocate indirect costs will be an important subject for CE managers. Further, because the CE organization is itself frequently the object of indirect cost allocations from the parent, a thorough knowledge of the theory and practice of dealing with "overhead" is valuable. This chapter will help you understand the ways in which indirect costs can be allocated to operating units or cost objects, and it will spell out the effects different allocation methods are likely to have on the behavior of members of the CE organization. The chapter will then turn to a discussion of promotion expenditure assessment.

WHAT ARE INDIRECT COSTS?

Organizations differ widely in what they decide to classify as indirect costs. One, for example, might treat all telephone expense as an indirect cost to be allocated to courses, perhaps proportional to the total direct expense of the course; another might require that long distance charges be assigned to courses as a direct cost. However, some common categories and examples of indirect costs can be cited.

An indirect cost pool is a group of naturally associated indirect costs that will all be allocated on the same basis. For instance, the indirect portion of telephone costs in the example just cited might be naturally associated with other kinds of office costs, such as supplies, office machine maintenance, reproduction charges, receptionist salary, office rent, subscriptions, and office janitorial service. One common and obvious category of indirect cost pools is service or overhead departments. All costs associated with a given department are often allocated as one pool or total. Of course, these pools can be combined to form even larger pools, and it might be appropriate to do so where several departments are to be allocated on the same basis. For example, registration, student records, and the cashier's office might be combined and allocated on the basis of number of enrollments. Other cost pools may be more difficult to identify. Programming departments have indirect costs of their own. Some CE units count programmers' salaries among indirect costs.

Another category of indirect cost pools is line item pools—costs that generally show up as line items on a budget. For example, administrative rent or classroom rent, where the rent charge is fixed over a specified period, may have to be spread over a number of cost objects. Colleges and universities also tend to treat fringe benefits as a separate line item overhead charge. Many line item pools present special difficulties because they require sequential allocation. For instance, as service departments all take administrative space, they incur administrative rental costs. Rather than allocating administrative rent directly to courses, it may make sense to allocate rent first to all departments, including the service departments, adding rent costs to the departmental costs, and then allocating total departmental costs, including rent, to the final cost objects.

All this complexity may evoke the question: Why bother? Why do indirect costs have to be allocated at all? Not making allocations is discussed later in this chapter. Indeed, in traditionally funded CE organizations—those more or less subsidized or those with fixed resources—indirect cost allocations are not required and would not be as useful as they are in self-supporting CE units. But it is worth the trouble to allocate indirect costs, even when it is not required, because such allocations allow an organization to carry out the "full cost" concept. Full costing in CE has the advantage (or, sometimes, the disadvantage) of displaying to all levels of the decision-making hierarchy, including, most importantly, the programmers, the total costs of courses and the relationship of the parts of the organization to the whole. Making the comprehensive financial structure of the organization concrete can have a positive effect on morale and the quality of communication.

Used wisely and with care, indirect allocation can also be an effective management tool. If indirect costs are built into the financial planning of every course, the organization is less likely to come up short at year's end. In financially self-conscious organizations, furthermore, the manipulation of indirect cost allocation algorithms can be effective in directing decisions. For instance, the elimination of the assessment of indirect costs to courses presented in rural areas may encourage more extensive programming in those areas.

CRITERIA FOR SUCCESSFUL ALLOCATION OF INDIRECT COSTS

Discussions, even arguments, about overhead allocations are so common that the term overhead has gained a negative connotation. Almost by definition, overhead costs, since they are not directly associated with the production process, are "unproductive." In organizations large enough to be segmented into departments, rivalries and resentment sometimes develop along departmental lines, and these rivalries may deepen when an income-generating department is "charged" for the costs of a service department. Resentment may increase further because allocations always carry with them a certain arbitrariness and are always, in some sense, unfair. Negotiations concerning overhead can be protracted, hard fought, and divisive, which makes them expensive to the organization.

Allocations can also be expensive in a more direct way. They require records, calculations, paperwork, clerical operations, and system design and operation. The more fair and equitable the allocation system is, the more complex and costly it is likely to be.

But by far the most important problem facing managers trying to design an indirect cost allocation system is that of avoiding distorted behavior caused by the system. An appropriate allocation method should reinforce behaviors that advance the goals of the organization and discourage those that do not. Allocation methods can become symbolic and frequently troublesome beyond their proper function. They can be misread and misunderstood, leading to unintended effects. The method and the rationale behind the methods should, therefore, be clearly articulated, and management should continually monitor the effects on decision making. When they make sense, exceptions should be made to the allocation rules. Courses that show a substantial margin before being burdened with overhead, or courses important for other than financial reasons, are possible candidates for such exceptions. A good allocation method avoids most of these problems by being

- consistent with the goals and objectives of the organization and leading to budgeting, financial, and programming decisions.
- viewed as fair and legitimate by those who must follow it.
- rational and easily understood.
- easy to calculate and inexpensive to operate.
- integrated with the budget and financial control system.

METHODS OF ALLOCATION

Three main categories of indirect cost allocation methods are available to CE managers—transfer pricing, cost allocations, and non- or "hidden" allocations. Within each of these general categories are a number of options.

Transfer Pricing

Strictly speaking, transfer pricing is not an allocation method at all; rather, it involves turning an indirect cost into a direct cost. A transfer price is the price of a good or service used in recording the passing of that good or service from one part of the organization to another. Thus, a service department using transfer pricing resembles an outside vendor, although there can be some significant differences. A common difference is that the internal department is often given a monopoly within the organization; other departments are not allowed to go to outside suppliers, as is possible in the open market. Another difference from the open market is that management can set the transfer price.

Transfer pricing can be used effectively where there is a clearly defined good or service provided, where a rate sheet or a pricing schedule can be developed, and where the using department can be easily determined. A reprographics department, a promotion department, a computer services department, and a classroom facility all are potential candidates for the transfer pricing method because their products can be identified. The director's office is not a good candidate because the "product," called management or administration, is hard to define and its consumption is hard to attribute to operating units. (I was tempted to end that last sentence with "because no one knows what the director does.")

The most significant advantage of transfer prices is their flexibility and the immediacy and directness of their effect. They can be set high to encourage efficiency, low to encourage use, or anywhere in between, and they can be changed frequently, often simply by publishing a new rate sheet. Transfer prices can be calculated in many ways.

Full Cost Plus Markup

This method requires that all costs of operating a service department, plus an amount in excess of cost of operation, be allocated to the products of the department. This method has the advantage of being similar to the method employed by outside vendors in arriving at prices, so that under some circumstances, especially where outside vendors offer comparable services, the relative efficiency of the internal operation can be judged by comparing its prices with those of outsiders. This comparison should be done with care, however, since the outsider cost structure may be significantly different from that of the internal department. For instance, internal departments may not have financing, promotion, or tax expenses, and they may be subsidized in other ways. Also, this method provides no incentive to service department management to keep costs low and remain efficient.

Budgeted Cost

Under this method, transfer prices are based on budgeted costs, with the goal being to "breaking even" at the year's end. This method has the advantages of being well integrated with the budget system and of having a clearly defined standard of success. Large deficits or surpluses indicate clearly that budgetary adjustments must be made. Transfer pricing based on budgeted costs is most appropriate where operations are relatively stable from year to year and no basis exists for external comparison. However, where budgeted costs are subject to debate and negotiation, they may not be a good basis for transfer prices. In cases where significant changes in the volume of activity may result in volume variances, prices based on budgeted costs may be off the mark. In most situations, budget-based transfer prices do not provide incentives for savings and efficiency.

Budgeted Cost Plus Markup

This variation of the budgeted cost method attempts to introduce the profit incentive. It has the advantage of providing a cushion (the markup) against a deficit, with the possible accompanying disadvantage of being unfair to the buyer (user). Performance can be judged by the size of the surplus (if any) at year's end.

Market Prices

Where service department products (including services) are similar to those offered by outside vendors, and where market prices for the products are easily determined, market prices can be used as transfer prices. Pegging transfer prices to the market has some clear advantages. First, it can reduce price-related user complaints, because prices are established by external forces. Second, it will bring quality issues to the surface. If a better product is available for the same price on the outside, management will hear about it. Third, it provides clear information on inefficient operations. If a service department loses money at market prices, something is wrong. The disadvantage of market-based transfer prices is that market prices, which must build in a profit and provision for costs not normally incurred by internal audits, may not be a good measure. A relatively inefficient operation, allowed to charge market prices but not subject to market cost structures, might continue undetected for a long period. Another difficulty is that true market prices are sometimes hard to determine. Outside vendors may "low ball" prices charged to a large organization in the hopes of securing business, raising prices after a relationship has been established. Furthermore, when market prices are used, the temptation is to make overly simple comparisons between outsiders and the internal department that may not recognize the hidden costs of dealing with outside vendors, such as the lack of control over quality and scheduling of work and the paperwork and administration that may be required. Internal units may also have less incentive to show loyalty to the internal department.

Negotiated Prices

Transfer prices arrived at through negotiation have the theoretical advantage of having the approval of the parties involved. Their disadvantages are that negotiations can be time-consuming and divisive and the prices arrived at may not provide management with a good standard for judging the operating efficiency of the service department. Since prices may or may not reflect the cost structure of the department and may or may not be set in a consistent manner from period to period, operating results will not tell a clear story.

Combination of Transfer Price and Pro Rata Allocation

Service department costs should sometimes be allocated through both a transfer price mechanism and an allocation scheme. This combination is common where, for the good of an organization, a service department must be subsidized or run at a loss or where a transfer price reflecting the full cost of operations would price the department out of the market. For instance, with advances in printing technology, small-scale printing or reprographics operations are becoming less and less economical because the cost of new equipment is growing, requiring higher volumes of work to justify the investment. However, to assure a dependable and timely source of promotion and course material reproduction services, CE management may want to maintain a printing operation. Under these circumstances, the transfer price should be made equal to prices set by outside suppliers, placing any deficit resulting from the use of this price "on the overhead" for allocation on another basis. Similarly, to encourage the use of a new classroom facility, management may set classroom rental rates artificially low, absorbing the excess of costs over (internal) income in some other way. It may also be appropriate in some cases to separate service department fixed costs from variable costs, using transfer prices to cover variable costs and allocations to cover fixed costs. Thus, the user department is charged directly for its use of the service, but "ready to serve" costs are distributed through overhead allocations.

Transfer pricing can be an effective management tool for making a service department more accountable. For instance, a large university recently placed its computer operations on a recharge (or transfer price) basis, removing the appropriation to support the computer center from its own, separate budget, while at the same time increasing the operating budgets of the computer user departments. Theoretically, this change made the computer center view users as customers rather than supplicants and thus forced it to become more responsive to user needs.

A counterbalancing disadvantage of transfer prices is the frequent difficulty of calculating them. This difficulty is especially true where there is a large "mix" of products or services. Thus, it may be fairly simple to compute an average "per impression" charge for a printing operation by dividing the total costs of the operation by the estimated total impressions produced. However, this average may not be a fair price because small jobs are more expensive per impression than large jobs due to setup and preparation time. Setting a price on this basis may encourage users to go outside with the large jobs the service department needs to keep its cost per impression down. Further, the printing operation may do other things—binding, cutting, folding—that are part of some jobs and not others, and to burden all jobs with the cost of these special services may not be fair. However, the process of computing fair transfer prices, despite its difficulty, can force service department management to examine operations for inefficient and costly processes that otherwise might go unnoticed. For many service operations, transfer pricing is an obvious and useful option.

Cost Allocations

Once indirect costs have been determined and cost objectives defined, a basis for allocation should be chosen. The allocation basis determines how indirect costs are to be grouped or pooled.

Fixed Cost Bases

Indirect costs can be made to behave either as fixed costs or as variable costs, and the choice can have profound effects. Fixed cost allocations usually specify a dollar amount per cost object or are tied in some way to existing fixed costs. For instance, we might allocate director's office costs to programs by dividing the total costs of the office by the total number of programs offered. We would then charge each course, say, $300. Alternatively, we might take an existing direct fixed cost, say, personnel costs, and allocate some indirect costs (e.g., telephone or office supplies) to total personnel costs. Fixed cost allocation methods are usually easy to compute and apply, and the rationale for their application is easily understood.

Another characteristic of fixed cost allocations is that their influence on decisions is either absent or subdued; they tend to "drop out" of calculations. If every course were charged $300 for director's office indirect costs, such allocation would play no part in deciding which course is more promising financially. This can be either an advantage or disadvantage. Indirect costs should often not play a part in decisions about courses or about the efficiency of departments because programmers and department managers rarely have any control over these costs. On the other hand, when programmers and department managers ignore the effects of their decisions on indirect costs, the organization as a whole and the operations of particular service departments can be adversely affected. For instance, an allocation method that charges every course $200 for the services of the registration office might encourage programmers to program high-enrollment, low-fee courses because they are not required to recognize that the costs of registration are tied to the number of students who will be registering.

Variable Cost Bases

Variable indirect cost allocation bases mean that the amount of overhead allocated to a cost object varies with the volume of activity, which becomes the basis for allocation. A few of the more common bases of variable cost allocation and the possible effects of employing them are listed below.

- **Number of Students (Enrollments).** Some indirect cost pools are naturally associated with the number of students or enrollments. Registration costs and cashiering costs are obvious cases. Generally, a "per student" cost is calculated and charted to each responsibility center or course. The more students that enroll, the higher the indirect cost charged. This calculation makes programmers aware of the real costs involved in registering the students. It is easy to compute, apply, and understand, and it has an air of fairness about it. Heavier users are charged more. However, it tends to discourage the presentation of high-enrollment courses because high per student charges force fees higher, thereby tending to reduce enrollments where there is elasticity of demand and, at the same time, decreasing the reward to the programmer for a successful program. Also, where registration services are underutilized and cannot be varied to meet changes in workloads, per student charges may act against the interests of the organization. A per student rate may also hide some inequities. For instance, credit enrollments may cost more to process than noncredit enrollments, since more care, more record keeping, and more counseling may be necessary. In such a case, student record-keeping costs might be segregated in their own cost pool and allocated to credit enrollments alone; or two rates, one for credit and one for noncredit courses, might be calculated.
- **Number of Courses.** Some costs, like program processing costs, classroom use costs, and perhaps administrative costs and certain types of indirect promotion costs, might be assigned to responsibility

centers on the basis of the number of courses offered (or attempted). This method is "variable" only for cost objects involving a grouping of courses; by the time such costs are allocated to individual courses, they behave like the fixed allocations previously described. Like the per student allocation basis, the per course basis can be adjusted for a variable mix of course type. Here, too, the credit or noncredit categorization may be most appropriate, or other categories, such as course format, geographical location, number of credit hours, or subject matter, may lead to a more equitable distribution of indirect costs. Per course allocations, like per student allocations, are easy to compute and understand and can result in fair division of costs. However, especially when they are assessed against attempted courses, such allocations may encourage a reduction in course offerings and discourage valuable risk taking by programming staff.

• **Percentage of Income.** Dividing the total (actual or anticipated) indirect costs in a particular pool by the total (actual or anticipated) income yields a percentage by which indirect costs can be allocated on the basis of income received. This simple, widely used method is especially useful where large-scale allocations must be made. Income is usually a readily obtainable figure, and in some systems it is known more accurately and earlier than any other factor, including number of enrollments. It can often be projected more accurately for the overall operation than other elements. In most instances, it can be used as a surrogate for the number of enrollments because it tends to vary proportionately with the number of enrollments.

However, this allocation method has some decided weaknesses. First, it appears to penalize behavior that would normally be encouraged, that is, the generation of income; second, it can result in significant inequities. Course fees are often artificially raised either to cover abnormally high costs or for the convenience of the student. For instance, a travel course fee may include a provision for student travel and accommodations. The full fee will be recorded as income in such a case but will include an element of cost that "passes through" the organization to the supplier of the services. Under the percentage of income method, this kind of course would bear an artificially high overhead burden, or else the income of the course would be scrubbed of the "pass through" element, a cumbersome task subject to error. Furthermore, the amount of income is directly associated with few, if any, elements of indirect cost. For example, it costs just as much to process a $35 enrollment as it does a $1,000 enrollment; low-fee courses therefore enjoy an unearned advantage under this allocation system, while high-income courses with the potential of generating a significant excess of income over expense may be penalized.

- **Percentage of Direct Expense.** This percentage is calculated in the same way as percentage of income, substituting total direct expense for total income. Certain indirect cost pools, like the business office, which processes invoices and other items associated with expense, and perhaps the director's office, are naturally associated with total direct expense. When indirect costs are applied on top of direct costs, an incentive exists to keep direct costs down, so desired behavior is rewarded. However, total direct costs have the disadvantage of being difficult to forecast, and actual direct expenses are usually determinable only late in the game when all the costs of a course are in. Furthermore, this method shares some of the inequities of the total income method: The cost of dealing with expense-related operations is more a function of the number of transactions than of total dollar volume. A high-cost program that brings in a healthy margin before overhead is applied can be completely smothered by this method.
- **Specific Items of Expense.** Overhead costs can sometimes be applied on the basis of specific items of expense. For instance, indirect promotion costs might be applied on the basis of direct promotion costs on the theory that the higher the direct costs, the more the indirect services were utilized. The cost of the personnel office might be applied on the basis of total direct salary expense or total number of full-time equivalent (FTE) employees. Direct labor cost or number of FTEs is a common basis for allocations because both can be associated with a variety of indirect costs, from whole service departments (director's office, personnel office) to line items (telephone expense, office supplies). This method can be effective where a direct relationship exists between a direct and a legitimate indirect cost. When it is used, however, programmers and managers generally try to keep direct cost as low as possible. This tendency may be positive, but it may also discourage the proper mix of program expenditures, say, in the promotion area, thus hurting some programs.
- **Program Days, Contract Hours, or Hours of Use.** Sometimes indirect costs are allocated on the basis of the period of instruction. This basis is usually appropriate for allocating overhead costs associated with the use of a classroom facility or a computer lab. Actual hours of use is usually the best basis to apply, but other measures that are surrogate for hours of use, such as number of credit hours (contact hours for noncredit programs) or number of days the course will meet, may also be appropriate. This allocation basis is fair in the sense that heavier users are charged more, and it is easily understood and calculated. However, where certain facilities are underutilized or management wishes to encourage the use of facilities, this allocation basis may not be the best. This method also requires that the hours of

use be recorded in a manner that may be difficult or expensive because measurement of such hours is not part of the normal financial recording system in the way enrollment or income figures are.

There are many more bases of allocation besides these more common ones. In an effort to arrive at fair allocations, some organizations have developed elaborate formulae, often combining two or more bases in a weighted average. But the more elaborate and complex the allocation method, the more expensive it is to calculate and understand. As with most management decisions, the choice of an indirect cost allocation method involves careful weighing of alternatives.

Non- or "Hidden" Allocations

In a large CE organization, charging all courses or responsibility centers on the same basis is often unfair. We might reasonably expect the business and management and engineering departments to contribute a larger proportion of their income to covering overhead costs than the community service and adult literacy departments. Trying to reflect this difference in the allocation scheme itself can raise problems, including organizational jealousies, excessively complex allocation formulae, and creation of "second-class citizen" departments. To avoid these problems, management might set "available for overhead" targets for each department based on a realistic expectation about what that department might be able to produce rather than on a predetermined formula. In this approach, management would calculate the total amount needed for overhead (including a cushion or contingency) and then apportion that amount among the responsibility centers. This method closely resembles the fixed cost allocation method. It places most of the burden for fairness on the subjective judgments of management, and its effectiveness will be related to the accuracy of those judgments.

In a few fixed resource organizations, especially those receiving full or partial support or subsidy, formal indirect cost allocations may not be required or necessary. However, to test the accuracy of management's assessment and to reveal the true contribution (and cost) of each center, some allocation method or methods should be employed. Allocations can be made in memo form or in special financial statements. The disadvantage of the latter procedure is that it shrouds overhead costs in mystery and relieves responsibility centers of the need to understand or help pay for indirect costs.

OTHER CONSIDERATIONS

Timing and Sequence of Allocations

Transfer prices and allocations may be computed in advance, on the basis of estimates (usually budgetary estimates or the experience of the immediately prior fiscal period), or in arrears, on the basis of actual figures. The advantage of computing allocations in advance is that the transfer price or allocated charge is known at the beginning of the period and can be used throughout the period, guiding decisions and facilitating accounting and financial reporting. The disadvantage is that an adjustment will probably be necessary at the end of the period to correct the estimates to the actual figures. The advantage of setting prices or allocations at the end of the period is that no such adjustment is necessary. However, using the latter method means that information on the effect of indirect cost allocations is not known during the budget period.

Determining the sequence of indirect cost allocations is especially important where several allocation methods are used. Until now, we have assumed that indirect costs are allocated immediately to the final cost object, either the programming department or the course. In reality, most indirect cost pools are added to other indirect costs. For instance, where administrative rent is assessed, all departments, including the service departments, should be assessed for the space they use. Similarly, the costs of the director's office should be borne by all the departments subject to the director's administration. Thus, allocations follow a certain sequence. First, the most universal indirect cost, rent, should be allocated to all departments on its allocation basis (perhaps square feet occupied). Then the director's office costs, which now include the cost of rent, are allocated on their basis (perhaps number of FTEs), and so on until all indirect costs have finally been allocated to the programming departments (or the courses). If all the rent were directly allocated to the programming departments, some of the intermediate allocation schemes and their carefully constructed purposes would be bypassed.

The advantage of a sequential allocation is that the full integrity, continuity, and rationale of the allocation process can be maintained. The disadvantage is that such a method can be complex and difficult to calculate. It also assumes no reciprocal relationships between service departments. For instance, the director's office may use the services of the personnel office, and, of course, the personnel office is administered by the director's office. Which department should be allocated to the other? Fortunately, in a CE organization such reciprocal relationships are usually few and relatively unimportant, so no large inequity will result from ignoring them.

Allocating the Cost and Value of Programmer Time

Finally, let us turn to the allocation of programmer time. (See Chapter 5 for a discussion of the two components of programmer time—cost and value.) Theoretically, the best way to handle both the cost and the value of programmer time is to charge each directly to the cost object, the course. (The discussion of ABC and MDB in Part 2 contains a full description of this theoretical objective.) An accurate direct system for charging payroll and opportunity costs to courses can be valuable to programmers, helping them allocate their time and decide which courses to develop. It is also an important factor in determining the ultimate profitability of a course. In practice, however, such direct charging is rarely done because it requires too much record keeping and time keeping or is too subject to estimation to be useful. Programmer time, despite its proximity to the course, is most often treated as an indirect cost.

The most common method of allocating programmer time as an indirect cost is the use of a per course basis. The total payroll cost of the programmer and related clerical staff is divided by the number of courses to be offered. This method at least allows financial assessment of an average of programmer time spent per course, a measure that can be easily understood and to which a realistic assessment of the actual time spent can be compared. For instance, a programmer planning a new course in a new subject area that can be offered only once would expect to spend more time in developing the course than the average and would therefore look for a higher potential return on that course. A variation on the overall average per course allocation is to divide courses into different categories and allocate different amounts per course to the different categories. For instance, previously offered courses might be charged less than new courses because new courses will take more time and effort. Although it might discourage new course development, the method could still be a useful aid to planning. Of course, the most desirable method is to assign programmer costs to courses based on the principles of ABC.

Because people work in different ways and think about their work differently, and because programmer productivity is related to so many factors, the treatment of programmer time is a touchy subject. For some workers, time is not really a good measurement of productivity, effort, or value; rather, their creativity and their ability to respond to the world around them are of value to the organization, and these abilities can never be quantified. Still, all of us have an interest in managing our time more effectively, and the system that can achieve this will pay good dividends.

ASSESSING THE COST-EFFECTIVENESS OF PROMOTION

Effective allocation of organizational resources to promotional efforts is an important and difficult CE managerial activity, primarily because the success of the enterprise is often determined by the success of marketing and promotional efforts; income and thus the bottom line depend on the number of people who know about and then are attracted to courses. Promotion costs have a number of other characteristics that make them important and hard to manage.

Characteristics of Promotion Expenditures

Promotion costs are sunk or up-front costs. They must be expended before there are any real indications that a course will be successful. They are often a significant portion of the CE expense budget, typically ranging from 10 to 20 percent. They are likely to be highly discretionary, and decisions about promotion are likely to be decentralized. Promotion costs are also important to CE management because responsibility for promotion decisions rarely resides with one individual. However, the characteristics that most demand the attention of CE management are the unpredictability of promotion results and the lack of obvious standards by which to judge the success or failure of promotion efforts. How much should be spent on promotion? How many enrollments should result from a particular promotion effort? These questions cannot be answered without experience and the use of both "hard" and "soft" evaluations.

Determining the cost-effectiveness of promotion involves the following steps:

1. Identifying costs
2. Attributing results
3. Choosing and calculating methods of measurement
4. Interpreting measurement

Identifying Costs

Many promotion costs can be identified easily, but identifying all the costs of promotion is impossible. CE managers must define the level of detail upon which they will base their definition of promotion cost. This definition should make clear which costs will be directly associated with a promotional campaign, which will be indirectly allocated to it, and which will not be recorded at all. Paradoxically, the unidentifiable costs and the results that cannot be properly attributed often lead to an effective promotion system. Each promotion campaign places the institution's name in front of people, automatically increasing recognition of that name and, in effect, promoting all course offerings. While results must be defined in relation to a particular campaign, the *total* promotion effort is larger than the sum of its parts, and any measurement of individual campaigns will leave something out.

Attributing Results

Just as costs of a particular promotion effort must be identified so must the results of that effort be identified. Most attribution schemes rely on a "tracking" system to add up responses and enrollments for each defined promotion effort. Untracked or "mistracked" responses are unavoidable. As a rule of thumb, schemes unable to track more than 65 percent of the responses or enrollments are likely to produce misleading data. Measures of promotion effectiveness usually assume that untracked responses are distributed among alternatives in the same proportion as tracked responses. In spite of the limitations and problems of interpretation associated with tracking systems, such systems are useful, even indispensable, in measuring promotion effectiveness.

Measuring Effectiveness

Once data are collected, we can begin to make analyses. Even before the data are accumulated, however, we should have a clear idea of our purpose so that we can choose appropriate evaluation measures. No one measure can answer all our questions, and usually the more analyses we make, the more questions we will encounter. A common error is to invest one measure with more importance than is appropriate.

Prospective Measures

Measures of promotion effectiveness are either prospective or retrospective. Prospective measures are made before promotion actions are taken. Because they deal with estimates of costs and results, they do not, in a sense, measure anything real. They are used primarily to compare one or more proposed alternatives of action. Often they are incorporated into or are reflected in the budget process. Typical prospective measures are reward/risk ratios and the cost of reaching 1,000 people or households (cost per thousand).

Retrospective Measures

Retrospective measures determine the results of past promotion expenditures, but their real purpose is to predict the future. Their usefulness is based on the assumption that the past is a good guide to the future, a notion that must be tempered by judgment. Retrospective measures can be divided into gross measures and detailed measures.

- **Gross Measures.** Gross measures determine the effectiveness of large aggregations of costs and results. They are designed to help managers form overall judgments of effectiveness rather than decide on specific promotion strategies. Perhaps the best overall gross measure of promotion effectiveness is the ratio of total promotion costs to total income. This measure works best with larger organizations where the nature of the courses offered changes little from year to year and variables tend to average out. A cost/income ratio of from 10 to 20 percent is fairly common for a self-supporting, non-degree-granting CE organization. This ratio is most useful when it is employed to compare the effectiveness of the same organization from one year to the next.

- **Detailed Measures.** Detailed measures are often structured as comparisons between promotion alternatives: Which of several radio stations is most effective in generating enrollments? Is it better to advertise a particular course in a general catalog or in a special brochure? Answers to questions like these can be determined most accurately by using a combination of some or all such measures as response ratios (responses/people reached), cost per inquiry, conversion ratios (enrollments/responses), cost per enrollment, and repeater rates.

Usually, the more measures used to calculate promotion effectiveness, the more accurate the results. However, all measures, even when used collectively, suffer from certain problems of interpretation. For instance, some expensive marketing campaigns can bring in enrollments in high-margin courses (contribution margin effects), the real effect of one campaign can be felt later on (spill-over effects), a high percentage of untracked items can cloud interpretation, repeater rates may not be available, and a host of unidentified costs and influences may distort interpretations.

Developing Informed Intuition

Evaluating the cost-effectiveness of promotion expenditures is hardly a science. There is no substitute for being close to students and potential students, knowing from personal contact what is important to them, what they need and want, and how to talk to them. All the quantitative techniques, questionnaires, and statistical analysis in the world cannot substitute for this kind of knowledge. However, it is important to accumulate and analyze promotion data in a comprehensive and organized way and at the same time to recognize the need to develop, exercise, and retain the intuitive skills of the organization's members. No definite formulae exist for achieving this kind of capability, but here are some suggestions that might be helpful.

Those involved in evaluating promotion effectiveness should have an understanding of both the usefulness and the limitations of the data and the measures they use. Each promotion decision should be viewed as an experiment. To gain the most from this experimental approach, the promotion decisions must be recorded when they are made, and the results of the decisions must be measured and recorded in some way that can be used later. Another technique is to carefully define criteria for a successful campaign in advance. Developing a priori criteria focuses attention on the questions to be answered, which can be helpful in planning the "experimental" promotion campaign.

SUMMARY

Intuition, the seat-of-the pants "feel" that guides so many decisions in CE promotion, can be aided by the use of quantitative techniques. CE managers need to establish a framework for gathering and interpreting information about promotion effectiveness. Key to that framework are individuals whose experience and analytic skills help build an institutionalized base of "informed intuition" to guide promotion decisions. Experienced CE managers understand that no matter what methods are used to allocate resources to promotion and to evaluate promotion expenditures, they can never know for sure that good decisions are being consistently made. These decisions are a matter of art, not science.

CHAPTER 15

Investments in Continuing Education: Beyond the Current Operating Cycle

Some of the most important decisions CE managers have to make involve long-term investments in facilities or programs, the expenditure of funds to produce value in future operating cycles or fiscal periods. Such investments might be made for tangible property like buildings, leasehold improvements on rented facilities, or equipment, or they might be for intangible property such as computer programs or systems development, the rights to media, or the development of programs, including but not limited to programs using such new instructional technology as computer-aided instruction. Decisions related to such investments are important because they often involve the expenditure of significant funds, signal new directions for program development, and predict audience preferences. Because they anticipate the future, they also involve considerable risk. Yet, most CE financial information and management systems are unable to soundly inform investment decisions or to report on their performance.

THE NATURE OF LONG-TERM CE INVESTMENTS

In the preceding paragraph, "tangible" and "intangible" describe different kinds of investments, but a more useful division may be the following three categories: administrative infrastructure, instructional infrastructure, and programmatic. This scheme is useful because each category defines a different relationship between the investment of funds and the realization of a return.

Investments in Administrative Infrastructure

Administrative infrastructure investments are intended to make the organization more efficient, provide better service, or, sometimes, simply enable the

CE organization to continue to operate. Such investments may be tangible or intangible. Examples are investments in enrollment systems, administrative office space, delivery vehicles, e-mail and other administrative computer systems, promotion production equipment, or, in some cases, long-range planning advice. Because these investments usually have only an indirect influence on the amount of revenue generated, they are often the last investments to be made and the hardest to assess. Because of this, such investments are sometimes forced upon the CE organization and need to be made in a hurry—the enrollment system is breaking down or the parent institution has decided to up-grade its computer systems. Administrative investments are frequently undervalued by CE professionals until serious systemic problems occur. The challenge to CE managers is to avoid serious problems by making timely investments in the administrative infrastructure even in the face of weak support for such investments inside the CE organization.

Investments in Instructional Infrastructure

Instructional infrastructure investments are intended to enhance the learning/instructional environment and are usually designed to benefit a number of programs rather than a specific program or group of programs. A few years ago, common examples were computer laboratories, classroom audio-visual equipment, libraries, and learning centers. With the advent of new instructional technologies, the possibilities for investment in instructional infrastructure have greatly expanded: investments in the use of the Internet and World Wide Web to aid instruction and facilitate communication among students and instructors; the purchase and installation of teleconferencing facilities; the establishment of servers capable of storing text and information, homework assignments, and learning exercises; and the building of multimedia course laboratories dedicated to enhancing instruction. Because these investments are made to benefit a large group of future courses, their association with specific income streams is difficult. However, because they are associated with the "products" in continuing education and intended to enhance their attractiveness, investments in instructional infrastructure can be identified with relevant courses, and recharge or transfer pricing schemes can be devised to match costs with income.

Investments in Program Development

In one sense, CE units continuously invest in program development. They must spend money and effort on the process before a course is offered and has a chance to generate income. The same situation applies to the hiring of a new CE professional; several months must normally pass before his or her efforts result in income. When such development efforts are costly and intended to produce programs that will be offered in several future terms, they should be called "investments." In the past, development of single courses rarely warranted consideration as investments because the investment was generally too small. Sometimes the development of a full curriculum was large enough to be considered an investment particularly if the development effort spanned an operating cycle. Such consideration applies particularly to independent study programs where the program offering, by design, is intended to extend over a long period of time. Now, however, with the increasing adoption of new instructional technologies, even the development of a single course can cost many thousands (even hundreds of thousands) of dollars. To justify the cost, these courses must be delivered to many students either at the same time or "asynchronously." These large-scale investments require different accounting and financial systems from those designed to deal with traditional classroom instruction. While it is relatively simple to associate such investments with specific courses and sources of income, it is frequently difficult to track both the investment and income over a number of periods.

PROBLEMS ASSOCIATED WITH LONG-TERM INVESTMENTS

Problems in this area are mostly associated with parent institution systems and those inherent in any investment decision whether in CE or in the business world.

Problems Associated with Parent Institution Systems

Several common characteristics of parent systems actively discourage long-term investments. Many CE organizations are subject to lapsing funding, which pulls any surplus generated at the end of the fiscal period away from the CE organization. Because few can use balance sheet accounts, CE organizations cannot create assets that can then be charged against revenue in future periods. These two characteristics mean that CE organizations have a hard time "saving up" for a needed investment. Also, rarely can they borrow from future revenue to fund needed investments, again not only because there may be no source of funds, but also because no mechanism exists for paying out future sums.

These parent system characteristics can distort CE management decisions even when investment funding can be found. For instance, suppose a CE unit has acquired a computer for its registration system. Usually this acquisition is made from some special fund set up specifically for such purchases (often called a reserve fund), or else it is acquired as a gift. In either case, it is "free" to the operation; no part of the acquisition cost will ever be charged against the registration operation, which has, in effect, received an unrecorded subsidy that will reduce the cost of operations for some time to come.

Registration operations will thus appear artificially cost-effective, and comparisons with other operations will be virtually impossible.

However, the registration system will eventually have to be replaced. What if there is no reserve fund or willing donor at the time? If the cost of the system had been recognized over the term of its use and reflected in the fee structure—or, even better, if the replacement cost had been so reflected—the organization might have been able to build up a reserve. At the least, the showing of deficits would have sounded a warning.

Recognizing these problems is the first step in solving them. When the benefits of a particular investment are clearly defined, most parent systems can be adjusted to permit such investments and their logical treatment. Reserves can be created, the balance sheet can be opened up to CE, and funds can be borrowed against future revenue, all with special permission or arrangements. However, even when these institutional obstacles can be overcome, a number of inherent difficulties remain in making investment decisions and monitoring their results.

Inherent Problems

While the business world, unhampered by fund accounting and other requirements imposed by most CE parent institutions, has worked out some of the mechanisms for dealing with long-term investment decisions, many problems are still unresolved. The principles of ABC can be applied to some of them.

One problem is deciding and then determining what costs should be included in a long-term investment. Such costs are said to be "capitalized," that is, segregated as a capital asset. The cost of computers and software to create a new computer lab should clearly be included in the long-term investment, but other costs may not be so clear cut or easy to determine. What about the cost of the consultant hired to help determine the best equipment or software, the administrative time involved in making and implementing the decision, and the lab monitor's time in working out bugs in the systems? A sufficiently detailed ABC system could provide some of this information.

Another set of problems is associated with the calculation, both prospectively and retrospectively, of the return on investment. The elements of this calculation are the total amount of the investment, the income expected from the investment, the additional expenses required to produce the income, and the period of the pay back. Estimating or measuring each of these elements presents problems to managers. Estimating future events is always difficult, and few accounting systems are set up to track returns on specific investments. Frequently, an investment is considered a "sunk cost," and interest in making careful calculations of returns diminishes. Unless factored into the period of the payback calculation, the risk of obsolescence is often ignored.

Finally, few investment decisions or measurement schemes take into account the time value of money.

MAKING INVESTMENT DECISIONS AND MEASURING THEIR RESULTS

Long-term investment decisions are often described as capital budgeting. Capital budgeting means planning the expenditure of funds for items that will be of benefit to the organization for longer than the budget period. Such budgeting may involve large expenditures for tangible property such as buildings, classroom facilities, or equipment, or for intangible property such as computer programs, the rights to media materials, or long-range program development. The methods of analysis described below may also be used for smaller long-term expenditures, such as audio-visual, multimedia, and small reproduction equipment.

Capital budgeting differs in several respects from the sort of budgeting examined so far in this book. First, it is often more important because it can commit the organization to a future plan of action involving a great deal of money and several years. Capital budgeting thus involves risk taking. Whereas adjustments can be made in day-to-day budgeting operations as conditions change, such quick adjustments often cannot be made with capital items. For instance, the decision to establish an instructional computer laboratory is fraught with risk: The technology might change, the market might diminish, competition might increase, software might change, and inadequate equipment, once delivered, cannot be returned. But these risks are balanced by the possibility of rewards, and this balancing is the purpose of capital budgeting. Second, capital budgeting is not so much a target against which actual results may be judged as an aid to deciding between one alternative and another. As with much of decision making, capital expenditure alternatives rarely present themselves in an orderly fashion. Should we spend $100,000 on a new computer lab? Capital budgeting attempts to put alternatives in some order and to clarify the real choices. Finally, capital budgeting deals with issues of finance, the outflow of present value for the inflow of future value. Present and future value as formal concepts are not widely addressed in continuing education.

Capital budgeting attempts to estimate the full effect of the proposed acquisition on the organization. To do this, it concentrates first on cash flows and the quantitative financial aspects of decisions. How much will the organization have to spend and when, and how much monetary return will it receive? Once these factors have been derived, the qualitative factors can be considered—better service to students, more accurate and quicker information, a more polished and professional organizational image.

Crucial to the understanding of capital budgeting are the concepts of incremental cash flow and internal rate of return. An incremental cash flow is the difference between the inflow and the outflow of cash associated with the investment. For instance, in acquiring a new registration system for $60,000, an organization may be able to sell some of its old cash registers for, say, $3,000. The incremental cash flow (in this case, an outflow) is then $57,000. This incremental flow is associated with the acquisition of the capital asset. Other flows are associated with subsequent operations related to the asset. For instance, the new registration system will have new operating costs associated with it—operator salary, systems support, paper costs, machine maintenance, and utility costs. But the new system may also save money by eliminating salaries or allowing present personnel to do other things. The difference between these two flows is the operating incremental cash flow.

The internal rate of return is the opportunity cost of any investment—the rate of return that an organization would receive by investing funds differently. It is used primarily as a benchmark against which to judge capital investment proposals. For instance, if our organization could earn a 9 percent annual return on its $57,000, then, all factors other than finance aside, the new registration system should return at least 9 percent per year. Arriving at an internal rate of return can be difficult where issues of finance are far removed from the CE organization, and they may not be relevant where the organization does not earn money on accumulated reserves. But even so, CE management should have some idea of an opportunity cost—a return goal for each investment.

Common Methods of Capital Budgeting and Capital Acquisition Analysis

Payback Method

The payback method is the simplest and the most widely used method for analyzing acquisitions. The payback period is the length of time it takes for an organization to recover its original investment through incremental cash inflows. Under the assumption of even incremental cash inflows, the formula for the payback period is as follows, where P = payback period, I = incremental investment, and CI = incremental cash inflow from the investment:

$$P = I/CI$$

Suppose we are considering the purchase of a new portable overhead projector costing $500, and are able to get a $50 trade-in on an old piece of equipment. We will be able to rent the projector to programming and other departments at $18 per day, and we figure that the cost of booking the equipment, inspecting it when it returns, and maintaining it will be $4 per booking. The payback period in this example is calculated as follows:

$$P = \frac{500-50}{18-4} = \frac{450}{14} = 32 \text{ days}$$

This calculation tells us that the investment will be "paid back" when the projector has been rented for a total of 32 days. By itself, that may be interesting information, but it is more useful if it is compared with other alternatives. For example, overhauling the old machine, say, at a cost of $200, might be an alternative to purchasing a new one. We will be able to rent the overhauled machine, because it is an older model, at only $15 per day, and we expect that higher maintenance needs will raise the cost of fulfillment to $6 per booking. In this case, the payback period is calculated as follows at 22 days:

$$P = \frac{200}{15-6} = \frac{200}{9} = 32 \text{ days}$$

If other things are equal, we will choose to overhaul the old machine because that investment will be paid back in a shorter period. Of course, we may need to consider nonmonetary factors: the new machine might be easier to use, create a better impression of our organization, aid in generating good will with instructors, or provide images of better quality. Also, the overhauled machine may not have much survival value and may soon break down.

Dealing with uneven cash flows is slightly more difficult; it usually requires a tabular analysis. Suppose we are considering the purchase of a $900 CD-ROM for our media library. We will rent it for $60 per showing. Because of the current popularity of the material, we expect to be able to rent it four times in the first month, three times the second and third months, and two times per month for the next six months. We have calculated our booking, inspecting, shipping, and overhead costs to be $15 per rental. The payback period calculated as follows, should be 8 months:

Month	Rental Income	Fulfillment Costs	Net Cash Inflow	Cumulative Inflow
1	$240	$60	$180	$180
2	180	45	135	315
3	180	45	135	450
4	120	30	90	540

Month	Rental Income	Fulfillment Costs	Net Cash Inflow	Cumulative Inflow
5	120	30	90	630
6	120	30	90	720
7	120	30	90	810
8	120	30	90	900

In the equipment rental example given earlier, the payback period was given in rental days, not actual calendar days; in this example, a calendar month is the payback period. This change is because we assumed that we had a captive market for the projector and that, whether old or new, it would be used at the same rate over the payback period. We could convert the rental day measure into a calendar day figure simply by computing how many times per month the overhead projector would be rented. Since we cannot assume this equality with other media, one CD-ROM may be booked much more often than another, booking frequency becomes an important element in the CD-ROM calculation.

The payback method has disadvantages. First, it does not take into account the useful life of the investment or its residual value at the end of that life. We would expect the new machine in the first example to last longer after the payback period than the older machine, and to have a higher trade-in (or scrap, or salvage) value. Second, it does not provide an indication of the profitability of the investment. For instance, at the end of the payback period for the older machine (22 rental days) the organization would have received $198 in surplus ([$15 – $6] x 22). After 22 rental days, the new machine would have provided $308 ([$18 – $4] x 22), and at the end of the payback period $448 ([$18 – $4 x 32). Of course, the older machine required an initial outlay of only $200 versus the $450 for the new machine, freeing $250 for additional investment. Further, the payback method does not consider the "time value of money."

Despite these disadvantages, the payback method can be useful as a screening device and for comparing parallel alternatives. It has the advantage of incorporating some measure of risk where the holding period of an asset is an important element of risk. A payback period of more than two years on microcomputer equipment, for instance, may indicate a poor investment because of rapidly changing technology.

Unadjusted Rate of Return

The unadjusted rate of return method incorporates a measure of profitability and is easier to interpret than the payback method. It is called "unadjusted" because it does not use the time-adjusted value of money. The formula for computing this measure is as follows, where R = the unadjusted annual rate of return, CI = the annual incremental cash flow, D = the incremental depreciation on the investment, and I = the incremental investment:

$$R = CI-D/I$$

Continuing education does not use depreciation but a substitute calculated by subtracting any residual value from the cost of the investment and dividing by the number of years of useful life. Although this formula is expressed in terms of years and annual rates, any period of time can be used as long as it is finally expressed as an annual measure.

Suppose we are considering the renovation of a computer lab, changing it from 386 PCs to 486 PCs. We determine that we could offer 32 more courses per year, each of which would net us $1,000. If we do this we must also pay an additional $3,000 per year in maintenance costs and drop four courses that presently net us $700 each (for a total of $2,800). The new machines would cost $70,000, and we could sell our old machines for $5,000. We estimate that the new machines would be used for four years. From this information, we can calculate each of the values for the formula as follows:

$$CI = \$32,000 - \$3,000 - \$2,800 = \$26,200$$

$$I = \$70,000 - \$5,000 = \$65,000$$

$$D = \$65,000/4 = \$16,250$$

With these values, we can calculate the unadjusted rate of return as follows:

$$R = \frac{\$26,200 - \$16,250}{65,000} = 15.3\%$$

This rate of return can be compared with other rates similarly calculated to arrive at the best investment decision from presented alternatives. Again, nonfinancial factors are not considered here but would have to be introduced before a wise decision could be made.

The disadvantage of this method, as with the payback method, is that it ignores the time value of money. For example, our $65,000 could be invested in the current year at today's prevailing interest rate. It would have interest added to the principal every year, and that sum would earn interest for the next year (that is, that sum would compound). Furthermore, the positive cash flows generated by such an initial investment could also be invested at prevailing interest rates each year and could thus earn interest.

Net Present Value Method

This method determines the present value of all cash inflows and outflows, then adds them together. A positive net present value indicates a worthwhile investment, while a negative net present value indicates that the investment should not be made. The specified interest rate may be the internal rate of return, or it may be a target rate of return (a time-adjusted annual rate of return). Using our computer lab renovation as an example, and specifying that our internal rate of return should be 14 percent (i.e., that we know other alternatives that can assure a return of at least 14 percent), we can compute the net present value of the proposal as follows:

	Years	Amount	Present Value Factor (at 14%)	Present Value
Net cash inflows	4	$26,200	2.914	$76,347
Initial investment	0	65,000	1	(65,000)
Net present value				11,347

The present value factor was obtained from a table, usually called "the present value of an annuity of one." It helps us calculate what we would have to invest now to receive an annual amount of $26,200 (principal and interest) each year for the next four years if we could invest at 14 percent interest. Since our initial investment is in the present, it has a factor of one. A positive net present value means this investment is better than the alternative of investing at 14 percent.

This investment can be compared to other proposals by using the present value index. This index is simply the present value of the cash inflows from the investment divided by the amount of the investment. From our example, the calculation would be as follows:

This index is useful because the investment with the highest net present value may not be the most profitable if it requires a disproportionally high initial outflow.

$$PVI = \frac{76,347}{65,000} = 1.175$$

The net present value method is theoretically sound and has no disadvantage except that it is more difficult to use than the previously described methods and does not give the real rate of return of a specific investment. It has the advantage of comparing alternatives to a predetermined investment target and is also flexible; in our example, we assumed an even cash inflow, but the method can be used with uneven cash inflows and outflows. Each flow need only be reduced to a present value.

Time-Adjusted Rate of Return

This method is a computation of the rate of return on an investment that incorporates the time value of money. The question it answers is simple: Using our example, what return, expressed as an annual percentage, would we get if we were to invest $65,000 today and get back $26,200 each year for four years? The formula for this calculation is as follows, where PV is the present value of the investment, F is a factor on the "present value of an annuity" table, and A is the annual annuity:

$$PV = F \times A$$

In our example we know the PV and the A and so can compute the F as follows:

$$F = \frac{PV}{A} = \frac{\$65,000}{\$26,000} = 2.481$$

By extrapolating from the "present value of an annutiy" table for four periods, we can determine that the rate of return is about 22.3 percent. When $65,000 is invested at 22.3 percent per year, the investor can get back $26,200 (principal and interest) per year for four years. This calculation finally reduces the capital budgeting decision to a single, understandable, theoretically sound number that can be compared to similar calculations for other investment opportunities both inside and outside the organization. Its disadvantage is that it is sometimes hard to calculate, especially where there are uneven cash flows. In such a situation, using tables requires a trial-and-error method of extrapolation. But, as with many complex calculations, such problems can be avoided by using computer programs designed to do discounted cash flow calculations.

Once a capital investment decision has been made, capital budgeting proceeds in theory much like any other budgeting. The assumptions that led up to the decisions are tested against reality: Was the initial investment estimated correctly? Are the cash flows what they were projected? The problem is that accounting and budgeting systems usually do not routinely track the elements of cash flow identified with an investment. Thus, except in extreme cases, decision makers often do not know how their decisions turned out and do not have this feedback to inform subsequent decisions. The challenge is to develop financial information systems that can provide feedback on long-term investment decisions on a continuing basis. An ABC system with appropriately conceptualized cost pools can provide this information.

CONCLUSION

Long-term investment decisions are likely to increase in frequency and importance in the working lives of CE managers. As CE organizations seek to provide students with a larger number of choices about what, when, where, and how to learn, the number of possible long-term investment opportunities will proliferate. In the past, these possible long-term investments were typically in administrative or instructional infrastructure categories; now they occur increasingly in program development areas. With the advent of new technology, program development requires larger and larger capital investments and larger and larger audiences to justify that investment. Spending $300,000 on the development of a course in hazardous materials management designed to be delivered electronically to individual desktop computers may well require a large investment in promotion to obtain an audience of a size sufficient to cover the cost. This increase in the scale of development and marketing efforts, the up-front, at-risk portion of the CE program budget, threatens to change the financial structure and measurement practices of the past. Small scale, risk-averse organizations may not be able to survive in every market. Long-term investment decisions are more likely than ever to be *strategic* decisions with profound implications for the future of the CE enterprise. These decisions need to be informed by careful analysis and information systems designed to support such analysis.

GLOSSARY

· · · · · · · · ·

ABC. *See* Activity-based costing.

Absorption costing. *See* Full costing.

Accrual accounting. An accounting method requiring costs to be associated or matched with the income produced by the incurring of those costs. Both costs and income must be reported in the same accounting period. *See also* Cash accounting.

Activity-based costing (ABC). A cost accounting system that assumes all costs can be assigned to activities and those activities can be associated with efforts to produce or improve products, serve customers, advance managerial goals, or reduce waste. In ABC, the cost object is an activity. *See also* Cost object.

Activity-based management. A system of management focused on the management of activities rather than on the resources activities consume.

Activity center. An entity in which the costs of a particular and defined activity take place.

Alternative level budgeting. A budgeting practice that requires budgets to be prepared according to universal assumptions, e.g., for several levels of activity or for certain increases above or decreases below the "base" of the previous budget.

Analysis of variance. A form of budget analysis designed to determine the underlying causes of variances of actual results from figures predicted by the budget. *See also* Variance.

Applications database. A database developed with a particular application in mind. *See also* Database; Subject database.

Autocratic organizations. Organizations led in a manner that discourages the exercise of initiative by those not in the top leadership.

Available for overhead. Income minus direct expenses, i.e., the amount left after all direct expenses have been covered. Also known as margin, surplus, or profit. *See also* Margin.

Balance sheet. A financial statement that lists the assets, liabilities, and ownership or fund balances of an accounting entity.

Balance sheet budgets. Budgets that project and control the values of assets, liabilities, and capital accounts or fund balances of organizations. Not frequently encountered in continuing education.

Base. Funding for the normal and continuing activity of an organization or program. Such funding can usually be considered secure from one budget period to the next. *See also* Incremental budgeting; Zero-based budgeting.

Batch mode. Accumulating data in advance and processing them into or within a computer as a group.

BEP. *See* Break-even analysis.

Break-even analysis. The determination of the level of activity (volume of sales) at which total income equal total expense. This level is called the break-even point (BEP).

Break-even point (BEP). *See* Break-even analysis.

Budget object. The item being budgeted. In this book, the budget object is usually the course (*see* Part 2), or the CE organization, or a segment of that organization (*see* Part 3).

Capital budgeting. The process of selecting and planning for the financing of the acquisition of capital items. *See also* Capital item.

Capital item. An asset or a proposed expenditure for something that will be of value to an organization for a period longer than one year.

Carrying cost. The cost of maintaining and servicing an inventory.

Cash accounting. A method of accounting for operations that focuses on the effect of the transactions on the cash balance. *See also* Accrual accounting.

Cash budgeting. The process of forecasting or planning the flow of cash into and out of an organization. *See also* Accrual accounting.

Centralized organizations. Organizations in which most important operating decisions are made by the highest management level. In the CE context, "centralized" means that jurisdiction and control over continuing education is concentrated in a single operating entity or organizational segment. *See also* Decentralized organizations.

Coded label. A database label that uses a code (letters or numbers in combination) to indicate elements of a category. *See also* Virtual label.

Collegial organizations. Organizations in which management decisions are arrived at through a process of discussion, participation, and negotiation involving a broad spectrum of the membership of the organization, including members of several levels of management. Also called participative organizations.

Commitment. A planned and definite outlay of funds that will occur before the end of the budget period. Unlike an encumbrance, it is not legally binding. *See also* Encumbrance.

Common fixed indirect costs. Fixed indirect costs that cannot be identified with the incremental volume brought by any one responsibility center. Also called "ready-to-serve" costs. *See also* Responsibility center; Separable fixed indirect costs.

Consumer surplus. The positive difference between what a consumer is willing to pay for a good or service and the actual price of the good or service.

Continuous budgets. Budgets prepared continuously throughout the year, say, every month, rather than only once. Usually, a new budget is prepared each month for the twelfth month and all other monthly budgets are updated. Also called rolling budgets.

Contribution margin. The amount over direct, variable cost produced by one additional unit sale—in continuing education, usually one enrollment.

Control structure. The sum of the methods by which management exercises control over the behavior of the members of an organization.

Controls. Checks built into a computer system that are designed to catch errors, protect data, control access to date, and prevent loss of data.

Conversion ratio. The ratio of the number of people who buy a good or service (in continuing education, the number of people who enroll in a course or program) to the number of people who express interest in it.

Cosponsorship. A situation in which more than one organization is involved in presenting a course of instruction, so that costs, income, and responsibilities must be divided.

Cost-benefit analysis. An analysis designed to compare the resources given up through a course of action with the benefits received from that course of action.

Cost center. A responsibility center in which the manager is assigned responsibility for controlling costs but not for generating income. *See also* Responsibility center.

Cost drivers. The cause of a cost or an increase in cost. An element, such as number of students, which, when it increases, causes costs to increase as well.

Cost mix. The mixture within one cost object of different categories of costs, such as fixed and variable, direct and indirect, or sunk and unsunk. *See also* Cost object; Direct costs; Fixed costs; Indirect costs; Sunk costs; Variable costs.

Cost object. The item or object for which an organization wishes to accumulate costs. In traditional methods, the cost object is usually either the course or the CE organization. ABC is based on the activity as the cost object. *See also* Activity-based costing.

Cost of goods sold. The amount of value, at cost, that an organization gives up in a sale, usually involving inventory.

Cost of programmer time. The total resources of the organization that must be given up to secure the services of a programmer. *See also* Programmer; Value of programmer time.

Cost per unit. *See* Unit cost.

Cost pool. *See* Indirect cost pools.

Cost workup method. A method of determining the price of a good or service by first determining the total cost of it and then basing the price on the cost.

Critical path method. A method for organizing the course-planning process whereby each element of the development of the course is plotted on a chart and its cause-and-effect relationship to each other element is shown.

Customer budget. The budget used to accumulate the costs of serving a defined customer group, such as "international students."

Database. A large collection of organized data accessible for use in more than one application. *See also* Applications database; Database management system; Subject database.

Database management system. A software system facilitating the creation, maintenance, and use of a database. *See also* Applications database; Database; Subject database.

Decentralized organizations. Organizations in which operating decisions are made by relatively low levels of management and responsibility is broadly delegated. In the continuing education context, "decentralized" means that continuing education is offered separately by a number of segments of the parent organization. *See also* Centralized organizations

Decision/process model. A conceptual framework for analyzing the potential financial return of a course throughout its development and implementation.

Depreciation. The amount of the cost of a capital item that is charged to the operating costs of a particular period, or the process by which the purchase of an item whose useful life will extend over several operation periods is allocated to those periods. *See also* Capital item.

Direct costs. Costs that can be directly and easily associated with (attributed to) a particular cost object. *See also* Cost object; Indirect costs.

Director. In this book, the person who is responsible for administering all or part of an organization that presents continuing education courses, regardless of actual title (dean, chair, chancellor, or whatever).

Discretionary funds. Funds remaining in the budget that are uncommitted and therefore may be expended at the discretion of management.

Distorted behavior. Behavior that runs counter to the overall welfare and objectives of the organization; such behavior may be caused by poor management or poor design of the budgetary and financial control system.

Down-side risk. The risk of loss that would arise from the complete failure of a project or course.

Economic order quantity (EOQ). The amount of inventory that should be ordered to minimize carrying and ordering costs. *See also* Inventory.

Elasticity of demand. The effect of price on the number or amount of the sales of a good or service (such as enrollments in a course). When a decrease or increase in the price of a good or service markedly affects sales, demand is said to be elastic; when changes in the price have little or no effect on the number of sales, demand is said to be inelastic.

Encumbrance. A legally executed, fully completed transaction requiring the future outlay of funds. *See also* Commitment; Expenditure.

EOQ. *See* Economic order quantity.

Expenditure. In accounting, a fully completed actual outlay of funds. *See also* Commitment; Encumbrance.

Expenditure budgets. Budgets that concentrate on where and how resources will be spent, ignoring where the funds came from and not explicitly calculating the effect on cash balances. *See also* Financial budgets.

Financial budgets. Budgets concerned with the financing of activities or with the disposition of an investment return on financial assets. *See also* Expenditure budgets.

First stage cost drivers. Generally the resources that are consumed by activities, often the equivalent of line items. Examples in CE are instructor compensation and promotion costs. *See also* Line item budget.

Fixed costs. Costs that do not vary with the level or volume of activity. *See also* Variable costs.

Fixed resource organization. An organization for which the amount of resources available in any period is fixed and known at the beginning of the period. Most subsidized CE organizations are fixed resource organizations. *See also* Variable resource organization.

Flexible budget. *See* Variable budget.

FTE. *See* Full-time equivalent.

Full costing. The practice by which the "full cost"—both direct and indirect costs—is assigned to cost objects. *See also* Cost object; Direct costs; Indirect costs.

Full-time equivalent (FTE). A measure of full-time workload against which workloads of part-time employees or students can be compared.

Fund accounting. A set of accounting rules and practices, followed by most nonprofit organizations, that segregates and accounts for expenditures according to the source of the funding of those expenditures.

Fund budgeting. Budgeting used in fund accounting to ensure that funds or groups of resources are used for the purpose for which the funds were established and that the funding limits are not exceeded.

Future value. The value of the receipt of cash in the future as opposed to the present at a specified rate of interest.

Gantt chart. A chart that shows the timing of activities and expenditures involved in a project, such as the planning of a course.

Go, no-go decision. The crucial decision about whether to go or not go ahead with the presentation of a course.

Hard money. A funding source that is relatively stable and can therefore be depended upon to fund line items, including salaries, from one budget period to the next. *See also* Line item budget; Soft money.

Hidden subsidies. Sources of funding for an activity that are not budgeted or disclosed in financial reports. In this book, hidden subsidies are resources (e.g., clerical time, office supplies) devoted to continuing education but paid from sources not formally associated with continuing education activity.

Incremental budgeting or funding. Budgeting or funding that concentrates on new activities as opposed to "base" activities or that deals primarily with increases or decreases in funding from one budget period to the next. *See also* Base; Zero-based budgeting.

Incremental cash flow. The difference between cash inflow and outflow related to a capital expenditure.

Incremental costing. A cost accounting method under which only the additional or incremental costs, rather than the full costs, associated with a cost object are attributed to it. *See also* Cost object; Full costing.

Indirect cost pools. Groupings of individual elements of indirect costs that are allocated by the same basis or method.

Indirect costs. Costs that cannot be directly or conveniently associated with (attributed to) any particular cost object. Often called overhead. *See also* Cost object; Direct costs.

Inelastic demand. *See* elasticity of demand.

Information center. Source of information that users need to make decisions. Similar to database. *See also* Database; Operations system.

Information overload. A situation in which the quantity of available information is so large that it clouds rather than clarifies issues about which decisions must be made.

Inputs. Data to be put into a computer.

Interface. The connection or linkage between two systems.

Internal rate of return. The rate of return on an investment, expressed as an annual percentage, that an organization sets as a standard against which to judge potential investment opportunities. *See also* Target rate of return.

Inventory. Usually the quantity of goods on hand to be sold, such as textbooks and course materials; courses themselves may also be regarded as a kind of inventory.

Investment center. An organizational responsibility center whose object is to measure and maximize the return on investment of a defined group of assets. *See also* Responsibility center.

Lapsing funds. Funds that will lapse if not spent or are returned to the funding source at the end of the budget period.

Lead time. The period of time between placing an order for a good or service and the time of its delivery.

Levels of financial success. Course financial break-even points, computed by calculating course costs at several levels. *See also* Break-even analysis.

Line item budget. A budget concerned mainly with the projection and control of "line items" or "natural classifications" of expense, without regard to the underlying purposes or objectives of the expenses. Examples of line items are instructional compensation, room rent, office supplies, and promotion expense. Line item budgets are used in traditional budgeting. *See also* Program budget.

Management by exception. A practice whereby management of an organization concentrates its time, effort, and attention on exceptional (usually problem) situations, segments, or processes.

Management by objectives (MBO). A strategy in which management clearly describes its objectives and assigns responsibility for meeting those objectives, then evaluates performance in terms of achievement of the objectives.

Management information system (MIS). The process or system by which information is provided to management for the purpose of making decisions.

Margin. The positive difference between the income and expense of an activity where the level of expense is carefully defined; used in this book instead of "profit." *See also* Available for overhead.

Marginal cost. The cost of producing one more item or, in CE, enrolling one more student.

Margin of safety. The "cushion" or contingency between projected revenues and projected expenditures.

Master budget. The largest, most inclusive budget in an organization.

MBO. *See* Management by objectives.

MDB. *See* Multidimensional budgeting.

MIS. *See* Management information system.

Montage funding. Funding of a particular project, organization, or entity from more than one source.

Multidimensional budgeting (MDB). A system of budgeting that seeks to plan the allocation of total resources using more than one categorization scheme simultaneously.

Multiple-source funding. *See* Montage funding.

Natural classification. Classifying or naming expenses according to the general reason for the expenditure, such as rent, instructor compensation, utilities, or promotion. *See also* Line item budget; Program budgets.

Net present value. The difference between present and future cash inflows and outflows, expressed as a present value at a specified annual interest rate.

Non-value added activity. Activities that do not contribute to the production or improvement of a product or service, or to the furtherance of a strategic initiative. In other words, waste.

Open-ended budgeting. A budget preparation policy that places no restrictions on the amount of money that can be requested for the next budget period.

Operating budget. The budget that projects and controls the day-to-day operations of an organization.

Operations system. A computerized system that serves the day-to-day processing needs of an organization, such as enrollment processing, cashiering, and mailing list maintenance. *See also* Information center.

Opportunity cost. The benefit foregone when one alternative is chosen over another.

Order cost. The cost of placing an order for more inventory, receiving and inspecting the goods, placing them in stock, and processing and paying the invoice.

Organization segmentation. The process by which a large organization is divided into smaller, more manageable parts for purposes of financial control (including budgeting) and assignment of managerial responsibility. *See also* Cost center; Responsibility center.

Outputs. Reports or other products generated by computers.

Overhead. *See* Indirect costs.

Parent. The larger institution of which a CE organization is a part.

Partial services. Services, such as registration or logistical services, that CE organizations may be called upon to provide for conferences sponsored by others.

Participative organizations. *See* Collegial organizations.

Partly variable costs. *See* Semivariable costs.

Pass-through costs. Amounts included in the fee for a course that are for cost items unrelated to instruction. They may be said to "pass through" the organization to vendors and thus cannot logically be included in income for the course. Student travel and accommodations in travel programs are examples.

Payback method. A method of capital budgeting that determines how quickly an organization will recover its investment in a capital item.

Pools, indirect cost. *See* Indirect cost pools.

PPBS. *See* Program planning and budgeting system.

Present value. The value of having cash now as opposed to later, given a specified interest rate.

Present value index. An index used to determine the relative profitability of alternative investments, obtained by dividing the present value of cash inflows by the acquisition cost.

Present value of an annuity. The present value of the right to receive a specified future pattern of cash inflows, given rate of interest.

Product budget. The budget prepared to accumulate the costs of producing or improving a particular product (in CE, usually a course).

Profit. *See* Available for overhead.

Profit center. A responsibility center in which the manager is concerned with generating income as well as controlling costs. *See also* Cost center; Investment center; Responsibility center.

Program budget. A budget that summarizes income and expense associated with a particular endeavor or responsibility center. *See also* Line item budget; Responsibility center.

Programmer. In continuing education, an employee responsible for planning or programming CE courses.

Programming department. A CE organization segment dedicated primarily to programming. *See also* Service department.

Program Planning and Budgeting System (PPBS). A budgeting system in which each budget submission requires justification of each "program" for which it seeks funding.

Project budget. A program budget covering the carrying out of a defined task. Usually project budgets span one or more operating cycles of the organization.

Promotion. The specific steps taken to get people to buy a good or service—in continuing education, usually a course of study.

Quota budget methods. Budget preparation practices that establish limits on the amount of money that can be requested in the next budget period beyond the "base." *See also* Base.

Ready-to-serve costs. *See* Common indirect fixed costs.

Relative contribution. The contribution toward the success of a project (say, the presentation of a course) as compared with the contributions of other elements.

Relevant range. The range of activity over which fixed costs remain fixed. *See also* Fixed costs.

Reorder point. The level of inventory at which more inventory should be ordered. *See also* Inventory.

Repeater rate. The rate at which new enrollees enroll in subsequent courses given by the same CE organization.

Residual value. The estimated value of a capital item at the end of its use or at its expected disposition.

Response ratio. The number of responses (inquiries or enrollments) produced by a promotion campaign, divided by the number of people (or households) estimated to have been reached by the campaign. The resulting percentage is a measure of promotion effectiveness.

Responsibility center. A segment of an organization that is assigned responsibility for carrying out a particular task and for which an individual is assigned managerial responsibility.

Responsibility structure. The formal system of assigning and monitoring responsibility in an organization.

Retention rate. The number of students completing a course of study divided by the total number of students who initially enroll.

Return on investment (ROI). The amount gained from an investment; technically, the percent of an investment returned per year.

Reward/risk ratio. The potential reward of a project divided by the potential risk (of loss) of the project. In this book, a common reward/risk ratio is the potential available for overhead divided by the sunk costs. *See also* Available for overhead; Sunk costs.

ROI. *See* Return on investment.

Rolling budgets. *See* Continuous budgets.

Safety stock. The amount of inventory that an organization keeps on hand to serve customers in the event that an order to replenish the inventory is delayed. An emergency supply. *See also* Inventory.

Second stage cost drivers. *See* Cost drivers.

Segmentation. *See* Organization segmentation.

Semivariable costs. Costs that contain both fixed and variable elements. Sometimes called semifixed costs. *See also* Fixed costs; Variable costs.

Separable fixed indirect costs. Fixed indirect costs that can be assigned to a particular responsibility center. *See also* Common fixed indirect costs; Responsibility center.

Service department. A CE organization segment dedicated primarily to serving the programming departments. The registration office, director's office, and cashier's office are examples. *See also* Programming department.

Soft money. A funding source available only for a stated period of time or one that is uncertain from one period to the next. Often arises from contracts and grants. *See also* Hard money.

Software. Computer programs that are often sold in "prepackaged" forms designed to do specific kinds of tasks.

Spillover effect. The effect by which a promotion campaign causes customers to buy a good or service (produced by the same organization) other than the one at which the campaign was aimed. Institutional advertising, for example, is not designed to cause students to enroll in a particular course but, by making students aware of the CE organization's name, to prompt a later enrollment.

Spreadsheet. A way of arraying data in columns and rows. Spreadsheets are one of the main kinds of packaged budgeting software available for computers.

Strategic budget. The budget used to accumulate the costs of a defined strategic initiative or goal.

Step function. The behavior of fixed costs that respond to large increases in volume or activity by moving upward in sharply defined "steps" rather than in smooth, continuous curves.

Stock out condition. A condition in which an organization cannot serve a customer because it does not have enough inventory on hand. *See also* Inventory.

Subject database. A database that focuses on one subject and incorporates as many attributes as are likely ever to be used in reports. *See also* Applications data base; Database.

Sunk costs. Past or previously incurred costs, especially direct course costs that must be expended before the decision about whether to actually present the course is made. Sometimes called up-front costs. *See also* Direct costs.

Surplus. *See* Available for overhead.

Systems analysis. The process of analyzing or designing a system with the goal of arriving at the most efficient operation.

Target rate of return. The rate of return on capital investments that the organization sets as a standard against which to judge investment alternatives.

Time-adjusted rate of return. A capital budgeting technique that determines the true rate of return on a proposed capital investment, considering the time value of money. *See also* Time value of money.

Time value of money. The idea that the value of a cash flow depends upon when it is received; the opportunity cost of not investing cash. *See also* Opportunity cost.

Top-down analysis. A way of approaching the design of a system that starts with the broadest objectives and proceeds "downward" through successive levels of greater detail.

Tracking system. A system for discovering the promotion campaign that produced each enrollment; used to determine effectiveness of promotion.

Traditional budgeting. *See* Line item budget.

Transfer pricing. A method of assigning costs within an organization in which one segment of the organization charges other segments for goods or services according to preset, often published, prices.

Unadjusted rate of return. A capital budgeting method used to estimate the return on a capital project without considering the time value of money. *See also* Time value of money.

Unit cost. The cost of producing one "unit." In this book, the unit cost is usually the cost per enrollment, which is derived by dividing a particular element of cost by the number of enrollments associated with it.

Up-front costs. *See* Sunk costs.

Up-side potential. The potential gain from a successful project.

Value of programmer time. The net amount of resources that a programmer can generate for an organization within a specified period; often seen as an opportunity cost. *See also* Cost of programmer time; Opportunity cost; Programmer.

Variable budget. A budget or series of budgets prepared for different levels of activity. Also called flexible budget.

Variable costs. Costs that vary with the level of activity. *See also* Fixed costs.

Variable resource organization. An organization in which the amount of resources available in any period is, at least to some extent, unknown at the beginning of the period and is usually dependent on the performance of the organization. Most self-supporting CE organizations are variable resource organizations. *See also* Fixed resource organization.

Variance. Positive or negative difference between figures projected in a budget and actual performance. *See also* Analysis of variance.

Virtual label. A database label that consists of letters or numbers that can be easily understood. *See also* Coded label; Database.

Volume variance. That part of the difference between budget and actual results caused by a difference between the budgeted volume of activity (e.g., number of enrollments) and the actual volume of activity.

Walk-away position. The limit beyond which one will not go in a negotiation. Programmers should calculate a walk-away position before discussing compensation with instructors, for example. *See also* Programmer.

Zero-based budgeting (ZBB). A budget method in which there is no "base"; every expenditure in the budget submission must be fully justified regardless of past practice or activity. See also Base; Incremental budgeting.

INDEX

· · · · · · · · ·

by Kay Banning

Opportunity costs
  capital investments and, 273
  course planning and, 96, 105
  definition of, 287
  instructor compensation and, 134
  promotion and, 127
  reward/risk concepts and, 78
Order cost, 287
Organization chart, 17
Organization segmentation. *See also* Cost
    center; Responsibility center
  definition of, 287
  financial management systems and, 156–
    61, 169
  program budgets and, 34, 36, 197
  traditional budgeting and, 23, 27
Organizational behavior, budgets and, 24–
    25. *See also* Distorted behavior; Re-
    ward systems
Outputs, 287
Overhead. *See* Indirect costs

Parent institutions. *See also* Continuing
    education organizations
  antiquated systems of, 218
  budget deadlines and, 172
  budget shortfalls and, 147
  budget form and, 19, 23, 30
  capital investments and, 270–71
  charges from, 8–9, 34, 149–50
  control structures and, 233
  cost-cutting efforts of, 9
  definition of, 287
  final budget approval, 186
  financial information from, xviii
  financial management systems and, 9,
    169
  function diversification and, 10–11
  hidden subsidies and, 149, 168
  indirect costs and, 150
  institutional environmental factors and,
    147, 148–53
  line item budgets of, 31–32
  management and, xix, xx
  management information systems and,
    17
  management theory and, 12
  markets and, 11
  organizational segmentation and, 159

reward systems and, 168
  service departments and, 157
  subsidies from, 149
Partial services, 121, 138–40, 287
Participative organizations. *See* Collegial
    organizations
Partly variable costs. *See* Semivariable costs
Pass-through costs, 9, 99, 101, 259, 287
Payback method, 273–75, 287
Payroll costs
  budget worksheets for, 198
  as committed costs, 221
  in line item budgets, 31, 34
  management information systems and,
    222
  product-driven activities and, 58
  reduction in, 185
  service departments and, 174
Performance standards, and budgets, 18
Period of instruction, and indirect costs,
    260–61
Personnel policies, 151–52
Personnel services, as service department,
    157
PERT (program evaluation and review tech-
    nique), 23
Political environment, 146–47, 153, 168,
    184
Pools, indirect cost. *See* Indirect cost pools
Portfolio management, 36–37, 82–83, 106,
    156, 158
PPBS. *See* Program planning and budgeting
    system (PPBS)
Present value, 272, 288
  of annuity, 278, 288
Present value index, 277, 288
Presentation costs, 223, 246
Price
  differential prices, 125–26
  market prices, 255–56
  price variances, 225, 230–32
  quality and, 124
Pro rata allocation, 256–57
Process. *See also* Budget process; Decision/
    process model
  of activity centers, 236–37, 243
  cost/budget object and, 26
Product budgets, 40–43, 205, 207, 288
Product costs, 106, 242–43